THE
SCRIBE
METHOD

THE BEST WAY TO
WRITE AND PUBLISH YOUR
NON-FICTION BOOK

THE
SCRIBE
METHOD

TUCKER MAX AND ZACH OBRONT

LIONCREST
PUBLISHING

THE SCRIBE METHOD

The Best Way to Write and Publish Your Non-Fiction Book

ISBN   978-1-5445-1406-2 *Hardcover*

978-1-5445-1405-5 *Ebook*

978-1-5445-1407-9 *Audiobook*

CONTENTS

PART 3: OUTLINE YOUR BOOK

PART 4: WRITE YOUR BOOK

PART 5: EDIT YOUR BOOK

PART 6: FINISH YOUR MANUSCRIPT

PART 7: DESIGN AND MARKET YOUR BOOK

PART 8: PUBLISH YOUR BOOK

WHY WRITE A BOOK?

I've never met you, but I'm gonna read your mind.

Not literally, of course.

I'm going to make an educated guess about why you want to write a book.

If I'm correct in my guess—it means this is the perfect book for you.

If I'm wrong in my guess—then I've just saved you a lot of time. You can skip this book; it's not right for you.

Here's my guess. See if it resonates:

You had a problem.

It was probably a difficult problem for you. You suffered for a long time because of it.

This problem might have even defined you as a person—at least for a while. You spent time, energy, and effort on it, and maybe even dedicated your career to solving it.

Finally, after a lot of struggle and work, you solved your problem. You found a solution, and you made your life better.

But you didn't just find the solution to this problem. You mastered it. You're good at implementing this solution. Yes, there are times you doubt yourself—as we all do— but part of you is even a little proud of yourself and what you've accomplished. You know some things (at least in your field).

Although you've never written a book before, you keep coming back to the idea of writing one, for two main reasons:

1. You want to share your hard-earned knowledge to help people solve the same problem you used to have. You want to give this wisdom back to others so it can impact them. Basically, you want to help people through your book.
2. You want some recognition for what you did. I am not implying that recognition is bad—quite the opposite. It is natural and right to want your peers and family and friends to know the real you and see what you've done. And you also hope this recognition will actually help

you in some way as well, probably in your career (and maybe even in your personal life too).

I'd bet you've been thinking about writing a book for some time. You've probably had people saying, "You should write a book!" long before now.

But you didn't acknowledge it, because the next step—writing the book—was too scary.

After all, you don't know where to start, or how to structure your book, or if your book idea is good enough, or if you have enough to say, or if anyone will care once you write it.

And then there's the worst fear of all, the one you don't want to talk about but always lingers:

What if you write a *bad* book?

You *might* have even started writing the book at some point, but you stopped. You probably had some good momentum at first and found it really rewarding to get your ideas out of your head. You thought about how people would receive the book, maybe pictured the eventual praise in your future.

But you hit an obstacle, and it stalled you. It brought up all your self-doubt and anxiety, and without a plan to get past that obstacle (or obstacles), you lost your momentum, and then you stopped.

It's probably frustrating that you aren't writing your book. You see other people—some of whom don't even know as much as you about your subject—who did write their books, who have credibility and authority in their field, who are getting increased visibility, and who have more clients and more opportunities, all from their book.

Most of all, you see the impact their books have on people. You know you could have that same impact—if you could just get your book done. Your book might not save the world, but it could change some people's lives for the better...if only you could get it to them.

Does this sound familiar?

Does it describe you?

If so, then *this is the perfect book for you.*

It was written specifically for people just like you, as you embark on your journey to writing and publishing your own book.

If you follow the steps, it will get you there.

If I haven't just described you, then like I said, this book probably isn't right for you, and you can put it down and move on to another book that is better suited for you. (If this story has nothing to do with you, yet you've already paid for it, then email me directly and I will give you your money back: tucker@scribemethod.com. I'm totally serious).

WHAT THIS BOOK WILL TEACH YOU

In this book, I will teach you everything you need to know to make sure you write a great book—one that impacts readers lives and cements your legacy. Here's just a sample of how-to topics you'll find in these pages:

- Pick the perfect book topic—one that both displays your knowledge and helps readers improve their lives (chapter 2.4)
- Make sure there will be an audience waiting to buy your book before you write it (chapter 2.3)
- Write a book to build your brand (chapter 2.2)
- Ensure your book gets you an ROI (chapter 2.2)
- Set yourself up for success before you even start writing your book (chapter 1.1)
- Figure out how much of your story should be in your book (chapter 2.1)
- Structure your book exactly so you get it correct—and so it's easy for you to write (chapter 3.1)
- Create the motivation and inspiration, on command, to sit down and write every day (chapter 4.1)
- Find the perfect book title (chapter 6.1)
- Price your book to maximize both sales and impact (chapter 7.6)
- Get an amazing book cover (chapter 7.4)

You'll also learn…

- What the most common writing obstacles are (chapter 1.2), and how to beat them (chapter 1.3)
- Once you start writing, how to make sure your audience will love your book (chapters 4.2 and 4.3)
- Editing techniques to ensure your book sounds exactly right (chapter 5.1)
- Exactly who to use to help publish your book (chapter 8.1)
- The key to writing book marketing copy that sells (chapter 7.1)
- And of course, the most important thing you can do to make your book a success, that most authors get wrong (chapter 2.1)

WHY LISTEN TO ME?

Because I know how to write, publish, and market books.

My name is Tucker Max. I cofounded Scribe (along with the coauthor of this book, Zach Obront), and I'm the primary author of this book.

I've written four *New York Times* bestsellers, three of which hit #1. These four books have come together to spend almost ten years combined on the bestseller list and have sold more than four million copies worldwide (as of 2018).

I'm one of three people, along with Malcolm Gladwell and

Michael Lewis, who've had three books on the nonfiction *New York Times* Best Seller list at one time. I was named in *Time* magazine's Most Influential list, and a movie was made about one of my books.

Before founding my current company, I worked with authors like Tim Ferriss, Robert Greene, Peter Thiel, James Altucher, Dave Asprey, Seth Godin, and dozens of others, to market their books.

All told, I've been directly involved in writing, editing, publishing, or marketing over twenty-two *New York Times* or *Wall Street Journal* bestsellers that have sold over 15 million copies combined worldwide.

Everything you'll read in this book has been tested over decades. This method has been proven to work at the highest levels of writing and publishing, and with regular people who are not professional writers.

The point is, you're in good hands.

If my educated guess resonated with your own story, this is the right book for you.

Now, let's get started.

PART 1

PREPARE
TO WRITE
YOUR BOOK

THE PROPER EXPECTATIONS FOR WRITING YOUR BOOK

"The art of good decision making is looking forward to and celebrating the tradeoffs, not pretending they don't exist."

—SETH GODIN

Before you start writing your book, let's talk about what you can expect during your journey.

At Scribe, we've helped over 1,000 authors write their books, and probably the number one thing that separates those who finish their books from those who do not is having the proper expectations going in.

Why?

Because writing a book is hard, and if you're not prepared

for that fact, you're far more likely to stall and even quit. But if you know the difficulty of what's coming, you can mentally prepare to get past those obstacles when they come (and *they will*).

These are the five major expectations you should have as you write your book.

1. EXPECT WRITING A BOOK TO BE HARD

Anyone who tells you writing a book is easy is either trying to sell you something or has never written a book (or writes really bad books).

Books are hard to write. And writing a good book is even harder.

Yes, this should be obvious, but there are many people who seem to think, if only subconsciously, that there is some "trick" that will make writing your book easier.

There's not.

There is no hack or trick or workaround.

Even with our system—which does make writing a book much easier and more efficient—expect that writing a book will require hard work from you.

2. EXPECT TO GET TIRED

Writing is tiring (especially if you do it correctly).

Expect to get tired when you write, and expect that it will drain you.

If you practice good self-care, you'll be fine. But it will tire you out at times.

3. EXPECT TO BE CONFUSED

Writing a book is inherently confusing. It is not easy to properly position and structure a book, not to mention to do the actual writing.

On top of that, I will tell you to do things you've probably never heard before or will give advice that seems counterintuitive.

What you'll find as you work through the Scribe Method process is that, while some of the things we recommend might *seem* unusual, they actually WORK really well— which is ultimately what matters the most.

If you approach the instructions here like Daniel did in *The Karate Kid,* you'll do great. If you didn't see the movie, in *The Karate Kid*, Mr. Miyagi had Daniel do a bunch of isolated tasks that seemed to have nothing to do with karate: painting fences, waxing cars, etc. Daniel got frustrated and annoyed. But then, when he started doing karate, he realized that those seemingly unconnected movements formed the basis for karate.

This book will be similar. The exercises I put you through might seem disjointed at first, but by the end, you'll see how they all come together. No effort is wasted.

The exercises are designed to build your book efficiently from the ground up the first time. As long as you have the discipline to walk through them and do them right, it'll work.

4. EXPECT TO BE EMOTIONALLY UNCOMFORTABLE AND AFRAID

This is a big one. Writing a book will unquestionably push you emotionally and expose fears and anxieties, and that's something that is very difficult for a lot of authors to deal with. (Don't worry, we have a whole chapter about what fears you can expect to experience and how to deal with them.)

A quick example: we worked with a UFC fighter on his book. This is a man who hits people in the face—for his job.

The book was about anxiety. He came into the process knowing he'd have to be vulnerable in order to really explore his subject matter, but being vulnerable was not something he was used to. In fact, any conversation that touched on him revealing anything personal or "weak" was, at first, totally outside his comfort zone. Quite frankly, he was afraid.

We helped him work through his fears and have those uncomfortable conversations, and he finally opened up about a mental breakdown he'd had in a way that truly benefited his readers. And in the end, it benefited him personally too.

I'm not going to ask you to step outside your comfort zone in this book. No, I'm going to ask you to EXPAND your comfort zone to include things you KNOW you can do but are not yet doing.

If you do that—if you work hard to expand your comfort zone, just like the UFC fighter did—you'll end up with a great book.

5. EXPECT THAT, IF YOU WRITE AND PUBLISH YOUR BOOK, THEN YOU'LL LEVEL UP

Even though the process of writing a book will challenge and stretch you, the actual product that you are left with—your book—will be an amazing addition to your life and career.

When you write your book, so much changes.

Once it's done, it's done, and it's with you forever. It shows you can commit to a difficult goal and then follow through to get it done. It will raise your authority and credibility in your niche. It will raise your visibility more prominently in your field.

And last, it will enable you to leave a legacy behind that impacts and helps other people. It's proof of your work and proof of your knowledge that will help and empower other people on their journeys.

This is no joke. Your life—and the lives of your readers—will be much better off when you write and publish your book.

"Nothing in the world is worth having or worth doing unless it means effort, pain, difficulty."

—THEODORE ROOSEVELT

THE SIX FEARS YOU (COULD) FACE WRITING YOUR BOOK

"Your inward conflicts express themselves in outward disasters."

—KRISHNAMURTI

Now that you're an author, you'll have to deal with all the fears and anxieties that come with writing.

You're not alone. All authors start where you are. We start insecure, unsure, and afraid. We start with fear, and sometimes even terror, gripping us. And sadly, for some authors, these fears stop them from ever writing their book at all.

I've been writing professionally for fifteen years, and the fears I'm about to detail are the same ones I've had to deal with in the past (and still deal with on a day-to-day basis).

This chapter will detail the common author fears, explain how they are destructive to books, and provide insight into how you can reframe those fears to help you. You may not have every one of the six I list below, but chances are you will deal with at least four at some point in the process.

(In the next chapter, I will show you a specific set of tactics for how to deal with the fears you face as you write so you can finish your book.)

FEAR: "I DON'T HAVE A BOOK IN ME."
ALTERNATE EXPRESSIONS OF THIS FEAR

- "I'm afraid there is no book in me."
- "I'm afraid I don't have anything to say."
- "What right do I have to be an author?"
- "Who am I to write a book?"

HOW THIS FEAR WILL IMPACT YOUR BOOK

It's very common for an author to be afraid that they don't have the knowledge in them to write a book.

For most people, this is a version of what's referred to as Imposter Syndrome.

Imposter Syndrome is when someone—even a very accomplished person with many credentials—believes they don't actually know what everyone thinks they know.

They believe that their ideas are either wrong or invalid or that everyone already knows what they know. People with Imposter Syndrome have this idea in their heads that everyone else has it figured out but that they are the imposter.

In the most extreme cases, Imposter Syndrome is when authors feel that their book will expose them as frauds or as fakers.

EXAMPLE OF AN AUTHOR WITH THIS FEAR

We worked with consultant Jonathan Dison on his book *The Consulting Economy*. He is a management consultant who has his own consulting firm that is doing very well. Hundreds of people he'd worked with throughout the years had asked him to write a book—one that would detail the method he used to help them transition from corporate employee to independent consultant.

Despite all these people asking him for the book, he put it off because he thought he was not enough of an expert to write a book. Even though he literally made the life-changing transition himself and had coached hundreds of people through it, at some level *he didn't believe he actually knew anything.*

HOW TO USE THIS FEAR TO HELP YOU

This fear is beneficial when it forces you to really think

about the value you're providing to the reader and focus your book on that.

I can't tell you how many times Jonathan said, "Tucker, I have no idea what I'm doing."

I would then walk him through how he helped people transition from corporate employee to independent consultant. I would have him explain his process to me and tell me about the people he'd helped and have him tell me what they told him about his advice (always gushing praise).

Then he'd admit, "Okay, yeah, I guess I do know something."

This fear can benefit you if you use it to think only about your potential reader.

Why would they find the book valuable? What do they get out of it? How will the knowledge in the book change their life?

Even if you believe you're an imposter, you can still recognize that someone else will value what you know. Then you can write the book for them.

That's what's so great about this fear. It's usually easy to understand if it's based in reality. Just ask yourself: *are people coming to me and asking me for, or paying me for, my knowledge?*

If so, then you clearly have a book in you as long as the book is just you sharing that knowledge with people. You can overcome your Imposter Syndrome by focusing on that fact alone.

FEAR: "I'M AFRAID MY BOOK ISN'T ORIGINAL ENOUGH."

ALTERNATE EXPRESSIONS OF THIS FEAR

- "I'm afraid everyone has already said all of this."
- "I don't think I have anything new to say."
- "Everything I have to say is stuff everyone already knows."
- "How will my book be any different from other books on this topic?"

HOW THIS FEAR WILL IMPACT YOUR BOOK

The funny thing with Jonathan Dison (from the example above) is that once he admitted that he knew something, he'd say, "But this is obvious. No one needs to be told this!"

This is a common feeling. And it's almost always wrong.

Many authors have the idea that a valid book must have a new insight that no one has ever considered.

That's ridiculous. Very few books are profoundly original, and the few that are tend not to be that valuable (because they are too esoteric).

A book is valuable if *the knowledge within it is accessible and usable to the audience.*

If you can write a book on a deeply covered topic, providing a unique perspective that sheds new light on the subject and helps your audience understand something they were missing, that is very valuable.

Even if you feel you don't have a brand-new perspective on the subject, if you have a unique voice and perspective around key concepts tailored for your audience, you will help them see old concepts in a way that finally clicks for them.

No reader cares if the idea is new or old. They only care if it's USEFUL TO THEM.

EXAMPLE OF AN AUTHOR WITH THIS FEAR

My favorite example of this is *Meetings Suck* by Cameron Herold.

How many business books are there on meetings? According to Amazon, there are over 50,000.

Surely, if there was one book that did not need to be written, it was this one, right?

That's what Cameron thought at first.

We walked through what he knew and helped him realize that though his methodology for meetings had no single insight that was truly original, the way that he combined all his insights and presented a complete plan for how to run a meeting was deeply useful to everyone he coached and taught.

With ninety-nine reviews and 40,000 copies sold, it's obvious that his take is engaging with people in a way that none of the other books on meetings have.

That's why *Meetings Suck* has done so well—because it explained a lot of old ideas in a way that no one else had before.

This fear is useful because it will force you to clearly define your audience and the value that you are providing to them.

This is a key aspect of the Scribe Method (which we'll get into in detail soon). We have our authors look deeply at who derives value from their knowledge, which helps the author define their audience. Once they know their audience, they can then think, "What did I teach those people that they found valuable in their lives?"

And your fear has led you to define both your audience and the value you provide them.

FEAR: "I'M AFRAID MY BOOK WON'T BE GOOD ENOUGH."
ALTERNATE EXPRESSIONS OF THIS FEAR

- "I'm afraid my book won't be perfect."
- "I'm afraid I put too much in."
- "I'm afraid I didn't put in enough."
- "I'm afraid I'm going to forget everything I want to say."
- "I'm afraid of leaving things out."

HOW THIS FEAR WILL IMPACT YOUR BOOK

This is almost always perfectionism. How is perfectionism related to fear?

As the author dives into the book, they become obsessed

with every detail. They fret over every word, every punctuation mark, and every phrasing.

This is not about trying to make the book as good as possible. Excessive obsession with every detail—beyond the point of reason—is a way of masking a fear that the book is not good enough. Authors will get stuck in one of the perfectionism rabbit holes so they can avoid publishing the book.

Books can get stuck here in various ways:

1. The author will try to put everything they know into the book, and this causes the book to bloat and become unmanageable.
2. The author won't stick to a subject and will jump around to different ideas.
3. The author's perfectionism becomes an excuse to delay or avoid actually working on the book.
4. The author edits and adds in never-ending cycles, spinning in circles and never actually finishing the book.

EXAMPLE OF AN AUTHOR WITH THIS FEAR

Deb Gabor is a great example of this. Deb is a brilliant brand strategist. She's worked with companies like Dell, NBC, and Microsoft on their branding strategy, and she wrote a book called *Branding Is Sex* about how companies can use branding in new and innovative ways.

She started the book confident in her knowledge and the value of the book to her readers. But as she moved further into the writing process, insecurity took hold. She wondered if anyone would find it valuable, and to compensate, she put more and more information into it.

As a result, the book, without any conscious intent, became far too big and unwieldy because she was trying to put everything she knew into the book instead of just focusing on what her audience valued and wanted to know. In order to compensate for her insecurity, she turned to perfectionism, and it almost ruined her book.

HOW TO USE THIS FEAR TO HELP YOU

Thankfully, Deb is smart and self-aware, and once we walked her through what she was doing, she recognized it and was able to get her book refocused and sharply defined.

That's the good thing about this fear: it forces you to define both your audience's needs very specifically and how your book meets them. By using this fear productively, you force yourself to focus exclusively on the audience and what they want and to stop thinking about yourself and how you look. This enables you to write a better book—one that gives the audience what they are looking for and, thus, gets you what you want.

Another thing we explained to Deb is the saying that "art is never done; it's only abandoned." The point is that being perfect is literally impossible. All you can do is the very best job you can right now and then put it out to help your audience and you're done.

FEAR: "I'M AFRAID NO ONE WILL CARE ABOUT MY BOOK."

ALTERNATE EXPRESSIONS OF THIS FEAR

- "What if no one reads it?"
- "What if there is no audience?"
- "What if my book doesn't impact anyone?"
- "What if this is a waste of my time and effort?"
- "I'll be embarrassed if people criticize my book."

HOW THIS FEAR WILL IMPACT YOUR BOOK

This is a pretty simple fear, and it generally comes up in people who are trying to find a way to avoid other deeper fears (like the "looking stupid fear" covered below).

Usually, this fear manifests by an author convincing themselves that no one will care about their book.

Paradoxically, this is almost always suffered by the authors who have the books that are most impactful on others. (The authors who *should* worry about this almost never do. Such is life, right?)

Dr. Douglas Brackmann grew up with ADHD and was told his whole life that he has a disability. He refused to see it that way. He spent his life seeking to understand where ADHD comes from (it's actually genetic and serves an adaptive purpose) and how to utilize the energy and focus the condition creates to improve his life.

He solved this issue in his life and then started training the highest performers—entrepreneurs, CEOs, pro athletes, inventors, and Navy SEALs—to learn how to perform even better using the techniques he had to learn to compensate for his ADHD.

But when it came time to write a book, he wasn't sure anyone would care.

Think about that for a second: he was ALREADY training some of the highest performers in the world, but he still wasn't sure that anyone would care about his book.

This sort of thing happens because when an author knows their subject so well, they often think it's obvious or easy, and so they discount their knowledge. They forget that the exact people they're writing for do not have this knowledge and are often desperate for it.

In Dr. Brackmann's case, this happened. Look at the Amazon reviews:

I could not put this book down...it was as if it was written directly to me...answering questions that I had held in my mind for over 4 decades.

Now that I've realized more of "what" I am...I have been more fulfilled, felt more joy over the same activities I was doing a month ago. My business, my family, my health are all improved...and most importantly...my SOUL finally feels like I've found my place!

I work with a lot of entrepreneurs, marketers, and high achieving clients from all walks of life...and this book has instantly been put onto the top recommendations I have when starting out with them.

The tools that Dr. Brackmann gave me, all of which you will find in his book, allowed me to find inner peace and happiness and realize my true potential...I could recognize my soul again, lift myself up and design the life I had always dreamed of. Dr. Brackmann helped me understand how my mind worked and helped me harness the Driven characteristics I had so that in less than 1 year I could build a 7 figure business with no outside help, find the girl of my dreams, and pursue a life of mastery in many different areas. I highly recommend this book for anyone that has a desire to find more peace while fulfilling their potential.

This fear can turn into motivation if you use it right. If you're afraid no one will care, then find someone in real life who *does* care about what you have to say, teach them what you know, and then look at the transformation in their life.

If you can see that, see the impact it makes on them, then it should be much easier to finish your book because it's no longer about you. It's about them and the other people like them.

FEAR: "I'M AFRAID MY BOOK WILL UPSET PEOPLE."

ALTERNATE EXPRESSIONS OF THIS FEAR

- "I'm afraid this book is going to make someone mad."
- "I'm afraid of being judged."
- "Will my friend be mad if I tell her story in my book?"
- "I don't want my book to upset my current clients."
- "I can't say these things about people."
- "What if my friends read it and hate it?"
- "What if I sound bitchy?"

HOW THIS FEAR WILL IMPACT YOUR BOOK

This fear is a major book killer. The fear of judgment is crippling to many authors and prevents them from either writing their book or from writing the book that they really want to write or from telling the stories they want to tell in their book.

Here's the simple fact about books: *if no one at all disagrees with what you are saying, then you aren't saying anything worth going in a book.*

A book should make new claims or reframe old information or take a position that stands in opposition to conventional wisdom or teach something new or different or contrary.

That's the entire point of a book—to help people find a new way to think about something or do something.

Let me say it again: **it's impossible to write a good book without taking some kind of risk.**

EXAMPLE OF AN AUTHOR WITH THIS FEAR

Shannon Miles is a great example of this. Shannon wrote *The Third Option*, a book that explains how women do not have to choose between a career and a family—that they can actually create a life that gives them both.

There are many women who will claim that a woman's career should come first, and there are many others who will say family must come first. Shannon took the position that neither is true, that you can have both—which is upsetting to both sides.

Because Shannon knew that she was going to be heavily criticized and attacked from both sides, she hesitated about whether to write her book at all. Once she made the decision to move forward, she still found herself censoring her views and holding back.

Eventually Shannon got past this worry. With the help of her Scribe, she focused not on herself but on her reader and realized that by withholding her views or stories, she was not serving them. She was failing them and betraying herself.

As a result, she wrote a book that has been extraordinarily well received. She did get some negative feedback, of course, but it was overwhelmed by all the positive responses and thanks from women who felt like she understood and spoke to them in a way no one else had.

HOW TO USE THIS FEAR TO HELP YOU

First off, it's okay to admit you feel bad when people say bad things about you. Even if what they say is wrong and unfair and even if they are straight up lying about you, that still hurts.

It's okay to admit it, and it's okay to feel all the terrible feelings that come with that. The human brain is designed such that it interprets social violence almost exactly the same as physical violence. It hurts when people attack you, and I will never tell you to block it out and pretend it doesn't bother you. That doesn't work.

But if this is a fear you are facing, you have the option to see it as a gift.

If there are people who will criticize your position, they can force you to examine it from all angles and make sure your arguments are rock solid.

Also, opposition also helps you find and galvanize your own audience of people, like Shannon did. If there are loud and angry people on only one side of a debate, it probably means the other side simply does not have a spokesperson. Your book puts you in that role.

Also, use this fear to make sure you are being fair to people and other arguments. It's okay to be conscious about the words you use and how they impact people. This does not mean you water down your position; in fact, your argument is strengthened when it is considerate of alternate viewpoints.

Finally, remember the iconic quote about this by Steven Pressfield:

> Making a judgment, taking a stand, and then acting against an injustice or acting to support excellence is the stuff of the everyman hero. If you are an aspiring artist and you wish to avoid "judgments," you'll find that you have nothing to say.

FEAR: "I'M AFRAID MY BOOK WILL MAKE ME LOOK STUPID."

ALTERNATE EXPRESSIONS OF THIS FEAR

- "I'm afraid I'm going to look stupid."
- "What if I get all one-star reviews?"
- "What if everyone who reads it hates it?"
- "What will people think if there's a typo?"
- "I'm afraid something will be wrong with my book and I'll look stupid to everyone I know."

HOW THIS FEAR WILL IMPACT YOUR BOOK

The biggest unspoken fear that I believe (virtually) every author has is that they will embarrass themselves. I saved this for last because almost every fear above boils down to this one.

This fear is actually not irrational. For many professionals, writing a bad book is actually worse than writing no book at all. This is because for someone with a certain level of status, a bad book will hurt their career.

For others, it goes even further. For some, the book is very attached to their identity. They see the book as an extension of themselves, and they are worried that the book isn't well-received, then it means they will personally look bad. No one wants to look flawed to their peers, especially with something as personal as a book.

This fear can get so bad that people will forgo the tens of

42 · THE SCRIBE METHOD

thousands of dollars they pay us to help them write a book—all because they're afraid to hit the final "publish my book" button.

I'm not exaggerating at all. We have authors who will work for months, do all the difficult editing and revisions, go through the entire publishing process, and then, when there is literally nothing left to do besides give the final approval, will completely ghost on us.

They can't face their fear that the book isn't good, so they avoid even talking about it.

EXAMPLE OF AN AUTHOR WITH THIS FEAR

Every author we've ever worked with—without exception—has had some version of this fear (and I've had this fear as well).

Joey Coleman is my favorite example. He even wrote about his fear in his book, *Never Lose a Customer Again*:

> But not long after that, I started to doubt myself, and I began to question my decision to write a book.
>
> *Did I really have a good enough message that could carry an entire book?*
>
> *Would the readers find as much value in the eight-phase process as my clients had over the last twenty years?*

Would I be able to explain all the nuances of the framework properly in three hundred pages?

Was I going to make myself look stupid?

As these thoughts of fear, doubt, and uncertainty flooded my mind, I grew distant. I started rescheduling planned phone calls with the team, pushing them off for both real and fabricated reasons alike. I used any excuse I could think of that would allow me to delay the next step in the process.

This went on for several months until one night when my cell phone rang unexpectedly. The caller ID indicated it was Tucker's cellphone, and a quick mental scan of my calendar let me know this was an unexpected call. I decided to answer anyway.

Tucker got me to open up and admit that I was having feelings of remorse and regret, and assured me that the emotions I was feeling were natural for any author. He told me a story about how he felt the same way when he released his first major book, which ironically enough went on to be a *New York Times* bestseller, selling more than a million copies worldwide since its release.

Tucker helped me see that I did indeed have a book in me and that he believed it would be valuable to many people. He persuaded me to trust the process, come back into the fold, and continue the work. That is how powerful buyer's remorse is.

Even though I deeply understood the perils of the cognitive dissonance that marks this feeling, even though *I teach this to companies*, I could not separate myself from these emotions when I was in that position.

Oops—I'm human too.

HOW TO USE THIS FEAR TO HELP YOU

Remember how I told you that fear is not in and of itself a bad thing? If you allow the fear to focus you and become motivation to focus and work hard, then it can help you. It can be fuel. It can help ensure you do everything necessary to create the best book possible.

But what about when that fear becomes overwhelming? When it seems like your fear—any of these fears—are too much? What then?

The next chapter deals with this exact question: how can you handle your fears once they come up and won't go away?

HOW TO BEAT YOUR FEARS (AND FINISH YOUR BOOK)

"Life is growth. You grow or you die."

—PHIL KNIGHT

THE PURPOSE OF FEAR

The first thing to remember about fear is that it's not necessarily bad. Fear serves a purpose.

On a primal level, fear is an adaptive response that helps us survive by motivating us to protect ourselves from danger. It is both *natural and helpful* in many cases. You evolved to fear things that can hurt you, and fear works to help keep you safe.

The problem with fear is when you let small or irrational

fears stop you from doing something you should be doing. Then fear is destructive, not protective.

Some of the fears you face will make sense, while others will seem ridiculous if you rationally analyze them. That's normal. Fears aren't always rational (nor are they intended to be).

Don't shame yourself if you feel any of these fears, even if they are irrational. Even if the reason is irrational, the feeling of fear is still real, and you have to address it in order to move forward with your book.

ALL AUTHORS FACE FEAR

At some point and at some level, you're going to be afraid of writing your book.

Don't feel bad about this. EVERY author feels the same way (including me). I've written seven books (so far), but should have written ten (maybe more). I've lost at least three books to fear.

I get it. I've been there. It's an awful feeling to know I had these books in me and never got to them, only because I was afraid to write them.

Don't beat yourself up if fear is holding you back. It's beaten me before, as it's beaten almost every author at some point or another.

You can win this fight against fear. How do you do it? And even more importantly, how do you prevent this fear in the future?

You train your emotional brain to reframe the fear you feel, and then use it as fuel to action instead of inaction.

Here are the steps to do that.

STEP 1: LIST ALL YOUR FEARS

Internally, we call this the "author scare card."

Ask yourself, what are you afraid might happen if you write a book? Write down the fears you are feeling. Write down every fear or anxiety.

Don't run from, deny, or minimize your fears. Really take a moment and pause to think about your fears and identify them.

If you are having a hard time articulating your fears, the last chapter discussed the most common fears. That should be a pretty good guide.

Don't worry if this list is long. It should have at least a few fears, and if it has a bunch, then so be it. In fact, the more you list (that are true), the better.

STEP 2: ASK YOURSELF, "ARE THEY REALISTIC?"

For each fear, ask yourself: "Is this fear realistic? Could it actually come to pass?"

Many times, people are anxious about vague and undefined fears. If that's the case, forcing yourself to name the fear and realize it's ridiculous can make it go away.

For example, someone could say, "I'm afraid that I'll write this book but that I won't be able to get it published." That's not a realistic fear. There are so many ways to publish now that anyone can do it.

This being said, most fears will be based on reality. For example, continuing with the above example, you could say instead, "I'm afraid that I'll write this book, and I will look bad, and it will hurt my professional reputation."

That's a real fear with real consequences. If you write a bad book, you *will* look bad.

For the fears that are unrealistic, disregard and cross them off the list. For the ones based in reality, keep going.

STEP 3: ASK YOURSELF, "IF THIS FEAR CAME TO PASS, WHAT WOULD THE CONSEQUENCES BE?"

For some of the fears, the consequences will be minor. For

example, if the fear is, "I'm afraid I'll sound bitchy," the consequences of that are probably benign.

For other fears, the consequences could be larger. For example, if the fear is, "I'm afraid that I'll write this book, and I will look bad, and it will hurt my professional reputation," the consequences might be substantial.

It's okay to think of the worst-case scenario here. In fact, it's preferable. If you articulate the worst thing that could happen, then you at least know what it is and can now move forward with a clear understanding of what there is to lose.

There is nothing wrong with this. Being realistic is a big part of defeating fear, so write down what the consequences are.

STEP 4: ASK YOURSELF, "WHAT'S THE PLAN TO AVOID THESE CONSEQUENCES?"

To start moving past your fear, you need to lay out precisely what the plan is to avoid or minimize the consequence.

This is because fears often partly originate from a subconscious reaction to a poor plan or a lack of a plan (this is also where procrastination comes from).

For example, if the fear is, "I'm afraid that I'll write this book, and I will look bad, and it will hurt my professional reputation," it's highly likely that fear comes from, in part, the fact that you're not confident in your writing skills and don't yet have a clear idea of who will help you edit your book. The plan might be as simple as having a professional editor and two colleagues review the manuscript before you decide to publish it to make sure you look good.

You may have to come back and fill in parts of this section later, and that's okay. For example, if the fear is, "I'm afraid I won't have time to write the book," well, right now you don't have a plan to make time to write the book (we get to that part of the plan later).

But don't worry. By the time you finish this book, you will have a specific, detailed, actionable plan so you can know for certain that, if you follow it, you'll get your book done.

STEP 5: ASK YOURSELF, "HOW CAN I USE THIS FEAR TO HELP ME?"

Fear can actually help you if you take the right perspective on it. Think about the physical symptoms of fear. What are they?

1. Heart rate rises (adrenaline increase)
2. Fight-or-flight response kicks in, you get jittery, break out into a cold sweat (cortisol surge)
3. You have tunnel vision, can't see or think beyond your fear (norepinephrine increase)

Now, let's think about the physical symptoms of excitement. What are they?

1. Heart rate rises (adrenaline increase)
2. Fight-or-flight response kicks in, you get jittery, break out into a cold sweat (cortisol surge)
3. You have tunnel vision, can't see or think beyond your excitement (norepinephrine increase)

Fear and excitement are the exact same physiological response.

Fear is excitement with a negative frame.

Excitement is fear with a positive frame.

Think of it like a roller coaster. Some people are terrified, some people love it, *but it's the same ride.* You cannot choose your physiological response to a roller coaster, but with some practice, you CAN choose how you *interpret* that physiological response. You can be afraid or thrilled, but the body treats it the same.

This means you can reframe fear into excitement and retrain your brain to not be afraid of writing your book— and in fact to harness that energy to help you write your book.

Did you notice in the previous fear chapter, each fear ended with a section about how to reframe the fear? That's for this section.

Now look at each fear you wrote, and ask, "How can I use this fear to help me?"

For example, if the fear is, "I'm afraid that I'll write this book, and I will look bad, and it will hurt my professional reputation," then you can use the energy of that fear to motivate you to put in the work to do a really good book to ensure that you do not look bad.

But don't stop with each specific fear. You can rethink each physiological response as excitement that benefits you. For example:

1. Heart rate raises (adrenaline increase): this helps you get the energy needed to sit down and write for an hour or two.
2. Fight or flight response kicks in, you get jittery, break out into a cold sweat (cortisol surge): this helps you take this seriously and really put your best effort forward.
3. You have tunnel vision, can't see or think beyond your excitement (norepinephrine increase): this helps you focus on your writing and block everything else out.

STEP 6: ASK YOURSELF, "WHEN I WRITE MY BOOK, WHAT BENEFIT WILL I GET FOR MYSELF?"

You could say, "If I write my book, then I will increase my authority and visibility in my field, get more speaking gigs, and be able to grow my business."

(Note: You're going to specifically define these benefits as the very next part of the process, but put something down now, even if you come back and refine it later.)

Then speak these benefits out loud, making sure to frame yourself as excited about them.

Literally say, "I should be excited because this book will get me increased authority, additional speaking, and a bigger business."

Do it three times.

And you MUST say it OUT LOUD. And make sure to phrase it as you talking to yourself.

I know, this sounds hokey, but saying it out loud has a very different impact on you then just thinking it. Without going too deep into the psychological explanation, saying it out loud makes it more real to your brain.

(If you want to know why saying this out loud makes such a difference, Google "inner speech of behavioral regulation" or "Von Restorff effect." Warning: these will take you down a serious rabbit hole.)

STEP 7: ASK YOURSELF, "WHO'S HELPED BY YOUR BOOK, AND WHAT DO THEY GET?"

Did you notice a trend with the fears you mentioned? What did they all have in common?

It's actually pretty simple: *all fear is selfish*.

When you're afraid, you are focused only on yourself and your own needs. Fear puts you into survival mode. Fear makes it impossible to see outside of yourself. Fear traps you inside yourself.

And even though you will benefit from your book, for many people, that's probably not the biggest reason why you want to write it.

Imagine the person you will be helping. Think of them very specifically. Imagine the pain they are in now. Feel the suffering they have because they haven't read your book.

How much of a difference will your knowledge make in their lives?

Your book is important to them. It matters to their lives. That's why you are writing it. They *need your book*.

Think about how much they need the knowledge you have. Imagine your audience after they've read your book. What will their lives be like then? How much better will they be because of your book?

Connect with that feeling. Can you do it—for them?

You want to write your book to help other people solve a problem that you used to have—one that's very painful to you. Helping those people is a big part of your motivation. So picturing those people in need, and you letting them down if you do not write your book, is a very powerful motivator.

Using this motivation turns out to be the ultimate fear buster. *Most people who can't be courageous for themselves will easily be courageous for other people.*

(And of course, if you just think about who your book is intended to help, you can focus on them. And if you do that—if you focus on the reader—you will actually end up looking good. We'll talk a lot more about this later in the positioning section of the book.)

STEP 8: ASK YOURSELF, "WHAT IF I JUST QUIT?"

This is about using your anxiety against itself. If you ask yourself, "If I do NOT write my book, what will happen? Who will suffer and how?" what you'll often see is that your brain reverses itself and begins to argue for writing the book.

This works because of the peculiar way that human brains work. Now that you have "seen" the benefits you can get from writing a book, picturing yourself quitting will trigger one of the strongest psychological reactions in humans: loss aversion.

Once you imagine yourself with all these benefits, and then you imagine yourself losing them, things shift in your brain. Your fear doesn't necessarily go away. It just takes a back seat to loss aversion.

This is one of the most replicated findings in social science. People are far more motivated by losing something than by gaining something. By already picturing yourself with benefits and gains, you now want to keep them.

PART 2

POSITION YOUR BOOK

WHAT IS BOOK POSITIONING (AND WHY DOES IT MATTER)?

"The task is not so much to see what no one has seen, but to think what nobody has yet thought, about that which everybody sees."

—SCHRÖDINGER

Positioning is the most crucial part of both writing and marketing your book. If you put in the work to properly position your book now, you will reap the benefits for years.

If you do not take this seriously and get your positioning wrong, then almost nothing you can do will save your book or make it successful. In fact, I would go so far as to tell you that *you can't write or market yourself out of a positioning problem.*

What is book positioning?

Simply stated, book positioning is ***the place your book occupies in the mind of your reader and how that reader perceives your book as fulfilling their needs.***

If you get it right, positioning acts as the business plan for your book. It makes both the writing and marketing of the book easy and ensures you get what you want from your book.

A (VERY) BRIEF HISTORY OF BOOK POSITIONING

For a hundred years in the old media traditional publishing model, every agent had to have the positioning discussion with an editor before they would buy a book.

Strictly speaking, in traditional publishing circles, the positioning discussion only revolved around how the book fit into traditional sales categories. That's where the term comes from. It's literally a discussion of what *position* on the bookstore shelves the book is supposed to go, because in the twentieth century, the market for books was essentially synonymous with the needs of bookstores.

This is obviously no longer the case. Most books are now sold digitally, categories don't matter as much, and the majority of physical books are not sold in bookstores but rather in nonbook retail stores like Costco and Walmart that don't even have categorized shelves.

Furthermore, when all book publishing was done by traditional publishing companies, the only positioning decisions they cared about concerned whether books would sell because that's how they made money.

MODERN BOOK POSITIONING

None of this is true anymore. Now, most books are published outside of the old traditional models, and most nonfiction books are not monetized directly.

Here is modern reality: **most nonfiction authors make the majority of their money from other things that a book gets them and *not from sales of their books*.**

You can always make money by selling copies, of course. But making money indirectly from a book means you're using your book as a marketing tool to get you something else that produces revenue.

For example, a book will help you elevate your authority, increase your visibility, and get you more clients. This strategy fundamentally changes the way books are conceived and positioned (more on this later).

At Scribe, we've adapted the old positioning process so that instead of serving the publishing company's needs, it serves your needs as the author.

POSITIONING DONE RIGHT ENSURES YOUR BOOK WILL WORK

I will lead you through our positioning process using the exact steps and questions we use to help authors refine and crystallize their ideas into well-positioned books that will get them results. These are the three sections:

1. Book Objectives: What result must the book produce for you to be a success?
2. Book Audience: Who is the audience that must be reached for your goal to be achieved?
3. Book Idea: What is your book about, and why will your audience care?

Everything is connected.

The objectives lead to the audience.

The audience has needs that must be met.

And if the book provides value to the audience, you'll reach the objectives you want to achieve.

It all ties together in a simple formula. If you follow it, you'll pick a book topic that provides value for both you and the audience.

HOW PEOPLE REALLY JUDGE A BOOK

I see authors spend years writing their book, finish the manuscript, and watch it never find an audience. It's incredibly depressing.

The worst part is that this is completely avoidable. In fact, *it's possible to know with a high degree of certainty whether or not your book will find an audience.*

To do that, you first have to understand how people judge books. After all, if the goal for the book is to find an audience, you have to understand how audiences perceive books.

This chapter will explain the mental process that a reader goes through when making a buying decision about a book, and will set you up to understand how to position your book to give it the best chance to reach the audience you want.

THE INFORMATION REAL PEOPLE USE TO JUDGE A BOOK

Let me lay this out for you in the starkest terms possible.

Almost every potential reader will judge whether or not to buy and read your book before they have read one single word inside the book.

Based on loads of empirical research and decades of experience in the book business, we have a clear picture of what happens in the mind of a potential reader when judging a book.

Even though we have a pretty good map of how people decide to buy a book (which we will outline soon), you must understand a key insight: *this process is almost never conscious.*

These buying decisions are a series of instantaneous and mostly unconscious judgments. They are made in less than sixty seconds, and they are made together, each influencing the other, not individually. The reader often doesn't know (or believe) they're evaluating the book this way, but they are. These judgments are real and substantive. In most cases, they are the main evaluation and purchase triggers.

A potential reader will consider these pieces of information about a book (usually) in this order:

1. The title

2. The recommending source
3. The cover
4. The book description
5. The blurbs
6. The customer reviews
7. The author bio and picture (depending on where the picture is placed)
8. The length of the book
9. The price (though this can come sooner)
10. The book text itself (the "see inside" function online)

We'll cover how to create each of these pieces in more depth later on. For now, let's walk through each step and unpack the reader's judgments around it.

1. TITLE

Most people think the cover is the first thing someone judges. That's only true if they're browsing a physical bookstore, which is rarely the case anymore. Most books are now discovered either by in-person word of mouth or online, and in both cases, what is the first piece of information they receive?

The title.

From that, people instantaneously assess if the book seems relevant, if it's for them, and if it sounds interesting. This is why I recommend spending so much time making sure you get the title right.

Let's be clear: A good title *won't* make your book do well, but a bad title will almost certainly *prevent* it from doing so. Many potential readers stop considering a book once they have heard the title and nothing else.

2. RECOMMENDING SOURCE

If Marc Andreessen or Bill Gates recommends a book, then thousands of their eager readers rush out to buy it. If a random person with no followers on Twitter recommends it, no one buys it.

This is because the *credibility of the source* is a hugely important piece of the recommendation puzzle. In most cases, people will transfer the credibility of the recommender onto the book.

It's all about *who is doing the recommending*. This applies to friends as well. If you have a friend who is very rich, successful and intelligent, you're far more likely to listen to their book recommendation than someone who is unemployed and living with his parents.

What's great about this is that if the credibility of the referrer is great enough, almost any title will work, and you don't have to worry about the rest of this list. But that is rarely the case, so you still want to make sure to give yourself the best chance you can.

3. BOOK COVER

If the reader is still interested after hearing the title and taking the referring source into account, they will now go to Amazon (or in rarer cases, a bookstore) and look at the book.

The potential reader makes more judgments about its relevance and their interest based on this information.

The most important thing at this point is that the reader not be repelled. Most people are looking for reasons NOT to buy the book, and you have to not give them any.

4. BOOK DESCRIPTION

At this point, if the cover hasn't repelled the reader, they will look next to the book description on the Amazon page (or flip over to the back of the book in a bookstore). The book description should give the reader a strong sense of what the book is about, making it interesting while not giving everything away.

5. BLURBS

If the reader still is interested, they will now look at endorsements (sometimes, for a physical book, they will do this prior to reading the book description).

Note that most readers look more closely at *who* the blurbs are from rather than what they say. They assume that the blurbs will be positive, so they want to see what level of social status the blurber is and whether it's someone they know and respect.

6. READER REVIEWS

If the reader is on Amazon (or BarnesandNoble.com or Goodreads, etc., but not in a bookstore), they now read the customer reviews.

They will usually first note the number of total reviews—as a gauge of popularity—and then look at the average rating. They may then browse the content of the reviews. If they do, they normally read (more likely scan) one or two of them, and if they are like most people, they skip the positive ones and read a negative one before going back to a positive one (if they even do that).

7. AUTHOR BIO AND PICTURE

Sometimes, but not always, people will look at the author bio. This is usually in situations where they have not quite made up their mind, are hesitant to buy the book, and need more information. Looking at the author page is about understanding the credibility and relative status of the author.

There are cases where this is one of the first things the reader looks at (when they've never heard of the author).

Some readers immediately want to know about the author and look at the bio first.

After collecting all this information, the vast majority of people have made their decision. Note that this is before they interact with *anything* inside the book. They have yet to read one single page, and they've already decided whether or not to buy the book.

8. LENGTH

This is one of those things that seems to be generational or divided by socioeconomic status. Some people, generally voracious readers, never even think to check length. Whereas other people always check length. Many people do not want to commit to a three hundred-plus-page book.

There's not much you can do here—your book is the length it is—but we've found in our data that, for nonfiction books, those between one and two hundred pages sell the best and are read the most.

9. PRICE

Some people will look at price. For some reason, it appears that people are far more price conscious for e-books than they are for physical books. The reason for this is value perception. Generally speaking, we recommend keeping your goals for your book in mind when you price.

10. THE BOOK TEXT

There are *some* people who actually use the "Look Inside" function on Amazon to check out the first few pages and engage the content of the book itself. If they're in a bookstore, they flip the book open and read a bit. They might even do more research to find articles online about the book.

These are the high information buyers, but they are a distinct minority. Probably fewer than 10 percent of your buyers do the thing that everyone says they want to do: judge a book by the content inside and not the cover.

HOW MUCH OF YOUR STORY SHOULD BE IN YOUR BOOK?

Every author struggles with how much of their personal story should be in their book. Some want to put a lot of their story in their book. Others don't want to put any of their story in.

So how much is correct? The basic answer:

Your book should have enough of your story to help the reader get what they want out of the book, *but nothing more*.

Let's examine both mistakes authors make with their story independently.

DON'T PUT IN TOO MUCH OF YOUR STORY

This is going to sound harsh, but it's the most important thing you'll learn from this book (and I will repeat this many times):

Your readers don't care about your book.

They don't really even care about you. Or your story.

They're not buying or reading your book for you. They are buying it and reading it to get something *they want*.

So yes, this means that your readers *only care about what your book will get them.* They view your book and you and your story in terms of that lens only.

We have some authors who want to make their book about themselves. They want to write all about their lives and their personal stories and go on and on about themselves, their fears, their anxieties, their accomplishments...no one cares.

You can absolutely write a book that is a monument to yourself.

But no one will read it or care but you. (Yes, there are some exceptions for certain types of memoirs, but that's beyond the scope of this book.)

I say that not to judge memoirs or books that are very self-focused. Just know that if you do that, you're writing that book only for yourself. If you know that and accept it, then it's fine. Go do it.

But if you want your book to find an audience and have an impact on readers, then you must start with the intention that the book is about what's relevant to the reader.

Yes, you are the author of your book...but it's not for you. It's for the reader.

PUT IN THE IMPORTANT PARTS OF YOUR STORY

The other side of this is authors who don't want to put any of their story in the book. They think it's arrogant, or they don't want to talk about themselves, or they are afraid to be vulnerable or to share emotions. These authors seem to think that there is a bright line of distinction between a memoir and business book and that a business book can't have anything personal in it at all.

This is not true, and in fact, a book with nothing about the author rarely works well.

If it helps the reader to understand why they should read the book and how the book can relate to them by hearing about specific parts of your story, then you should absolutely put those parts of your story in the book.

This is because of a simple fact of human biology: humans learn through story and example.

Readers pick up your book because it has knowledge and information in it that can help them solve a problem they have or get something they want.

But they read it and engage it and use it because of the stories in it that teach them, inspire them, motivate them, and help them actually understand and apply the knowledge.

As much as possible, your book should encase your teachings and wisdom and lesson in stories. Those can be your stories, or they can be stories of other people. Either one works.

WHAT PARTS OF YOUR STORY SHOULD BE IN YOUR BOOK?

This is a pretty simple test to help you understand whether a specific story should go in the book:

> *Does this story add value for the reader?*

Literally just ask yourself, who am I telling this story for, and what do they get? If it's not the reader, then you're wrong, and it doesn't belong in the book. If it is, then it stays in.

The exchange between you and the reader is they're giving you their attention and you're giving them a knowledge and wisdom they find valuable. So your story needs to embody that and display that, and if it does, it's in.

HOW VULNERABLE SHOULD YOU BE? HOW MUCH EMOTION SHOULD YOU SHOW?

The other thing authors ask is how vulnerable they should be in their stories. The answer is, again:

Be as vulnerable as you need to be to write the most impactful story for the reader.

For example, if you write a book about managing money, it would be great to tell a story about how you had to file for bankruptcy. That's a hard thing to admit and is a vulnerable thing to say in a book.

Telling that story in a book about managing money will greatly benefit the reader. It will make them trust you, help you seem credible, and let them know that you've been there and can help them get over their shame and their issues of money.

But if the book is about knitting, I'm not sure how much sense it makes to talk about bankruptcy. That doesn't give the reader anything. In that case, it feels like emotional dumping for the author.

This being said, for a lot of authors, showing emotion—

especially in writing—is very hard. I can't tell you how many times we've worked with authors and they describe a horrific scene, some sort of major trauma, with total detachment.

Maybe they had a bankruptcy where they lost everything, or they had someone in their family die, or they lost a business to a cheating partner, and we'll hear them talk about this, and they'll just describe the facts. They won't talk about how they felt or how it affected them.

We'll push these authors to then talk about their feelings. When that happened, what did you feel? What was it like? How did it affect you? If you are going to tell stories like that, then you should absolutely talk about your emotions—to the extent that it is relevant.

In fact, for many authors, we have to first tell them that their story deeply impacts us before they give themselves permission to talk about their emotions and feelings.

And when you do that as an author, you give the reader the permission to feel that emotion and engage with that emotion. That is what you're trying to accomplish with your book.

You are not there as an author to just give the facts. Facts are great. Facts are important. Facts are the bedrock of your book, but people don't learn through facts, and people don't engage through facts.

People learn through story and example. They make decisions about how to change their life with emotion. And that's what you need to do to have a great book. It's got to have both of those things in it.

If you're unsure about this, answer these questions:

- What's your favorite book?
- What is your favorite part about your favorite book? What was the thing that impacted you the most?

Right now, you're probably thinking about a part that was a profound moment in the book and that elicited a deep emotion in you.

It wasn't a fact. It was a story or an anecdote or a scene that brought something up in you.

Do the same thing with your book. Tell stories and anecdotes that elicit emotion because that will draw the reader in and make the facts stick to their brain.

The more you show the ugly stuff, the more you say the things that everyone thinks and no one says, the more you show your true self and true thoughts, the better your book will be.

All of this being said, the book should never be a place for you to dump your emotions on the reader.

If writing the book is therapy for you, that's okay. But you should not ask the reader to be your therapist.

Think about it like any sort of sharing with a friend. If your friend has a bad day and tells you about it, you listen and empathize. Then if you had a bad day, you share that as well. You're sharing, you're empathizing with each other, that's okay, right?

But if you just talk about all of your problems, and then once they start talking, you get up and leave, that's not empathizing. That's dumping.

There is a big difference.

FIGURE OUT YOUR BOOK OBJECTIVES

"Focus on the target, and you'll hit it. This gets you the trophy. Focus on the trophy, and you'll miss the target. This gets you nothing."

—JEREMIE RUBY-STRAUSS

At Scribe, we start book positioning with objectives. Once you know what you to accomplish with your book, it ensures you focus on writing the correct book.

Three basic questions help our authors discern the proper objectives.

QUESTION #1: HOW DO YOU WANT YOUR BOOK TO SERVE YOUR READERS? WHAT WILL THEY GET OUT OF IT?

While your book can get you myriad benefits, *the content of the book is not for you; it's for the reader.*

Readers are the audience for the book, and they will support and share your book (which helps you) only once they've gotten real value from it.

We begin by having our authors identify how they see their book serving readers. Once you can pinpoint the benefit your readers will receive, you'll see how to connect their support to your goals.

QUESTION #2: LET'S DEFINE YOUR FUTURE SELF: IMAGINE IT'S A FEW YEARS AFTER YOUR BOOK HAS BEEN PUBLISHED. WHAT HAVE YOU ACCOMPLISHED BECAUSE OF THE BOOK THAT MADE THIS EFFORT WORTHWHILE?

There is an almost infinite array of benefits a book can get for an author, but most of those benefits fall into one of these six popular objectives:

1. Raise Visibility/Profile: Books can increase visibility in any number of ways, like making it easier to gain media exposure or raise your profile in your niche.
2. Increase Authority/Credibility: Books help an author establish authority and gain credibility within their field.
3. Get New Clients/Opportunities: Books can easily help generate new business and other opportunities across a variety of platforms and venues in multiple ways.
4. Speaking Engagements: A book is almost a necessity for becoming a paid speaker or often getting booked for any public speaking at all.

5. Leave a Legacy: A book can help establish a legacy and pass your story on to others.

6. Impact Others: This is somewhat covered by the first question, but you can put it here as well. For some authors, this is often the main benefit to them. They either do not care about what they'll get from their book, or they care about that only as a secondary benefit. Note that for any book to be effective, it has to impact others. It's just that some authors place a much higher emphasis on this than others.

Obviously, the details of each of these depend on your specific field and profession, but any of those objectives can be very realistic.

If you want to see more examples of exactly how a book can benefit an author, read the reference chapter "How to Make Money with Your Book."

WHAT ARE UNREALISTIC OBJECTIVES?

Of course, everyone secretly hopes their book will sell millions of copies and be a breakout success, but if you make that your objective, you are setting yourself up for failure. Those are not realistic goals. If you set realistic goals, you give your book a chance to actually succeed.

In fact, the most important thing you can do with this

question is kill your fantasies and set objectives that are achievable. These are unrealistic objectives:

- Sell a million copies the first year
- Be asked to do a TED talk
- Become a famous author
- Be a *New York Times* bestselling author
- Get on Oprah/Ellen
- Fill an ill-defined emotional void

I know these sound silly, but they are all common answers we get from authors.

Here's the thing about these objectives: they are not literally impossible. People have accomplished them all. We've had a few of our authors do them.

But they are exceedingly rare, and most books have no shot at these objectives.

If you want to really dive into more about this, read the reference chapter "Don't Write a Book If You Have These Four Unrealistic Expectations"

QUESTION #3: WHAT'S THE *SINGLE EVENT* THAT WILL HAPPEN BECAUSE OF THE BOOK THAT WILL CAUSE YOU TO SAY, "THIS WAS ALL WORTH IT!"? THE THING THAT WILL MAKE YOU "BREAK OUT THE CHAMPAGNE" AND CELEBRATE?

We ask this question to check on alignment. If your "champagne moment" doesn't match any of your stated objectives, then you need to really ask yourself why, and examine your alignment.

Good Examples:

"When I book my first speaking gig."

"When I get my first client from the book."

"When my book is finally published."

BAD EXAMPLES:

(Note: These are real things authors have said to us.)

"When I sell a million copies and get on every bestseller list and Malcolm Gladwell asks me to co-write his next book and Oprah wants me on her show."

"When I keynote TED and sell my company for a billion dollars."

"When my dad tells me he loves me."

DON'T WRITE A BOOK IF YOU HAVE THESE FOUR UNREALISTIC EXPECTATIONS

One of the most common problems we see from authors are unrealistic expectations about what a book will get them.

So many authors have fantasies in their head surrounding their book, and those fantasies lead them to make bad decisions about their book. A book is a wonderful thing and can help both you and your readers immensely, but it doesn't work well unless you have realistic expectations for what it can get you.

I'm going to walk you through the most common unrealistic expectations authors have, then explain realistic expectations for a nonfiction book.

UNREALISTIC EXPECTATION #1: "MY BOOK WILL SELL MILLIONS OF COPIES!"

The first fantasy that authors usually have is about book sales. Some authors truly think that their book will sell millions of copies.

This is deeply unrealistic. Let's look at some numbers.

- According to the best estimates, the average nonfiction book is now selling less than 250 copies per year and less than 2,000 copies over its lifetime.
- The competition for sales is fierce. Bowker estimates that in 2015, there were about one million new books published (that is total books, not just nonfiction).
- Other estimates put the number at about 500,000 books published—just in America.
- This is in addition to the 13 million-plus that are already in print (again, all types of books).
- There is large supply but not a big market. The total market of nonfiction book sales is only 256 million print copies sold in 2013 in America, and that includes all adult nonfiction categories combined. That's a little under one book per person sold in America.
- According to BookScan, only about 250 books per year reach 100,000 copies sold.
- The books that sell one million per year is even fewer, probably around twenty (and almost all of those are fiction).

- The list of books that have sold 10 million copies in history is so small there is a Wikipedia page about them.

The facts are clear: very, very few books sell a lot of copies. The reality is, if you sell even 10,000 copies of a nonfiction book, that is very good, and you should be very happy with that.

For most nonfiction authors, the return on time invested is horrendous if you measure it only in terms of the expected value of book sales. It's basically the same thing as saying that your retirement strategy is to "play the lottery." In fact, your odds of winning most lotteries are better than selling a million copies of your book.

What's worse, even if you sell a decent number of copies, you can't charge enough for books to generate good revenue. The highest you can charge for a book is usually about twenty-five dollars, give or take. Even the greatest book ever written, if priced higher than that, won't get picked up. People have a low limit on their perceived value of books.

There is only one group of people who must focus on how many copies they sell: professional writers (novelists, fiction writers, etc.). They need to worry about selling copies of books because *book sales are their main source for making money!* They don't have anything else to sell but a copy of the book.

But this isn't true for most authors.

REALISTIC EXPECTATION: "MY BOOK CAN MAKE ME MONEY IN MANY DIFFERENT WAYS."

The good news is that a book can make you money if you look at it from a different perspective. This is how most of our authors look at books:

> *A book is a multipurpose marketing tool with the special ability to create authority and visibility that authors can turn into profit.*

For entrepreneurs, consultants, professionals, and other business people, the book itself creates credibility and authority that is the means to selling other, larger opportunities that can be very profitable.

For example, if you're a consultant and have skill or knowledge that is very valuable to people, the best way to get more clients and charge them more money is by writing a book about what you know. This establishes you as an authority and gives you credibility, as well as giving you a consistent pipeline of people looking for the exact type of skill and experience you offer.

For example, you can also use a book to get clients or paid speaking gigs, promote your company, raise money for a fund, or launch a brand. There are dozens of examples of ways to use a book to make money here.

UNREALISTIC EXPECTATION #2: "MY BOOK WILL BE A *NEW YORK TIMES* BESTSELLER!"

The *New York Times* Best Seller list is the most prestigious list (though for dubious reasons). Generally speaking, you need to sell about 10,000 books the first week to be certain you will hit the list.

The thing most people don't understand is that the bestseller list is, plainly put, a racket. The only way to get on it is to have a traditionally published book, then either have a large preexisting audience to sell to (in order to organically sell that many copies), or do what most authors do and cheat by buying their own books through bookstores to make it look like their book is more popular than it is.

This is not impossible. It can and does happen. We've even had some authors we worked with do it. However, hitting the *New York Times* Best Seller list is expensive, time-consuming, and an immense amount of hard work.

Here's the worst part of hitting a bestseller list: it does not get you much.

Just like having the line "These pretzels are making me thirsty" in a small indie movie isn't going to make you famous, having a book that spends a week on the *New York Times* Best Seller list does not mean you're famous. It barely gets you any attention at all.

Here's a fun game that shows this:

- What are your three favorite books?
- Were any of those books bestsellers?

When I ask this to people, there's usually a stunned silence, and then the inevitable answer, "Wow. Yeah...I have no idea."

REALISTIC EXPECTATION: "A BOOK WILL GET ME AUTHORITY AND CREDIBILITY IN MY NICHE."

A lot of people like to say that "a book is the new business card." I disagree. You can go to Office Depot and get business cards.

You can't go to Office Depot and author a book.

What I like to say instead is that "a book is the new college degree." It used to be, about forty years ago, only about 15 percent of people had college degrees. If you had one, it was a major signal of credibility and authority. It meant something.

But now that more than 70 percent of people go to college,

a college degree doesn't signal credibility much anymore. Everyone has one.

But a book is a credential that is credible and meaningful. Why?

Because it is hard to write and publish a book—especially a good book.

It's easy to write a bad book. You can even pay someone to write an okay book for you.

But you can't fake your way into a good book. Either you know what you're talking about or you don't. Either your book is professional or it's not.

A book gives people the opportunity to see your knowledge and evaluate it. A book shows you can commit to something and follow through. It shows you get things done—things that are hard and prestigious and require a lot of skills.

Yes, asking to be judged based on your book is risky, but that's why you get so much credit for a good book. A book puts you in a place that most people are unwilling to go—being judged—and it usually requires a lot of work to do.

That's where the credibility and authority come from: the difficulty of pulling it off well.

UNREALISTIC EXPECTATION #3: "A BOOK WILL MAKE ME FAMOUS."

Lots of people want to be famous, and they think a book will accomplish that.

It won't.

First off, there are very few famous authors. Start naming famous authors, and you'll realize quickly that 80 percent or more of your list are dead (Hemingway, Twain, Lee, Tolkien, etc.).

The other people you name will be famous for something else, and you probably read their book because of their fame in another area.

Writers simply aren't celebrities in America anymore. In fact, it goes the other way around in most cases: people get famous for something else first, then they write a book that becomes a bestseller.

Being famous is usually *why their book sells*. They don't get famous from their book.

In fact, there are only about fifteen, maybe twenty, living people who are famous only for writing (and nothing else). Malcolm Gladwell is one. J. K. Rowling is another. You can probably name a couple more.

Not ten more. Definitely not twenty.

There are a lot of famous people in America, but virtually all of them got famous in some way other than writing books.

REALISTIC EXPECTATION: "A BOOK WILL RAISE MY VISIBILITY AND HELP ME GET MEDIA COVERAGE."

A book—by itself—will not make you famous. But this is not to say a book will not help you become more well known. It can and it will.

Think about it: when a media outlet wants a comment on something, who do they go to? The expert, right? And how do they know someone is an expert?

Because they wrote the book. Once you have a book, media coverage is ten times easier to get.

And it goes beyond books. "Has a new book" is a required box to tick for the gatekeepers who control access to areas of the arenas you most want to enter: lecture halls, television studios, podcasts, boardrooms, media pages, special events, people's minds.

Larry King doesn't say, "My next guest has just posted a cat video."

How many people in your field have you seen get a lot of attention simply because they wrote a book? Even if you knew more than they do, they got the attention that you didn't—only because of the book.

If you want media coverage and visibility in your field, being the authority and the expert is key. And if you want to build a big brand or platform, a book by itself won't get you there, but it is a big part of a larger campaign that most definitely will.

UNREALISTIC EXPECTATION #4: "THIS BOOK WILL TRANSFORM MY LIFE."

People have a lot of fantasies about what a book will do for them, and almost all of them are not going to happen. I think this is summed up perfectly by Hugh Macleod, the renowned cartoonist and author:

> A successful book agent I know tells me that at least half the people he meets who are writing their first book, are doing so not because they have anything particularly interesting to say, but because the idea of "the writer's life" appeals to them. Tweed jackets, smoking a pipe, sitting out in the gazebo and getting sloshed on Mint Juleps, pensively typing away at an old black Remington. Bantering wittily at all the right parties. Or whatever. Anybody who wants to write books for this reason deserves to suffer. And happily, many of them do.

Doesn't this seem like so many other things? We all say we want to be rich, lose weight, start a business, etc.

But it's *the idea* of being rich or skinny or an entrepreneur that's more appealing than actually putting in the work to do it. The idea sounds glamorous, and we want glamour.

Here's the thing: we don't get glamour by "living the writer's life" or by wearing the best gym clothes or by playing the "startup game."

Glamour is the result of hard work and doing something that other people find valuable. Notice what's missing when people say that?

Actual writing.

REALISTIC EXPECTATION: "THIS BOOK WILL OPEN DOORS AND CREATE NEW OPPORTUNITIES FOR ME."

One of the things we've seen consistently is that books provide authors all kinds of opportunities—both ones they anticipated and ones they did not.

The ones they did anticipate are great, but often it's the other that take them by surprise. Here's usually how this works.

The number one search engine is Google. Number two is YouTube. You know what number three is?

Amazon.

And even more relevant to entrepreneurs and business people, it's the number one search engine when looking for products and services (with 44 percent of searches for products and services starting there). This means it is literally the *largest search engine for professionals*.

Think about it. How many times have you had a problem and tried to solve it by finding a book about it?

Well, what if you were the person who wrote the book on how to solve that problem? Then you're going to get all those people coming to you.

That's how it works. *Having a book brings people to you.*

It lets them know exactly who you are and shows them how you can help them. It's the best marketing tool you could ever use—not just to build your brand, but to attract clients.

Let me give you a personal example: when we started our company, Scribe, we realized we had a rocket ship that we didn't know how to fly. We needed to learn how to scale our company.

What did I do? I went to Amazon to read books on the subject.

Turns out, there are not a lot of great books out there about how to professionally manage and scale a fast-growing company. The best I could find was written by Cameron Herold (it's called *Double Double*, and he has two more called *Meetings Suck* and *Vivid Vision*).

I read the book and thought, *This is genius. But I need more. I need this guy to coach me directly.*

I reached out to Cameron, and he now advises our company (and owns a piece of it). That's how valuable he's been.

It all came about because he had a really good book that led me to him. There are probably five hundred other people out there who could have taught me the same things, but Cameron is the only one that had a great book that I could read and use to determine that he was the guy to teach me.

I never would have listened to a sales pitch or paid attention to an ad. I had to see proof, and his book was it. It caused me to come to him.

The point is, a book is not something magical that will make you rich, famous, and important. But it can help you accomplish a lot of other goals, if you use it correctly.

This means writing a book that has knowledge that is valuable to a specific set of readers and delivering it in a way that serves them.

In fact, if you do that, you can get a lot of benefits and

maybe even make some money and be well known—at least in your niche.

WHY DO UNREALISTIC EXPECTATIONS HURT YOUR BOOK?

You might be wondering right now, "Well, what's wrong with dreaming about hitting it big? Some books sell millions of copies and become bestsellers. Why not hope for the best?"

There is nothing wrong with wanting your book to do well. The problem with turning an unrealistic expectation into a goal is that it impacts your decision-making about what book to write, and it usually gets you a worse book.

For example, if you decide you want to write your book to sell millions of copies, you will try to make it as wide and accessible a topic as possible. But that trades off with reaching a niche audience, which is the key to getting authority and credibility.

Or if you want to write a book to be famous, you'll worry about how the book makes you look instead of focusing on your audience, which is what makes a good book and gets you visibility.

Getting the most out of a book is very much like the zen koan about the target and the prize:

Focus on the target, and you'll hit it. This gets you the trophy. Focus on the trophy, and you'll miss the target. This gets you nothing.

Books work the same way. If you focus on your audience and what they need, you will write a great book, and that will get you all kinds of great results. But if you have unrealistic expectations, then you'll focus on those and get nothing.

HOW WRITING A BOOK CAN BUILD YOUR BRAND

Note: Since this is a reference chapter, it does cover a lot of the same ground as a previous chapter. Feel free to skim this if you think it is repetitive.

If you're trying to build your personal or professional brand, what's the best way to do that? Basically, how can you stand out?

There are a lot of ways to do that, but one of the very best is pretty old school: write a book.

How does writing a good book help build your brand and elevate your career?

There are six different ways a book can help you:

1. **Increase Visibility and Raise Profile:** Books can increase visibility in any number of ways, like making it easier to gain media exposure or raise your profile in your niche.
2. **Establish Authority and Credibility:** Books help you establish authority and gain credibility within their field.
3. **Get New Clients and Opportunities:** Books can easily help generate new business and other opportunities across a variety of platforms and venues in multiple ways.
4. **Speaking Invitations:** A book is almost a necessity for becoming a paid speaker, or often getting booked for any public speaking at all.
5. **Legacy:** A book can cement your legacy and pass your knowledge and your story on to others.
6. **Create Impact:** Probably the very best long-term way to build your brand is to actually impact others, and there is no better way to scale your impact than to write a great book that really helps other people.

Let's break down each of these and see exactly how they work.

1. A BOOK INCREASES YOUR VISIBILITY AND RAISES YOUR PROFILE

Whenever any media want a comment on something, who do they go to? The expert, right?

And how do they know someone is an expert?

The experts are the people who wrote the book on the subject.

A book is the number one signal of expertise. Media want to talk to experts, and they judge expertise by who wrote the book on the subject.

Could you use more visibility in your field and media coverage? Write a book that establishes you as an expert, and media coverage will be ten times easier to get.

This is EXACTLY how Jonathan Siegel's book got him so much coverage. He wrote a good book that detailed a lot of the fallacies of conventional wisdom in tech startups, and dozens of media outlets like *Inc.*, *Business Insider*, and others wanted to cover him. He was already an expert in his field, he just needed a book to be the book to get him coverage.

The same thing happened with Stephan Aarstol. He wrote a book about the innovative culture at his company that allowed them to work five-hour days, and the media could not get enough of him and his book. Now he's all over the media, with articles in *Inc.*, *Forbes*, *Entrepreneur*, *Fast Company*, CNN, CNBC, Fox News, and others. Everyone in his world knows who he is.

I know you know this. How many times have you seen someone in your field get a lot of attention simply because they wrote a book?

Even if you know more than they do, they got the attention that you didn't *because of their book.*

2. A BOOK ESTABLISHES YOUR AUTHORITY AND CREDIBILITY

A lot of people like to say that "a book is the new business card."

That's wrong. Everyone has a business card. You can go to Office Depot and get business cards.

But you can't go to Office Depot and author a book. What I like to say instead is **that a book is the new college degree.**

It used to be, about forty years ago, only about 10-15 percent of people had college degrees. If you had one, it was a major signal of credibility and authority. It meant something.

But now that everyone (more than 70 percent) goes to college, it doesn't signal as much. So what is a signal of credibility and authority now—one that's reliable and difficult and rare?

A book.

A book shows you can commit to something and follow through. It shows you gets things done.

And most importantly, it shows the world what you know. A

book sets you up to be judged by your actual knowledge and work. It's really easy to skirt by and still get a college degree. It's really hard to manipulate your way into a good book.

Yes, being judged is risky, but that's why a book is a valid credential: it IS a risk.

By writing a book, you are in a place that most people are unwilling to go—being judged—and it usually requires a lot of work to get there. It requires you to prove you actually know something.

This is exactly what Bob Glazer did with his book. He wrote about a hard subject that has a lot of baggage (affiliate marketing) but wrote in a very open and vulnerable way, and shared his knowledge about his industry. He got tons of credibility and authority from both the media and clients because of how good his book was, how much of his "secrets" he shared, and how honest he was.

Same with John Ruhlin. He is a gifting expert and shared all of his best secrets in his book. As a result, the book not only took off, but John now does more than twenty keynote speeches a year and has seen his company double in size.

Most people are NOT willing to take that risk. They're afraid of sharing their knowledge or showing the world what they know.

This is why we are very upfront with our authors: you can't just vomit out nonsense, call it a book, and reap the benefits.

To get credibility and authority from a book, you have to share valuable knowledge and ideas with your readers.

If you can do that, you will rocket past all your contemporaries who do not have a book, even if they are just as smart and accomplished as you are.

3. A BOOK GETS YOU NEW CLIENTS AND OPPORTUNITIES

The number one search engine is Google. YouTube is number two. You know what number three is?

Amazon.

Even more relevant, it's the number one search engine for professionals (ranking even higher than LinkedIn).

When people look for a credible expert or authority, what's the first thing they think about? Same as the media—*everyone wants the person who literally "wrote the book" on the topic.*

Having a great book lets people know exactly who you are and how you can help them, and it brings them right to you. It's the best marketing tool you could ever use—not just to build your brand, but to actually attract clients.

Here's a great example of how this works.

When we started Scribe, we got a lot of early traction and quickly realized we had a rocket ship we didn't know how to fly. So what did I do? I went to Amazon to read books on how to scale a company.

Turns out, there aren't a lot of great books out there about how to professionally manage and scale a fast-growing company. The best I could find was written by Cameron Herold. It's called *Double Double*. The title isn't so great, but the book itself is amazing. I read the book, and thought, *This is genius, but I need more. I need this guy to coach me directly.*

I reached out to Cameron, and he's now my executive coach and owns a piece of my company. That's how valuable he's been.

There are probably five hundred other people out there who could have taught me the same things, but Cameron is the only one that had a great book that I could use to determine that he was the guy to teach me. His book was the best sales pitch. I had to see proof of his knowledge, and his book was it. It caused me to come to him.

Search creates create inbound opportunities, but books also facilitate the best marketing there is: word of mouth.

When someone you trust tells you to use something, you

listen, and you use it. Anything that helps other people talk about you and your business is the best marketing tool possible.

A book enables word of mouth better than almost any other marketing.

This is because a book lets you put your story into people's mouths, so when they talk about you, they're literally just saying what you want them to say. If you have a good book, people repeat your terms, phrases, and ideas to other people.

If you can write a book that is valuable to a group of people, they will WANT to talk about your book at a cocktail party to someone else who shares that problem.

Why? Because it makes them look better. That's how word of mouth works.

There are so many great examples of this. Melissa Gonzalez's book, *The Pop-Up Paradigm* created a topline sales gain of 33 percent year over year, and Melissa estimates that 75 percent of her clients know about her book before they hire her, and over 30 percent have even read it.

Because of this, Melissa has reversed her sales process. Now clients come in wanting to pitch Melissa on working with them.

Author Douglas Brackmann has had a similar experience:

> Since publishing, my world has become a lot bigger really
> quickly. I'm reaching people who I didn't think I could reach,
> and that's allowed me to be much more selective about who I
> work with. Lately, I've actually slowed down on the speaking
> and media because I can't handle all the business. I don't
> know what to do with all the phone calls.

Same with financial planner Mark Baird, who explains the book-to-word-of-mouth referral chain very well:

> You speak, you talk about the book, you sell a few copies, and
> they refer you to more people. It's a referral chain, and it's
> been very gratifying. I don't think it would have happened
> without the book.

4. A BOOK HELPS YOU GET ON STAGES

If you want to do any sort of public speaking, especially paid speaking, a book is a near necessity.

This is because a book is a basic credential for a speaker. A book is the way people know for sure you are qualified to speak to their group on your topic. And then once you get on stage, your brand changes.

This is what happened to Robin Farmanfarmaian. After writing her book on disruption in the medical space, she was booked to speak at over fifty conferences, including Singularity and TEDx. Not only that, but all of that speaking exploded her brand and got her a new position at a medical startup:

> The very first company, Invicta Medical, I jumped off stage and walked right into the founder. He's seen me speak, and we got to talking, and I was an advisor within the first couple meetings and a vice president within a couple of months.

For Lorenzo Gomez, his book had a profound impact on him, mainly through his speaking. His book details the struggles he went through going from a high school graduate to major tech CEO, and he was asked to speak to all kinds of audiences, including keynoting the commencement of the University of Texas–San Antonio:

> If I had known someone would ask me to give a commencement speech, I would have never written a book in the first place. I was terrified, and I'm still terrified just thinking about it, but it was one of the most gratifying moments of my life.

5. A BOOK HELPS CEMENT YOUR LEGACY

All of these previous examples have something in common: by sharing the knowledge and experience of the author, they result in people seeing the author differently.

This is quite literally the definition of legacy.

Legacy is what you leave behind. It can be good, bad, or indifferent.

And there is no better way for you to really cement what your legacy is—at least in business—than by writing a book.

This is what happened for Kirk Drake. Kirk is the foremost marketing and business consultant for credit unions, and his book got him all the benefits stated above. But it also did one more thing: it cemented his place in his industry.

This picture was snapped at the biggest credit union function of the year, when someone asked Kirk to sign their book and take a picture with them.

Of course, Kirk does not have the type of fame or celebrity

that would get him in *People* or TMZ, but he has something that is more important to him: a legacy in the field that he dedicated his life to and wants to make better.

(By the way, this is precisely why a niche book is better than a broad book: it helps you focus. There are many "marketing experts" but no "credit union marketing experts," so Kirk was able to differentiate and brand himself quickly by dominating that single niche.)

The same is true for Shannon Miles. She cofounded the virtual assistant company Belay Solutions with her husband because she wanted to create another option for mothers and other types of women who wanted to have careers and work but wanted the flexibility to stay at home.

Her book *The Third Option* laid out her vision and helped define this role and space for women who want to take this "third option." Her legacy as a woman who has helped women find new ways to work is now secure.

6. A BOOK CREATES REAL IMPACT ON PEOPLE

Even though I put this last, for many authors, this is the most important thing: ***how does their book actually impact the reader and change their life?***

Look at some reviews from the books I've mentioned. From *Driven* by Douglas Brackmann:

Justin

⭐⭐⭐⭐⭐ **I highly recommend this book for anyone that has a desire to find more peace while fulfilling their potential!!!**
September 12, 2017
Format: Paperback | Verified Purchase

I've worked with Doug Brackmann personally...I showed up at his doorstep broken, living in fear, estranged in most of my relationships, with self destructing habits and unsatisfied with who I was and what my place was in the world. He may recall me "convulsing" in his chair as I felt weak and alone. The tools that DB gave me, all of which you will find in his book, allowed me to find inner peace and happiness and realize my true potential...I could recognize my soul again, lift myself up and design the life I had always dreamed of. DB helped me understand how my mind worked and helped me harness the Driven characteristics I had so that in less than 1 year I could build a 7 figure business with no outside help, find the girl of my dreams, and pursue a life of mastery in many different areas. I highly recommend this book for anyone that has a desire to find more peace while fulfilling their potential.

From *The Third Option* by Shannon Miles:

 Tandy S. Hogate

⭐⭐⭐⭐⭐ **If you work from home or are considering it (or if you would really like to) please do yourself a favor and read this ...**
April 27, 2018
Format: Kindle Edition

This book seriously rocked my world. As a long-time VA, I made the decision to work from home years ago. But I lacked the confidence and wisdom to be wise with my skills and my time.
Shannon spoke to my heart on several occasions in the book by building up and encouraging me as the reader to be confident in my value as a VA. If you work from home or are considering it (or if you would really like to) please do yourself a favor and read this book.
On my bookshelf of hundreds of books, this one is one of my favorites.

From *The Cilantro Diaries* by Lorenzo Gomez:

 Amazon Customer

⭐⭐⭐⭐⭐ **Wonderful Book!**
October 29, 2017
Format: Kindle Edition | Verified Purchase

I wish I had this book when I was younger! Most business development books begin with, 'After I graduated from Harvard..' This is the book for the rest of us. This book has actual useful advice that you can put into practice immediately. If I had this book earlier in life there is more than one situation that I would have handled better.

From *The Five-Hour Workday* by Stephan Aarstol:

 Wade Galt

⭐⭐⭐⭐⭐ **Start Living More and Working Less NOW**
August 3, 2017
Format: Kindle Edition | Verified Purchase

Already taken my daily work hours from 8 1/2 to 5 1/2 hours in 1 month... All while hosting summer play dates for my kids and their friends. Have been working a 4-day work week for a few years, but still more hours than I like. Thank you, Stephan, for reminding me how possible this is. This is why I became an entrepreneur.

From *The San Francisco Fallacy* by Jonathan Siegel:

 Charles Johnson

⭐⭐⭐⭐⭐ **Learn these fallacies and avoid them or suffer the consequences**
February 21, 2018
Format: Kindle Edition   Verified Purchase

This book blew me away – I've lived and worked in San Francisco's startup culture and the fallacies Jonathan warns us about are all too common in living in the tech world of SF.

The author's personal story is inspiring and may just give you the kick in the pants needed to keep going in your own life struggles, but its the fallacies and the solutions he offers to address (or prevent) them that make this book so valuable.

I personally know people who have failed business ventures that potentially would still be alive and thriving today had they read this book.

There are literally thousands of these. Reviews from real readers who were deeply impacted by books.

Remember: ***the very best books are win-win.***

When the author really works hard, puts their best knowledge and stories in their book, and commits to delivering real value to the reader, then both the reader and the author come out better off.

HOW A BOOK BUILDS YOUR BRAND

It all sums up to this:

> *A book is a multipurpose marketing tool with unique and special abilities to create attention for you that you use to build your brand and career in multiple ways.*

HOW TO MAKE MONEY WITH YOUR BOOK

One of the most common questions I get from potential authors who are about to write a book is something along the lines of:

> How do I use my book to make money? How can I make sure I get an ROI on my investment of time and money?

It's a reasonable question.

The bad news is you will probably not make (much) money by selling copies of your book.

The good news is there are so many other ways you can make money with a book—and usually a lot more money than you'd make by focusing on selling copies.

I'll run through the most common ways, with examples for each.

1. CONSULTING SERVICES

At Scribe, our largest client base is consultants. Once they reach a certain level of success, they can't really go much higher without a book. A book is what establishes a consultant as authoritative and raises their visibility about the competition.

Ashley Welch and Justin Jones were in this predicament. They had taken their sales consulting firm, Somersault Innovations, to a high level, but they were not standing out until they wrote their book. This got them a speaking slot at Dreamforce, where they signed AT&T as a client.

Kirk Drake owned a successful consulting firm that helped credit unions learn to market and sell better. He was doing fine, but it wasn't until his book came out that he was able to command high six-figure fees and sign the biggest credit unions in the industry.

Joe Mechlinkski used his two bestselling books *Grow Regardless* and *Shift the Work* to sign major Fortune 500 clients and was named the Ernst & Young Entrepreneur of the Year.

For a consultant, a book is the best marketing you can do.

2. PAID SPEAKING

One of the major ways to make money from a book is through speaking engagements.

It's challenging to become a professional paid speaker without a book. People have started speaking careers without books of course, but almost all professional speakers eventually write a book, and when they do, the fee they can command usually triples.

John Ruhlin is a terrific example. He was a successful corporate gifting expert but was only able to charge about $5K for an engagement. He published *Giftology* and now regularly books keynotes for $30K or more.

This is because a book is a credential for a speaker. It's a basic necessity. A book is the way people know for sure you are qualified to speak to their group on your topic.

Kevin Kruse is another great example. His blog *An Authorpreneur's First $100K* details how he made money in his first year as an author. While he did $70K in book sales, he made $170K in speaking fees.

3. PROFESSIONAL SERVICE (MEDICAL, FINANCIAL, ETC.)

One of the best ways to use a book is to establish your authority in your field of service and then use that authority to generate new clients.

The fact is, most people have no idea how to pick a doctor or a financial advisor or any other related professional service practice. They don't know anything about the skills necessary, what to look for, what to avoid, or how to think about the service. A book is a great way to establish your authority and show people what it would be like to work with you. Beyond that, it does a great job educating your clients on what they should expect, making your job easier.

Dr. Michael Lewis has a specialized practice centered around traumatic brain injury. His book *When Brains Collide* is a great introduction to traumatic brain injury and how to treat it, so much so that his practice has grown over 30 percent in size since the book came out.

Sam Marrella saw something very similar happen to his financial planning firm. After writing his book, he got a barrage of local media and speaking requests and saw his assets under management double. This is fairly common for financial planners, as there is always a need for good financial advice and services.

4. COACHING SERVICES

If you are a coach of any sort, chances are that people have problems differentiating between you and any other coach— what makes you the expert and why they should work with you.

A book is a great way both to display your expertise and to explain what your work with them would be like.

A great example of this is Ben Bergeron. He is one of the best CrossFit coaches in the country but was somewhat under the radar. So he wrote a book about coaching the top CrossFitters in the game, and now he has to has too many opportunities to keep track of.

This is not just true for athletic coaches. Take Cameron Herold for example. He's one of the most renowned CEO coaches in the world and has clients like the CEO of Sprint—and got there by putting everything he knew about scaling and running companies into four different books.

5. CLIENTS FOR YOUR AGENCY

Every agency owner knows what a pain client acquisition can be. A book doesn't magically solve this problem, but it does make it much easier to both find and close new clients.

Deb Gabor had this problem with her branding agency and used a book to not only solve that problem but to catapult her agency to the next level. She now works with companies like Dell, NBC, and Microsoft, and she credits her book as the reason her agency stood out from other agencies.

Melissa Gonzalez did the same thing for her design and pop-up retail agency. She put most of what she knew about pop-up retail in her book, and it doubled her business in two years. Plus, it was the reason she got hired by many major retailers. Macy's, Chanel, and Marc Jacobs have all worked with Melissa since her book came out.

6. SELL A PHYSICAL PRODUCT

Go search Amazon under books for "lose weight" or "eat paleo." You'll see thousands of books, and a lot of them are essentially buyer's guides for physical products like supplements, food companies, or one-off products.

Mark Sisson is one of the best in this space. He started Primal Blueprint and has published nearly a dozen books about his version of the paleo diet. They're great books. He sells them on Amazon and even gives many of them away on his site.

Not only do they help people eat right, but Mark also has a complete line of Primal Blueprint supplements and food that people can buy. They don't have to buy these products, but they're there and easy to purchase, and the books and products dovetail perfectly.

Think about it—would you respond to an ad about supplements? Probably not.

What about a book that teaches you what supplements to take, when, and why? If you trust the book, you'll trust the supplement recommendations.

Mark has great books on eating that you trust, which automatically give his supplement recommendations more credibility.

7. PAID COMMUNITY/MASTERMIND GROUPS

There are many people who have paid mastermind groups. Many of their clients want to join because they've written books that show everyone how much they know and what they can gain from joining their group.

James Maskell runs the Evolution of Medicine Summit and mastermind group, where tens of thousands of health professionals meet and discuss topics. His book *The Evolution of Medicine* has been a great way for him to find and recruit new members.

Ari Meisel runs the Less Doing mastermind group. Many of his clients find out about him and his group through his books.

8. FREELANCE CLIENTS

If you're a freelancer, writing a book is a no-brainer. In fact, the problem is that as soon as you do a book, you get so slammed with work you can't handle it all.

This is exactly what happened to David Kadavy. He wrote a book called *Design for Hackers*. He wrote it for a very niche audience, and it ended up crushing him. He was flooded with design work. He had to create an agency and hand everything off by hiring someone to run it for him (and he created a course that does very well too).

If you're a great freelancer, if you have a specific skill that you sell, writing a book that explains how you do it creates an almost uninterrupted supply of clients.

Think about it—if I'm looking for a freelancer, I have no idea how to pick one over the other, no idea what I'm supposed to look for or how to decide.

Why not pick the one who wrote the book?

9. WORKSHOPS AND GROUP TEACHING

In addition to speaking, many consultants and speakers also do "group workshops." A business brings them in to teach their method to employees and train them over a day or a series of days. It's quite easy to get relatively larger businesses to pay you to teach their employees what you know in a one-day workshop.

Most employers know that if they pass out a book, their employees aren't going to read it. However, if they get the author to come in, give a presentation, and answer questions for a day, they can teach the stuff.

Mona Patel wrote the book *Reframe* and now holds workshops based on applying the principles in her book. They routinely sell out, and both the book and the workshops reinforce each other. The book leads people to the workshop, and she sells copies of her book to people who come to the workshop.

10. RAISE MONEY FROM INVESTORS

It's hard to raise money for projects from investors. They are trusting you with their assets, so they want to know you and understand who you are and what you believe. Once they do, they're much more likely to want to give you their hard-earned cash.

For Jorge Newbery, this was a revelation. He was a successful real estate investor who'd fallen on hard times, then worked his way back to success, but he couldn't get investors to understand this. So he wrote a book about his journey, *Burn Zones*.

It was so successful that Jorge now has the problem of raising TOO MUCH money. That's a problem all entrepreneurs wish they had.

11. RECRUIT PEOPLE TO WORK FOR YOUR COMPANY

This only applies to business owners and high-level executives, but for them, there is almost no better way to get great people to work with you than by laying your vision for your company out in a book.

Stephan Aarstol used his book *The Five-Hour Workday* to lay out his vision of a different way for a company to work. His vision struck a chord, and as result, he was flooded with both attention for his company and product sales. But most importantly, he received a deluge of applications. Thousands of people rushed to apply to work with him.

Another great example of this is Jeff Kavanaugh's book *Consulting Essentials*. Jeff is a partner at Infosys, a large consulting firm, and an adjunct professor at the University of Texas, Dallas. He wrote this book to help his students understand what consultants did and how to do it, and it's had the unintended consequence of attracting hundreds of very qualified applicants to his firm.

12. PROMOTE "DONE FOR YOU" SERVICES

Bob Glazer has an amazing company that he!ps big brands use affiliate marketing, but this is really hard to message. So he put his ideas into a book. And in less than a year, he signed up dozens of major brands and grew his company to over one hundred employees.

The same thing happened with Phillip Stutts. He runs a marketing agency that helps politicians use digital marketing. He realized that his tactics work extremely well for businesses, so he wrote a book about how most marketing companies don't serve their clients and how a company can audit them to get better results. What happened? The corporate side of his business more than doubled in a year.

13. SELL A VIDEO COURSE/INFORMATION PRODUCT

If your book teaches something for which there is a high ROI for the reader, you can create what amounts to an advanced version that is delivered as a video course, charge much more money for it, then use the book to push people to that course.

One of the main benefits is that while people will not pay more than about $25 for a book, they will often pay $500 or more for a video course of the EXACT SAME material.

This is rational because many people learn more easily from video and audio materials than they do from books.

Josh Turner wrote a book called *Connect*, which hit the *Wall Street Journal* bestseller list. His book is about how to use LinkedIn to drive sales in your company, and the book, along with being very good, ends up driving many people to his advanced video course.

Jason Fladlien did the same thing. He has the very best video courses and online training in the world about webinars, and he used his book as a "top of funnel" lead gen to sell millions of dollars of his courses.

14. SELL A SOFTWARE/SAAS PRODUCT

A book is a great way for a company to sell software, especially SaaS software.

The best example is HubSpot, the company that invented inbound marketing. What did they do to promote it? Among other things, they wrote a book called *Inbound Marketing*.

The book minimally pitches HubSpot and is instead a massive advertisement for their method of marketing (inbound marketing) and guess what?

Using their software is the easiest way to actually do inbound marketing. Not only does the book provide real value to the reader, but it also ends up converting a lot of readers to customers.

Another example is Mark Organ. His company, Influitive, helps companies and brands harness the power of their fans to create new "advocate marketing" channels. The software they have created to facilitate this is very powerful, but it often takes a mental leap for people to understand how "advocate marketing" really works. Mark wrote his book *The Messenger Is The Message* to explain this, and he has seen incredible growth since its release.

15. CHANGE CAREERS

Even if you have no business of your own or entrepreneurial

aspirations, a book can help you substantially advance your career, either within your current company or by helping you switch careers entirely.

Simon Dudley did this with his book *The End of Certainty*.

He was a big influencer in the video teleconferencing space, but because of various technological changes, he didn't believe in the field anymore. He thought they were going to be disrupted and didn't think companies there would change.

He wanted to move out of video teleconferencing, so he wrote a book about his theories on technological change and how to adapt to it, never mentioning teleconferencing. That way, he could go to other businesses and pitch them, saying, "Listen, I know exactly how you're being disrupted. I can help you."

He created a firm called Excession Events, and now he's successful as a consultant on technological change. He essentially created a new career.

Here's the supreme irony: no one in the teleconferencing business listened to him before he wrote the book. Since he wrote it—and though he never mentioned teleconferencing in the book, the parallels were obvious—half of his consulting business is made up of the firms in the teleconferencing business that wouldn't hire him before.

Jeb White is doing the same thing. He was a very successful lawyer, but it no longer served him, and he wanted a new profession. So he wrote a book about something he did in his spare time: helping poor and underprivileged kids get into top schools.

Jeb's book has led to now earning six figures a year as a college consultant and enabled him to quit his job as a lawyer.

16. GET INVESTING OPPORTUNITIES AND BE ASKED TO JOIN BOARDS

Consider Cliff Lerner's book *Explosive Growth*. Cliff was one of the original growth hackers, having turned his tiny dating company into the fastest growing public company a decade ago.

He wanted to coach startups, but it wasn't until his book was released that people understood what a genius he was and how much he could help them.

So he wrote a book explaining how to do what he did. Next thing he knew, he was being asked to join the boards of companies and to angel invest in hot startups: exactly what he was interested in.

Nearly the same thing happened with Jonathan Siegel. He had started and sold almost a dozen software companies and was looking to get into investing. So he wrote a book about all the mistakes and bad information out there that was designed to help new founders.

Now, he has his pick of investments and companies to help.

17. PROMOTE A FACILITY OR CONFERENCE

The founders of the Kentucky Entrepreneur Hall of Fame wanted to get more attention for their cause, so they wrote *Unbridled Spirit*, a book about all the famous Kentuckians who started great companies.

It took off, and they doubled contributions and increased media attention nearly ten times, just as a result of the book.

Books are an underexploited marketing avenue for conferences. We helped a conference called the LDV Summit, which is about vision technology and pairs venture capitalists in that space with the inventors and thought leaders, to write a book about their conference.

Then, the conference host did two things:

The conference owner (Evan Nisselson) sent copies of the book to LPs or potential entrepreneurs, and he got all the benefits of writing a book without having to be the one who actually wrote it.

He included a copy of the book when he mailed out the physical applications for each year's conference. It has tripled his re-up rate.

By spending $5 to mail a nice book to past participants, he gets them to spend $500-plus on a conference that is more than six months away. Pretty good deal.

TED does this as well. They even have their own publishing imprint.

18. ATTRACT HIGH NET WORTH CLIENTS

If you are in the business of selling to high net worth people, you know how hard they can be to attract and sell to. Having a great book makes that job much easier.

An example is Alex Andrawes, a high-end wine broker who helps people invest in fine wines. He was successful before writing a book, but after he published his book on investing in fine wines, he doubled his inbound leads and tripled his highest net worth clients—in only a year.

Nik Tarascio owns an airplane brokerage business. There are very few people who can afford to buy an airplane, and he used his book to help him both attract and close numerous buyers.

19. TAXES AND WRITE-OFFS

This is a counterintuitive way to make money on your book that far too few business owners use—and you can use in addition to any of the above strategies.

If you are using your book as a legitimate marketing tool to promote a business, the out of pocket costs of production are 100 percent deductible. That means everything you spend money on that is part of creating the book can be deducted, like:

- book cover design
- layout design
- all printing costs
- editing and proofreading
- any professional services you use to help create it
- etc., etc., etc.

It's all 100 percent deductible as business marketing expenses. Just like you can deduct what you spend on Facebook ads and website designers, a book falls into the same category.

Note: I am talking about tax laws in America. Though this is what my CPA and many other tax lawyers have told me, you should never take legal advice from someone who does not know the laws of your specific jurisdiction. Not only that, I live in Texas. It's legal to shoot wild hogs with machine guns from helicopters here. We're different.

20. BOOK SALES

I said earlier that book sales are not the best way to make money. I never said you can't make ANY money from them.

Once you have a book that appeals to a specific crowd, there are lots of ways to help spur book sales:

1. Facebook ads can often convert into book sales.
2. With bundled promotions, you can give free things away to incentivize people to buy books.
3. You can sell live at events (where you are a speaker, for instance).
4. Guest posts that feature key lessons from the book can also draw book interest.

I'm not going to spend much time talking about how to directly implement these things because, quite honestly, it's not worth the time for most authors.

If you positioned your book properly, you don't need to worry about selling copies. You only need to worry about how the book converts to what really matters to you.

But hey, if people buy it, you have a marketing tool that makes you money. That is pretty great.

FIGURE OUT YOUR AUDIENCE

"The only way on earth to influence other people is to talk about what they want and show them how to get it."

—DALE CARNEGIE

You can absolutely write a book without caring who your audience is. But don't expect it to do well.

In fact, there's a name for a book that is written without an audience in mind. *It's called a diary.*

If you want your book to be successful and reach the objectives you set out for it, you need an audience, and you need to think about and define that audience beforehand.

Let's start with a definition of what an audience is for the purposes of a book.

An audience is a single group of people that share the specific problem your book solves.

Why does this matter? Because they key to writing a good book is actually narrowing your audience down as much as possible to only the people your book is intended to help.

AUDIENCE MISTAKES

Authors make three big mistakes when thinking about their audience.

MISTAKE #1: GOING BROAD INSTEAD OF NICHE

Some authors start by thinking their book can potentially reach everyone. They dream about the millions of people that "could possibly" find their book appealing.

Don't do that. There is literally no book ever written with an audience of *everyone*.

Not the Bible. Not the Koran. Not the Torah. Not *Fifty Shades* or *Harry Potter* or any other book.

If you think your book is for everyone, you are flat wrong.

In fact, even thinking that your book appeals to a wide audience is probably wrong. There are very few nonfiction books published each year that have an audience of more than even 100,000.

The fact is, the large majority of books are completely unappealing to most people.

And that's perfectly okay.

BETTER FRAME: THE RICHES ARE IN THE NICHES

Imagine you are searching for oil. Do you want to dig down one inch over a square mile? Or do you want to go down a mile into the earth? Which is going to strike oil?

Of course you go a mile deep and an inch wide with your digging.

A book gives you the same choice, and almost all authors are better off putting their book into the "inch wide, mile deep" category.

How does this make sense? Why go niche with your audience instead of broad?

First, it's very hard to write a book with wide appeal. Even professional writers who sell books for a living don't try to write overly broad books. They define a clear audience and then go after that audience.

The second reason is that attracting a wide audience doesn't help you. Getting your book in front of a very specific audience of people who want what you are selling is the only thing that does.

If you're like most nonfiction authors (and all of our clients), your goal is to use your book to help increase your authority, raise your visibility, drive new leads and clients, and possibly get you speaking engagements or other opportunities.

Your book is a marketing tool, not the product or service you care about selling.

You can absolutely appeal to multiple audiences, but generally speaking, the more audiences you try to reach, the worse your book will perform.

A focused book that appeals to a small audience is much more valuable than a broad subject book that is only marginally appealing to many audiences. This is because broad subjects, like general life advice, tend to not only be well-covered already, but also tend to not be very actionable for people.

Most people read nonfiction because they expect it to provide a positive impact or ROI in their lives. They know it's specifically for them and directly actionable for their lives.

Compare this to a book about a broad, general topic, like "how to be happy." You might think everyone cares about being happy, and that is true to some extent, but unless you are really knowledgeable and already an expert about this subject AND you have an angle that has never been explored, it will be very hard to convince people that your book about happiness—as opposed to the thousands already out there by experts—is the one to read.

MISTAKE #2: THE AUTHOR DOESN'T KNOW WHY THEIR AUDIENCE WILL CARE

Here's the most important thing you must remember about your book:

> *Your audience doesn't care about your book; they only care what your book GETS THEM.*

Readers won't care about your book if you cannot compellingly explain why it provides value to them.

Think about yourself when you decide whether or not to buy a book. Do you ever care about the author's goals as a reason for buying the book?

Of course not. You only buy a book if you think that *buying this book will help you.*

Well, that's precisely what your audience is going to do when they see your book on a shelf or on Amazon or on their friend's Facebook page. So you had better be able to answer that question.

Why does your book matter to them?

BETTER FRAME: IMAGINE TEACHING SOMEONE PAYING FOR YOUR HELP

If you aren't sure why your book matters to your audience, then chances are very high you have made your book about you and have not spent any time thinking about who would read it. It's a common mistake that many authors make.

So instead, get back to the roots of why this book matters to you, what we talked about in the introduction: how can your knowledge help alleviate the pain and suffering of someone else?

Picture the exact person who you can help most. What would you say to them? How would you teach them what you know? How would that help them? Where would they be after they learned what you know and applied it?

If you can picture that, then dialing in your audience should be fairly simple.

MISTAKE #3: MIXING UP PSYCHOGRAPHICS AND DEMOGRAPHICS

One of the common mistakes that authors make in targeting their audience is they focus too much on demographics and not enough on psychographics.

Demographics explain "who" your buyer is, while psychographics explain "why" they buy. To summarize:

Demographics = Who People Are

- Sex
- Age
- Race
- Marital status
- Social class
- Income

Example demographic information:

- Female
- Aged 45-65
- Married, with children
- Dealing with issues of weight gain, diabetes, lack of energy, or hormonal imbalance
- Household income $100K+

Psychographics = How People Think

- Emotions
- Values/beliefs
- Attitudes
- Interests
- Opinions
- Tribal/group affiliation

Example Psychographic Information:

- Concerned with health and appearance
- Wants a healthy lifestyle but doesn't have much time
- Enjoys going online in the evenings, big fan of Pinterest
- Tends to favor quality over economy
- Finds fulfillment in her career and family
- Values time with a small group of friends

Understanding the difference is important in modern marketing. The reality is that demographic data used to be all you needed to target and understand audiences because so much of the market fell into predictable patterns based on demographics.

Digital media has exploded consumer options and made demographics less predictive of human behavior. Now, psychographics work better.

The differences between how people think are now more important in (most) marketing than who they appear to be.

BETTER FRAME: USE PSYCHOGRAPHICS TO UNDERSTAND EXACTLY YOU ARE TARGETING AND WHY THEY CARE

When you focus more on psychographics, what you are doing is deeply focusing on the emotions and values and problems of the people you envision your book targeting.

Psychographics force you to understand your audience, to walk a mile in their shoes metaphorically.

The best authors use both to deeply understand who their audience is, what they want, and why, and once they understand that, they write a book for a small group of people.

This is true even if you want to write a big book that appeals to a bunch of people. To do that, you must start with a small, specific audience. Every book that sells lots of copies starts with Kevin Kelly's idea of "1,000 true fans," which is the microtribe that *believes* in the idea and champions it to others. That small group of people is the launching pad for all famous books.

This is why we always tell authors to focus on the microtribe *first*.

There's a famous concept in innovation called "crossing the chasm." It's where a product tilts into the mass market. It cannot cross the chasm unless you *start* with your microtribe of "innovators" and "early adopters."

The people who believe in your idea and spread it to others are all you should be concerned about at the beginning, because they are the ones who will push your idea into the mainstream. If you truly want to change the world and reach tons of people, this is how you do it.

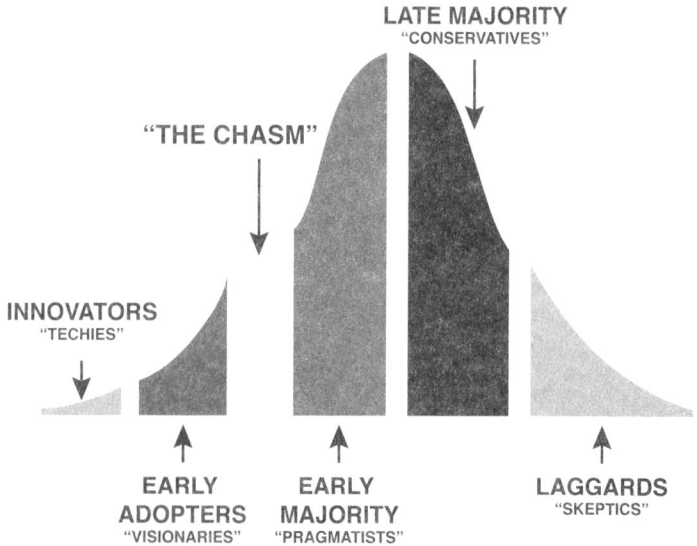

I'll give you two examples.

The first one is my own number one *New York Times* bestselling book, *I Hope They Serve Beer In Hell*. That book started as emails to my nine friends from law school. The first half of that book is literally cleaned up emails I sent to my friends. I only cared about making them laugh. It turned out that my friends represented a large group of people, and by making them laugh, I was able to make millions more laugh.

Or how about the Tim Ferriss story of how he launched 4HWW at SXSW. He didn't try to reach every white-collar worker sitting at home watching the news. He started with the tech crowd that would get super excited and actually implement his ideas. The ones who send hundreds of emails per day. They started using his email signature system he described in the book, and the book caught like wildfire. But he started with a *microtribe.*

And he did the same thing with defining his audience that we recommended above: define your primary audience as tightly as possible.

He false-started the 4HWW twice because he couldn't get the tone and voice right (and threw away many draft chapters). He finally decided to write it as an email to two twenty-nine-year-old friends of his—exactly the kind of people he thought would benefit from it. He actually opened an email and started typing the book to really hammer home that this book was aimed directly at that very explicit audience.

He believes the discipline of creating a super-specific avatar is what made the book so powerful. It made it authentic and legitimate.

Like I said above, many authors object to this idea, saying, "But I want to write a book for a broad audience."

Well, Tim goes on to explain, "The target is not the market."

It's a pithier way of explaining that you have to succeed with a core group before you have a chance at a larger audience. Before you can help them get clear on what they are doing and for whom.

This is why it's so important to not only nail your audience, but to make that audience very tight and specific.

HOW TO FIGURE OUT THE AUDIENCE
AUDIENCE QUESTION #1: WHO IS THE PRIMARY AUDIENCE?

We recommend starting with the smallest possible audience you must reach to make your book successful. For most authors, the smaller the better. Your total audience is a series of concentric circles. The primary audience is the bullseye.

When I say small and niche, I mean literally ask yourself, "Who makes up the smallest group of people that my book is specifically designed to reach and influence?"

By starting small, you can ensure that your book will definitely reach SOMEONE. This niche focus ensures that your audience will get excited about your ideas, they will implement your ideas, and they will share your ideas with their peers. Anyone who doesn't meet those criteria is not in your microtribe.

The audience you need to reach is directly tied to the results you want, and you can reverse engineer precisely who your audience is by understanding who *needs* to know about your book to make your results happen.

This process is no more complicated than asking yourself a very basic question:

> *"Who MUST know about my book in order for it to get the results I want?"*

For example, if your objective is to speak at a major oil and gas conference, then your audience is the people who book the speakers for that specific conference (and the attendees).

If your objective is to raise your authority in the CTO space to get clients for your CTO coaching business that caters to small-to-midsize companies, then chief technology officers from SMBs are your primary audience.

If you want to get visibility in your community to drive clients to your chiropractic practice, then your audience are the people in your community with the health problems that you can address.

Pretty simple.

Good examples:

- "Chiropractors who own their own practices, looking for better ways to market their business."
- "Accredited investors looking for how to get into wine as an investment."

- "Women executives, aged 30–45, who want to have kids but don't want to compromise their career."

Bad examples:

- "Women 20–70, suffering, that want to feel better."
- "Any executive who wants to be a better leader."
- "Young men and women looking for something more in life."

AUDIENCE QUESTION #2: WHO IS THE SECONDARY AUDIENCE?

Once you've identified your primary audience, you can then think about a larger secondary audience that your book *might* reach.

This is kind of like a "wish" audience. Identifying a secondary audience not only helps you focus on your niche audience; it also helps you see the path from small to larger for your book, and it will help you with the next exercise: identifying your ideal reader and envisioning how your book will help them.

Notice how the following examples relate to the previous primary audience examples, expanding out from the bullseye in a logical way.

Good examples:

- "Any medical practice owners who are looking for better ways to market their business."
- "High net worth individuals looking for a way to diversify their investments."
- "Any woman who wants to have kids and a career."

Bad examples:

- "Any women who want to feel better."
- "Anyone who wants to be a better leader."
- "Anyone who wants something more in life."

AUDIENCE QUESTION #3: WHO'S THE PERSON WHO MOST NEEDS TO READ YOUR BOOK? DESCRIBE THEM.

This should be a description of a specific person in your primary book audience. It can be a real person who is representative of your audience, or it can be a made-up composite of several people. It's essential that you describe a specific person, as it makes positioning your book more real. Don't describe a group or a type or a set of characteristics: create an individual with a name and a story.

This person is literally whom you are writing the book for. They are your perfect reader.

The point of creating an avatar is to set you up for the next two questions, which are about digging into your audience's pain and the benefits they will get from reading your book.

Clearly understanding both serves as a yardstick against which you can measure the value of your content when you begin writing.

If possible, pick someone who energizes you—either a real person or a composite of real people. Someone you really want to help, maybe someone who reminds you of yourself before you knew everything you know now (the "younger you" can be a great avatar). The more you envision a real person who you can help, the more excited you will be about writing this book for them.

Example:

> *Jenny works every single day as a consultant in her independent business. In between taking care of her children, she is taking care of her clients.*

> *She is staying up late at night to make sure the work gets done, waking up exhausted each morning and can't seem to increase her income no matter what she does.*

> *When something happens in the family, she is the only one holding it all together.*

> *She feels guilty because she loves her business and she loves her children and her husband, but two always seems to suffer when she spends time with the other. She feels like she not only can't get ahead, but she can't even get balanced.*

She's exhausted, she's frustrated, she's resentful, she's angry, and she feels guilty because she can't be present with her children and family, although that is WHY she decided to start her business to begin with.

AUDIENCE QUESTION #4: WHAT PAIN IS THIS PERSON EXPERIENCING BECAUSE THEY HAVE NOT READ YOUR BOOK?

This step is about expressing your avatar's pain. How are they suffering? What are they missing out on? What do they not have that they want? They are depressed and suffering—how, specifically, and why?

Your answer should only be about the problems they currently have, not the solutions. Your book is the cure, but we first have to know what ails them.

Example:

Nothing is working. Jenny is frustrated, physically tired, in the worst shape of life, and she avoids looking in the mirror and wears bigger clothes to avoid seeing this fact. Her marriage is crumbling, she hasn't had sex in months, and she feels unsupported, unseen, and unloved. Her children are acting out at school and home, which only adds to her physical toll and frustration/fear.

She feels like she is completely failing everyone around her and like they are failing her.

She's afraid to try something different because she is afraid of people not understanding, judging her, and abandoning her, which leaves her feeling more alone than she already feels now.

AUDIENCE QUESTION #5: WHAT BENEFIT WILL THIS PERSON GET FROM READING YOUR BOOK?

Once your avatar reads your book and implements your ideas, what happens? Do they only stop experiencing the pain described above, do they get more benefits, or both? What good things will happen as a result of reading your book and implementing your ideas?

Example:

Jenny will receive the tool kit to overcome her fears, frustration, guilt, shame, and anger.

She will understand who she is on genetic level, which will give her self-awareness, self-acceptance and then love of self.

She will understand how crucial her happiness is to the happiness of everyone around her and how her suffering contributes to the suffering of those around her.

She will understand how to center herself, how to make herself the priority, how to take care of herself physically, and why having amazing sex and allowing herself to be supported actually strengthens her relationships.

She will remove all resistance in her life. Everything will feel effortless and abundant most of the time.

And even in the moments it does not, she can look around and recognize how everything has brought her to this moment, and she'll know she can handle it—that she's never truly alone.

Most importantly, she will realize suffering does not equal love.

She will also understand her children and husband on a genetic level and help them do the same. She will love and accept them for exactly who they are, not who she thinks they can/should be, which releases the tyranny of expectation. This will allow her to build a partnership with her children and husband, and release herself from the pressure of PARENTING—which is true freedom as a mother.

REAL EXAMPLE

This is real audience targeting for an author of ours, Phillip Stutts, for his excellent book *Fire Them Now*:

1. Primary audience (microtribe you *must* reach):

Small to medium business owners (approximately $2 million to $100 million in revenue) or marketing leadership (directors, CMOs, etc.) in large organizations who are tired of paying out too much for bad results from conventional digital marketing agencies.

2. Secondary audience (group you'd like to reach):

Any leader who is unable (due to lack of skill, knowledge, or resources) but willing to innovate their marketing strategies in order to stay ahead of their competition.

3. Describe the avatar of your primary audience. Who is this person?

Harold is fifty years old and the CMO of his large regional insurance company. He has always relied on outsourcing his digital marketing and advertising because "This is how we've always done things."

4. Describe what pain this person is experiencing because they haven't read your book:

The agencies he's hired in the past consistently overcharged and underdelivered. Though this worked a decade ago, with competition increasing, it no longer cuts it. He has tried most of the agencies he can find, and they all do about the same. He wants to find an alternative but has no idea where to look. He's also heard much about AI and automation and the uncertainty about a changing agency landscape. Declining revenues are creating a significant amount of stress in his life.

5. Explain what benefit this person will get from reading your book:

After reading this book, he will know exactly how to evaluate and assess all the different digital agencies and options, and better understand and negotiate with them for their services. He will learn how to change, adapt, and innovate his marketing strategy by learning the right ways to invest in digital marketing, which will help him grow the other areas of his business as well. He will now also know of a new option where he can take his business: political digital agencies.

6. What do you want them to do after they read your book?

I want them to have the tools necessary to really look at the results their digital agencies are producing, critically examine them, and if they are lacking, know how to press them to get better results or, even better, come to my firm as a client.

See how this focuses completely on the reader, articulates a clear problem that pains them, and then directly connects it to how the book solves the problem?

After reading this, you know exactly who Phillip's book is for.

FIGURE OUT YOUR BOOK IDEA

"Explaining things that matter: Be simple. Simpler than that. Just say what happens. The part of reality that any given person needs to know is naturally riveting to them."

—ANNE HERBERT

Now it's time for the fun part: nailing down your book idea.

Book ideas often shift once the objectives and audience become clear, so we leave this task for the end of the positioning process. It's much easier now to get your idea right because you know exactly what you want to accomplish and what audience you must attract with your book to reach your objectives.

Before you write down your book idea, be sure to avoid the biggest mistake that authors make:

Don't write the book you think your audience should read. Instead, write the book your audience wants to read.

This is a subtle yet very important distinction. If you can answer the next two questions well, then it should be positioned properly.

BOOK IDEA #1: IN TWO HUNDRED WORDS OR LESS, DESCRIBE YOUR BOOK

Write a one-paragraph description of exactly what the book is about. DO NOT worry about writing the perfect description. Just get something down *in less than two hundred words* that answers these three questions:

1. What is the book about?
2. Who is the ideal reader for the book?
3. What will the ideal reader get?

You don't have to get it perfect at first; you just need to get something down that gets you pointed in the right direction. You will have plenty of time to polish rocks later, so to speak. For now, distill the book idea in two hundred words or, better yet, less. If you can't do it in two hundred words, you don't actually know what your book is about, who it's for, or why they will care.

If you are struggling with this, then think about your favorite book. Tell me in a few sentences what your favorite book is about. Okay, what would that description be for your book?

1. *This book will be an informative, easy-to-digest guide to hand safety in construction and manufacturing workplaces. The author will share what companies can do to educate their teams on hand safety and how to reduce hand injuries amongst their employees outside of just purchasing gloves. The author will explain the methodology and safety tips needed to prevent hand injuries before they happen and what to do if they do happen to prevent them from coming up again. He will include case studies, helpful tips, and practical applications that safety managers can use to prevent the majority of hand injuries in these companies, which is a huge risk each day.*

2. *Bob Glazer is the founder and managing director of Acceleration Partners, a company that was just named the number four best place to work in the United States by Glassdoor. He knows the importance of company culture and how very few people stay in the same job for their whole lives anymore. Several years ago, his company decided to make a radical move by eliminating the dreaded "two-week notice" problem. They decided that if upper management had an issue with a current employee or if a current employee had a problem with their role, it would become a discussion early on rather than waiting until it really became a problem or an employee decided to search elsewhere for work and give their two-week notice. This has completely shifted his company's culture and overall workplace happiness and results. This book will explain this concept of mindful transitions, how to rethink employee departures, and why you should eliminate the two-week notice. It will then* *give a blueprint for how to best follow this model for your own company.*

After you read the examples above, you could explain to someone else what the book is about, who it is for, and what they will get out of it.

EXAMPLE OF A POORLY WRITTEN BOOK IDEA

Jim Smith is known as the "deal maker of business." He got his start at the age of eighteen and hasn't stopped since. Now, with seven bestsellers and a reputation for his success as a digital nomad, Jim is looking to become a big deal with entrepreneurs.

In his book, Jim will reveal his country roots and his struggle with education as a high school student to set the stage for his readers to understand that the only thing holding them back is their mindset. Though he is known as a real estate success and has written extensively about cornering that market, this book will pull back the curtain to reveal that Jim's success isn't about real estate alone—it's about the self-awareness required to do well in all areas of life, not just business.

Jim will challenge his readers to give up their throne as the King of Dipshits, to surround themselves with people who challenge them, to identify and own the things they are not great at, and to stop working like $10/hour employees when they are running a million-dollar business. Most of all, Jim will use his experi-

*ences and his humor to bring fresh insight to entrepreneurs who
want a life like his but aren't sure how to get it.*

What's this book about? Who is it for? What will they get?
I couldn't say with confidence, and I doubt you can either.

BOOK IDEA QUESTION #2: WHAT'S THE "COCKTAIL PARTY PITCH" FOR THE BOOK?

This question is a check on your book idea. The goal is to
make sure it works well.

Picture your ideal reader in your head, the exact person
for whom you wrote your book. Now, imagine they're at
a cocktail party, drinking with friends. They mention the
topic that your book is about.

Another person perks up because they've read your book.
Now they are about to recommend that this person read your
book as well since it is on the exact topic they are talking about.

What do they say to recommend it?

This is the one-sentence explanation that *a real person would
actually say out loud* to describe your book to their friends,
not what you want them to say. That's the cocktail party
pitch.

This is NOT your book description. This is NOT ad copy.

This is about getting outside of yourself and describing your book in the way that a real person would.

EXAMPLES OF COCKTAIL PARTY PITCHES

Grain Brain

Good: "The book explains why bread is poisonous to humans and makes us fat, and then tells you what to eat instead."

Bad: "This book is a scientific, systematic, and detailed examination of the health problems caused by eating grains and grain-based foods, and a thorough, detailed plan for what foods best replace grain-based foods."

How to Trade Options

Good: "It tells you exactly how to easily trade options. I can barely add, and I got it. It's made me a bunch of money."

Bad: "The book explains why the simple options trading system is the greatest trading system there is and is proof that the author is a genius."

WHAT'S NEXT?

If you are ready to write your book description, do it now.

If you need more guidance, then read the next three reference sections, "How to Pick the Perfect Book Idea," "Don't Put Everything You Know in One Book," and "Advertorial vs. Editorial Content." They dive deeply into the book idea and will help you understand all the complexities of settling in your book idea.

"If a man writes clearly enough, anyone can see if he fakes.

Remember this too: all bad writers are in love with the epic."

—ERNEST HEMINGWAY

HOW TO PICK THE PERFECT BOOK IDEA

One of the most common questions I get from potential authors is:

> *"I know I want to write a book, but I'm having trouble settling on the exact subject matter. How do I narrow down and pick my book topic?"*

The truth is that there is no "one true method" for figuring out what your book should be about.

In this chapter, I will cover the three main approaches we use. These work very well, and in fact, you can use each one to examine your book idea from different angles, and ensure that it's the right book for you.

(Note that these three overlap a lot and can be used in conjunction. Do not see them as mutually exclusive but more as supporting each other.)

METHOD 1: THE SCRIBE METHOD

This is the exact three-step process we use with our authors.

1. OBJECTIVES: WHAT DO YOU WANT YOUR BOOK TO ACCOMPLISH?

The first question you have to ask yourself is: *what result must the book produce for it to be a success?*

This question can confuse a lot of people, so the way we frame it for our authors is to ask them this very specific question:

> *Imagine it's a year after your book has been published. What's happened over that period to make writing your book worth it to you?*

What this does is force you to think ahead and focus on objectives that are specific, measurable, realistic, and achievable.

Here are several popular (and reasonable) objectives that authors mention:

1. **Raise Visibility/Profile:** A book is fantastic at helping an author get more visibility in any number of ways, like making it easier to get media or other forms of attention.

2. **Increase Authority/Credibility:** A book is great at helping an author establish their authority and credibility in a field.

3. **Reach New Clients/Opportunities:** A book is very useful at helping generate all kinds of new business and opportunities, in multiple ways.

4. **Obtain Speaking Engagements:** A book is a necessity for becoming a paid speaker, or even getting booked for any speaking at all.

5. **Create a Legacy:** A book can help establish a legacy and pass your story on to others.

6. **Impact Readers' Lives:** Obviously a book can help people, and this is usually a primary goal of authors.

Of course, the details of each of these areas depend on your specific field and profession, but any of those can be very realistic objectives.

The goal you should probably stay away from is book sales. I'm serious. Selling lots of copies of your book is usually an unreasonable goal for authors.

In short, here's why: last year, there were almost **500,000 new books published** in America. BookScan, the company that measures all book sales, says that only about **200 books per year sell 100,000** copies or more. The number of books that sold **1 million copies last year is even fewer, probably close to ten** (and almost all of those were novels).

You *can* make a lot of money from a book, but that is done by using a book as a marketing tool. If you want to learn more about specific ways to use a book, I talk about several different ways to make money with a book here.

2. AUDIENCE: WHO MUST THE BOOK REACH?

Once you know what your objectives are, you need to get clear on precisely who the audience is that must be reached for your goal to be achieved. Here's an example.

Let's say your goal is to speak at human resources conferences. In that case, the audience your book must reach is the people who attend those human resources conferences and the people who book speakers for those conferences.

Or if you want to generate more business for your consulting firm that helps credit unions market their services, then you need to raise your visibility and authority with executives at credit unions.

This is pretty straightforward and simple: the audience is dictated by the objectives you select for your book.

3. IDEA: WHAT WILL YOU SAY, AND WHY WILL THE AUDIENCE CARE?

The final question is the key: *What is your book about, and why will your audience care?*

This should be a direct line from your audience. What they want to know about becomes the book subject. Here are some real-life examples.

Mark Laughlin wanted to help raise his visibility and establish his authority in the franchise coaching space, where he had a consulting practice. In order to do that, he needed to reach people who wanted to learn more about how to start and run a franchise, so he wrote the book *How to Succeed in Franchising* that explains exactly that.

Tyler Cauble wanted to establish his authority and generate leads for his commercial real estate business. In order to do that, he had to reach small business owners who were interested in finding and leasing space. He did that in a book called *Open for Business: The Insider's Guide to Leasing Commercial Real Estate* that reveals all the information small business owners need to understand commercial real estate.

Jonathan Siegel wanted to raise his visibility and profile in the tech and startup scene, get speaking gigs, and generate deal flow. To do that, he had to reach tech entrepreneurs and investors. He did that by writing *The San Francisco Fallacy: The Ten Fallacies That Make Founders Fail*, which recounts Jonathan's experiences building and selling a dozen software companies.

CHECK THE ANSWERS AGAINST EACH OTHER TO MAKE SURE THEY WORK

Once you answer the three questions, the key is to check each of the three against each other. If you don't have anything relevant to say to the audience you need to reach, then you need to reexamine your book objectives to reach an audience you can help.

Or if your objectives are so broad they require you to reach an audience that is not within your grasp, you need to narrow them down to something smaller so you can find an audience you can actually reach.

Everything ties in together.

Everything is connected.

The objectives lead to the audience.

The audience has their needs that must be met.

And if the book provides value to the audience, you'll reach the objectives you want to achieve.

It all ties together in a simple formula. If you follow it, you'll pick a book topic that provides value for both you and the audience.

METHOD 2: THE "TEACH THE PAIN YOU SOLVED" METHOD

This is a method that I've seen work really well for a lot of authors, especially for the types of authors we work with at Scribe (entrepreneurs, business owners, inventors, consultants, coaches, etc.). It's a deceptively simple process. This is how it works.

First, identify a problem you had—one that created real pain for you.

Second, describe the solution you came up with to solve that problem.

Third, ask yourself, "Is this a problem for other people, and if so, would they find my solution valuable?"

If the answer is, "Yes, there are people who would like that knowledge," then you probably have a good book idea in you.

I told you, really simple.

Let me give you some examples of how this works with real books.

USING YOUR PAIN TO HELP OTHERS

Driven by Dr. Douglas Brackmann is an excellent book that teaches driven people, specifically people with ADHD, how to master their gifts and get what they want from life.

Dr. Brackmann wrote this book because he grew up with the diagnosis of being ADHD and was told his whole life that he has a disability. He refused to see it that way. He spent his life seeking to understanding where ADHD comes from (it's actually genetic and serves an adaptive purpose) and how to utilize the energy and focus the condition creates to improve his life. He now spends all of his time training the highest performers—entrepreneurs, CEOs, pro athletes, inventors, and Navy SEALs—to learn how to perform even better using the techniques he had to learn to compensate for his ADHD.

He learned a new skill to solve his personal problem, built a business out of that, and then wrote a book to share this knowledge with others who were suffering from the same issues he was.

And if you look at the reviews, you can see the impact his book has made on people.

LEVERAGE TOOLS YOU'VE MADE FOR YOURSELF TO HELP OTHERS

Meetings Suck by Cameron Herold is the definitive text on how to run a business meeting. It quickly and succinctly explains every aspect of running a meeting, from setting an agenda to what to do if someone is late.

Herold became an expert at meetings because when he was busy growing three companies to over $100 million in revenue, no one in any of his companies knew how to run a meeting. As a result, huge amounts of time and money were wasted. It wasn't anyone's fault. There was no training, no resources, not even a pamphlet for people to refer to.

So he figured out best practices, taught his direct reports, and saw the productivity of his company explode.

This is basically what *Meetings Suck* is—the training manual he created to make the meetings at his companies enjoyable and effective.

PROBLEMS YOU SOLVED ARE VALUABLE TO OTHER PEOPLE

How to Run Away from Home: And Bring Your Family with You by Adam Dailey is about how, after he sold his company, Adam wanted to travel the world. The problem: he was married with four kids.

Impossible, right?

Nope. Adam and his wife became experts at traveling with children: knowing what airlines and hotels are best, learning how to find schools, navigating daycare and meals in strange places with six people, and creating the right mindset in your family for travel.

You see the pattern?

The author had a problem that created real pain for them.

They solved that problem in their lives.

They then shared their solution with other people through a book.

The reason this works so well is because it does two things:

1. It forces the author to ground themselves in reality and focus on something they actually did. It ensures they are offering real value to the reader because it's not theory; it's their actual solution to a real problem they had.
2. By focusing on a problem that other people also have, the author is making sure they have an audience ready for the book before they even write it.

METHOD 3: THE "COCKTAIL PARTY PITCH" METHOD

Even if you can come up with a book idea, a big fear many authors have is a very valid one:

Will anyone care about this book?

With over a decade of experience in writing and publishing books and working with authors, I've found one test that nearly always works to help authors answer this question.

I call it "the cocktail party pitch." It's very simple to do:

Picture your ideal reader in your head—the exact person your book was written for. Now, imagine they're at a cocktail party and they're talking about your book to their friends. What do they say?

This question works so well because it gets at the heart of the author's fear. If you can't imagine anyone talking about your book to their friends, that means it's not very useful to them, and the book might not be worth writing.

But if you can imagine your ideal reader talking about it to their friends in a *realistic and natural way*, then the book is probably a good idea.

The key to answering this question is self-awareness. Anyone can make up a silly story about how someone might recommend their book. That's unhelpful.

For this to work, you have to be honest about how people actually talk to their friends about recommendations.

There is a very specific pattern to how and why people recommend books to their friends. Generally speaking, people only recommend nonfiction books (or anything) for two reasons:

1. They took a lot of value from the book
2. Sharing the book makes them look good

For example, if a book helped them lose fifty pounds, they'll often recommend it to their friends because people will praise them for losing all that weight and sharing how they did this will raise their status among their friends.

If the book is about how to travel the world for $50 a day, they'll talk about it because it tells the world that they are travelers (which reinforces their identity) and makes them look good to their friends (who are probably also travelers).

In essence, they want to share books that will make them look smart, educated, and cutting edge to their friends.

This test goes both ways. It also helps you identify when your book might be something people do **not** want to share. People do not share things that:

1. Are hard to explain and make them feel stupid
2. Make them look bad to their friends

For example, if the book title is hard to pronounce or confusing, people won't say it out loud at a party because they will feel stupid for not knowing how to pronounce it.

If the book is something that is looked down on by their friends—for example, if they are into CrossFit and the book is on how lifting weights is bad for you—they probably won't admit to reading it, even if they really enjoyed it.

Even if the book is great, but the reader struggles to easily explain what it's about, they are less likely to recommend it or talk about it. Their inability to explain it easily will make them feel stupid.

If you can't imagine your ideal reader actually recommending your book to a similar reader at a cocktail party, then no, it's not a good book idea.

But if you can imagine that—by creating a plausible conversational scenario—then yes, that's a good book idea.

DON'T PUT EVERYTHING YOU KNOW IN ONE BOOK

Meatballs are delicious.

Ice cream is delicious.

But when you combine them into a "meatball sundae"... that's disgusting.

Even though they're great separately, they don't go together.

This is what many authors try to do with their book: create a meatball sundae. They do this by mashing several different distinct ideas into one book.

This never works.

First of all, it creates a bad reader experience. People read books in order to get expert knowledge that will help them solve a specific problem they have. No one reads books to get a firehose of unconnected information.

Second, having too many different angles and too much information in the book makes it harder to position and market. In fact, most positioning issues we see come from the fact that the author is trying to combine two or three different books into one and, thus, speak to multiple different audiences. This makes it almost impossible to have clear positioning.

Most authors try to combine everything they know into one book because they think they don't have enough information for one book. They're insecure about the book and try to compensate by cramming it with everything possible.

As I've said, that's the worst thing you can do. It results in a bloated, meandering mess that is hard to describe to people and has no natural audience.

AN EXAMPLE OF A MEATBALL SUNDAE

We worked with a pair of authors, Bryan and Shannon Miles, who together had built the most successful VA (virtual assistant) company in America (Belay Solutions) by connecting great VAs with a process that works at scale for companies and busy entrepreneurs. They also had built an incredible culture at Belay, being named the number one company culture in America by *Entrepreneur* magazine, and had also provided an incredible set of opportunities to mothers who wanted to work from home.

They were rightly proud of all three things and had a vision of a book that talked about how VA will change work, how to build a great VA culture, and how to use that culture to attract more women. They had a broad but very vague idea of how their book could talk about all three things.

This was not going to work. These are three different and very distinct ideas. We went around and around with them trying to find a positioning for one book about this, until I finally told them:

"I think you have at least two books here, maybe three. There is a book about how VAs will revolutionize work. There is a book about how to build an amazing company culture. And there is a book about how women can use VA work to change their lives.

They're all great books, but they are three different books, not one."

They agreed, and Bryan worked with us to write a book about how VAs will change the modern workforce, called *Virtual Culture*.

Shannon wrote her own book about women and VA work, *The Third Option*.

As an added benefit, by writing two books instead of one, they more than doubled the impact on their company.

Each book created a separate and distinct media campaign for their book. And each book served a different purpose. Bryan's book did a great job bringing them clients, and Shannon's book did an amazing job bringing them qualified VAs to serve those clients.

(Another important point that ties into positioning: they ended up deciding NOT to write the book on company culture and instead worked many of those ideas into Shannon's book. The reason for this is because we helped them see that doing a book on company culture would result in them getting a lot of speaking requests and consulting requests from people, which is actually something *they did not want*. They wanted to only focus on their business instead.)

HOW TO FOCUS ON ONE BOOK

If you're doing this in your positioning—combining two or three books into one—don't get down on yourself. It's very common.

In fact, it can often end up being a good thing (once you fix the positioning).

It's a good thing because it will both help you focus on finding the best book for you, and then it will help you see your next book(s).

The key here is to focus on your reader and how to best help them. If you're crystal clear about what reader your book will serve and how they will be served, then the ideal book idea to reach that audience should emerge. Once you have that, it's easy to see if other ideas fit or not and then finalize your book idea.

The reality is if you're an accomplished professional with deep experience in your field, you probably have multiple books in you. It's okay to have several books that are specific, focused, and deliver different things. In fact, that's preferable.

Almost every author we've worked with has more than one book in them, if they choose to write it. You can always write another book.

Don't try to put everything you know into the first one. Focus on what book makes sense for you first, then focus on how to make that book the best possible for the reader.

ADVERTORIAL VS. EDITORIAL CONTENT

Do you like when people blatantly try to sell you something? Especially when that's not what you want to hear about?

Of course not. *Everyone hates that.*

Yet, when it's time to write their book, so many authors will forget this universal truth and instead use their book to pitch their product or service.

This is obnoxious, annoying, and worst of all, it's ineffective.

No matter what your book is asking readers to do next—*especially* if you'd like them to buy your products or services—it's critical that the content of your book not only *doesn't* sell, but it educates and informs instead.

In book writing terms, this is called "editorial" rather than "advertorial" information.

Editorial content provides readers with information about a topic or explains something to them. It educates readers and provides them with value. Editorial content, at its core, is about *providing value to the reader*.

It is through editorial information that you share your expertise with readers and give your valuable information to them. You have given readers information they can put to use, which will earn their trust and, in turn, actually drive more sales to you than overt selling. It will do this by making you memorable and trustworthy.

Contrast this to advertorial content, which is an overt sales pitch. Rather than providing readers with the information they bought your book to acquire, you are telling them to buy. It's the worst way to accomplish your goal because readers will feel taken advantage of. They will not trust you. They will be pissed off, and you will look bad. Your readers will sniff out authenticity, just like you do when you read.

This is the key thing to remember: readers buy your book under the implicit contract that you will respect their decision and give them value for their investment of money and time. When you push something on them, they feel as though you've betrayed their trust.

If you do a great job in your book and provide knowledge and information that benefits the reader, you've accomplished your most important goal.

They'll respect you, and they will trust what you say. Some portion of them may come to you at some point in the future, whether it's to book you as a speaker, hire you as a consultant, or purchase your next book. They are also likely to recommend your book to other readers who will also be interested in your ideas.

The best way to accomplish this is by making your value clear to readers by providing information they can immediately put to use.

HOW MUCH DO YOU "GIVE AWAY" IN YOUR BOOK?

This is simple: put as much of your knowledge as you can in your book.

I say this again, without reservation: **put as much of your knowledge as you can in your book.**

The reasons for this are twofold:

1. If you actually care about serving your readers, this should be obvious. You are writing the book for them, and to serve them, you must actually give them all the knowledge you have.

2. But even better, giving them everything you have usually helps you reach your goals.

Just like the "advertorial vs. editorial" conversation, your book is about building trust with your reader. How can you do that if you don't show them what you know, and how it can help them?

This book that you're reading right now is a great example of what I'm talking about.

Scribe is a company that sells several different services to help people write books. However, at no point in this book have I pushed those services on you or even implied that you should buy them. In fact, I only even mention them in passing to set up stories that give examples to my teachings (like I am now).

To go even further, this book gives away every "secret" we have. You can follow the instructions in this book and accomplish everything that we do.

Why would we do that as a company? Why would we "give away" the process that we sell?

For several reasons:

1. **Authority:** If we are not willing to fully explain what we do, if we cannot show a reader what we know, why

would anyone trust or hire us? This book is the best possible proof that we are good at our jobs.

2. **Credibility:** If we were to try to sell you, it would greatly diminish the credibility of the book, the information in it, and ourselves. If you believe we're writing this only for our benefit, then you won't pay attention, and you won't find us or the information credible—nor should you.

3. **Reputation:** If we do, in fact, provide great information, then readers will respect us and speak highly of us. That is the type of word-of-mouth marketing that is incredibly effective and cannot be bought. It must be earned.

4. **Client Vetting:** Our services are expensive. Most people cannot afford them. Why sell to people who can't afford us? The type of people who hire us do so for two reasons: (1) we are experts who provide high-level book guidance (which this book helps to prove), and (2) they want to save time, and this book helps them see how time-consuming this process is and how valuable our services can be. For the type of people who hire us, this book sells us without ever trying to.

5. **Self-Respect:** We believe that everyone with knowledge to share should write a book. The mission of our company is to "unlock the world's wisdom." If we actually believe that, then how could we write a book that was anything less than everything someone needed to write a good book? To do that would be intellectually dishonest, and we could not live with ourselves if we did that.

I cannot tell you what to do with your book, but I will invite you to take a similar approach to your book. Put your best knowledge in your book, and do not try to sell people. Let them come to you because your knowledge is that useful to them.

Not only is it the ethical thing to do, but it's also the most effective.

THE NORTH STAR CHECK

This is what the entire book positioning has been working towards. This sentence should be able to sum up all the book and precisely how it will work.

This is the template:

> *"My book will attract [primary audience] by teaching them [insert primary audience benefits gained/problems solved], which will lead to my ultimate goal of more [desired result]."*

EXAMPLES OF GOOD NORTH STARS

My book will attract **people who lead sales teams** by teaching them **the neuroscience of how to effectively train and run a sales team**, which will lead to my ultimate goal of more **corporate sales consulting and training**.

My book will attract **HR managers from midsize businesses** by teaching them **how leveraging automation can revolutionize their experience with once repetitive and tiresome HR chores,** which will lead to my ultimate goal of **getting paid speaking and consulting engagements as an expert in the HR automation space.**

My book will attract **small market advertising professionals** by teaching them **five traits their brands can embody if they want to compete with (and beat) category giants,** which will lead to my ultimate goal of **gaining new clients for my advertising firm.**

I will use my book to target **mature startup founders** by **shifting their mindset from chasing VCs to building a revenue-focused business,** which will lead to my ultimate goal of **expanding my entrepreneur coaching programs across Canada and the US.**

If this sentence describes the book you want to write, then your positioning is good. Move to the next section.

If this sentence does not, then go back and work on your positioning until you get it right.

PART 3

OUTLINE YOUR BOOK

CREATE YOUR BOOK OUTLINE

"If you can't describe what you are doing as a process, you don't know what you're doing."

—W. EDWARDS DEMING

Your outline is the structure of your book and, thus, incredibly important. If you start writing without a structure, the process will take forever, and the product will be haphazard and incomplete. Worse, having no outline often leads to not finishing your book *at all*.

The outline is also your best defense against fear, anxiety, and writer's block. With good positioning and a good outline, the actual writing of the book becomes fairly easy. These two steps are where you think and plan; writing is where you execute. So focus, nail this, and you'll be more than halfway done with your book.

STEP 1: BRAINSTORM THE CHAPTERS FOR YOUR BOOK

The first step in brainstorming is to figure out the major points you want to discuss or teach in your book. Then, turn those points into chapters. While there are numerous ways to do this, here are the two frameworks that work best.

FRAMEWORK 1: WORKSHOP PRESENTATION

This framework works very well for people used to formally presenting their knowledge. Just imagine that you are giving a speech, presentation, or workshop over your material. What would be part 1? What would be part 2? How would you break up the days? Basically the structure of the workshop or presentation becomes the chapters of the book.

FRAMEWORK 2: TEACH YOUR BOOK

For this model, begin with your ideal reader, someone who is in your primary audience that you described in your positioning. Now, imagine teaching them everything in your book. What are the major lessons? What is step one? Step two? Write it all down.

If you get stuck in this model, your avatar is your motivator. Picture your ideal client, friend, or student in your mind: How would you explain your process to them? What would they get confused about? What points do they struggle with? What lessons have you conveyed to them? What did they find particularly helpful? What questions do they ask you? The beauty of "teaching your book" is that it's an excellent frame to articulate the knowledge you have that you may take for granted.

FRAMEWORK 3: WHAT NEEDS TO BE SAID?

Write down the main ideas, concepts, arguments, and principles that you want to make in your book. Don't get too granular. This is not about fleshing out every detail. This is about getting down the major points.

Warning on brainstorming: we've seen some authors start this and instead begin to write the book, producing pages and pages and getting frustrated. Don't go down that rabbit hole. Your list of key points and arguments shouldn't run longer than a couple of pages.

If you're writing more than that at this stage, you're getting in too deep too soon. Stay at the 30,000-foot level. Keep your descriptions to short phrases or single sentences so you're forced to stick to main points. Don't worry about capturing all the details that come to mind. You won't forget what you know. Instead, this is about clarifying what you know, down to the basics that you want to describe to your reader.

Whichever model you choose, understand that this part of the process can take some time, but do not get too bogged down in it. The point here is to find the major ideas and themes—the chapters. You can always come back and change things later if necessary.

Helpful Note: When you are brainstorming your chapters, have a section of your page called the "parking lot."

Put all of the good ideas you have that don't seem to fit into the parking lot. It's a place for you to keep those ideas without having to throw them away. This also helps you free your mind from any random ideas and keeps you focused on the main idea of your book, and gives you a place to put the seeds of your future books for later harvesting.

STEP 2: ORGANIZE INTO CHAPTERS

What is a chapter? It's basically a single cohesive idea, fully explored. Depending on how you organized our book, it can be a step in the process or one of several principles or anything like that.

Once you have what you think are your chapters, then write the thesis statement for each chapter. A thesis statement is a short summation of the main point you want to make in the chapter. DO NOT overwrite these. It should be one or two sentences. That's it.

What you'll often find at this stage is that you need additional clarity regarding what should go into the book. You may also find that you've repeated yourself. That's all fine. This is part of the outline creation process.

Keep working your list of chapters—adding, subtracting, moving—until you have the major points you want to explain, in the basic order you want to explain them.

Don't worry too much about the order at this point—they will change.

Also, don't spend too much time worrying about chapter titles. Just put something in. You can change it later.

TABLE OF CONTENTS EXAMPLE

How many chapters should there be? If there are at least five and no more than fifteen, that's normal.

If you have less than five or more than fifteen, that is not necessarily wrong, but it is very unusual. If you do that, you'd better have a good reason—one that makes a lot of sense to the reader.

STEP 3: FILL IN THE OUTLINE STRUCTURE

Using the Table of Contents you created, fill in the template for each chapter.

Below is the outline structure we recommend. It lays out the various elements you'll need for each chapter. Just fill in the information, which you will use as your guide to write the book.

Chapter X: [INSERT WORKING TITLE]
- Setup
  - This should be a personal story, a historical anecdote, a question to the reader, a shocking statement, or anything that draws the attention of the reader and sets up what is about to come in the chapter.
  - Do not be intimidated by this. All you really need to do here is tell a good short story or anecdote or introduce a fact that is engaging.
  - The best setups tend to be emotionally intense or some sort of mistake (which is usually emotionally intense).
  - The best way to start a setup is by "coming in late," as is said in screenwriting. Begin with a scene or a

quote or something that jumps right into the point you are making.

- Thesis of chapter
  - Once you have a setup, then you plainly state what will be taught/discussed in this chapter.
  - Essentially, you tell them what you're going to tell them.
  - This should be the same as the key takeaway in the Table of Contents.
- Supporting content
  - List all the key points/evidence for argument/factual content.
  - This is the bulk of the section. You can do this quickly and succinctly, but the outline of the chapter should be laid out fairly well.
  - Don't go too in-depth by writing every detail, but do be specific and thorough. You are creating an outline, after all. If you see you've written paragraphs, you're getting ahead of yourself.
  - Make sure these are ordered in a logical way so that they're building their point or argument like a pyramid, providing the basic foundational information first, then building up from there.
  - Make sure you look at this section from the vantage point of your reader, rather than your own. Your reader is not the expert, you are, so this section needs to be tailored to them.
- Stories
  - This is where you list the stories you think you want

to tell in this chapter. Effective stories are crucial to the success of a book. They are a great way to make the book and its specific takeaway points more memorable. Many readers forget facts after they read a book, but anecdotes and stories stay with them. They're often more "sticky."

- Make sure your stories are specific and highly relevant. You are not looking for a generic story in these points; rather, this should be a story that fits precisely here and demonstrates the message you want to convey.

- This does NOT mean that, in your book, you write your supporting evidence and THEN your stories. Of course you will integrate stories and supporting content.

- We recommend separating them in the outline, simply because it's not always clear which stories you want to use and where. Listing these separately allows you to figure this out as you go.

- Reader's key takeaway
  - This should be the summary at the end of the chapter. It clearly lays out what the reader needs to know from this chapter.
  - Essentially, you tell them what you just told them.

- Callback to/wrap-up of opening setup, plus a segue to the next chapter
  - This is an optional section, but most books benefit from tying the end of the chapter back to the setup and then giving some sort of segue to the next chapter.

EXAMPLES

CHAPTER 3: HOW CAN WE IMPROVE PUBLIC HEALTH?

1. Hook	American Public Health Association quote about public health.
2. Thesis of chapter	No other healthcare space can benefit more from the application of anthropology and design thinking than the public health sector.
3. Chapter content	The current problems within healthcare Why design thinking alone is not the solution (every patient requires their own individualized approach) What does educational assistance look like in public health? What we can learn from public health experts (What is their process, and what tools do they use?) How anthropology and design thinking come together to benefit public health
4. Key takeaway	While public health officials try to understand the problems patients are facing, they will always miss the mark as long as they fail to start by understanding the patient. This is why design thinking and anthropology are so important in the public health space.
5. Callback to hook	American Public Health Association quote about how public health can be addressed.
6. Segue to next chapter	The public health space is complicated. Understanding this, and that the space is further complicated by cultural barriers, enables to work harder to find solutions that fill these gaps.

CHAPTER 6: RECRUITERS WILL BE REPLACED BY TECHNOLOGY

1. Hook	Google search shows over one million articles about how technology is going to replace recruiters.
2. Thesis of chapter	AI will replace millions of jobs, but it will CREATE millions more. Technology will NOT replace recruiters. Rather, it will create more demand for recruiters with the RIGHT SKILLSETS, which is what this chapter is all about.
3. Chapter content	How to pump the brakes on automating a broken system until the underlying problems are fixed What readers need to consider in terms of their process before they go about implementing new technology How to develop the kind of skills that technology will never be able to replace
4. Key takeaway	Technology is only a tool. In and of itself, it can't fix a broken process.
5. Callback to hook	Despite all the discourse and panic, there will be great new opportunities for readers who make themselves invaluable and invincible.
6. Segue to next chapter	Now that you understand how technology will help recruiters, it's time to look at how to use technology properly.

OUTLINE THE INTRODUCTION

"Don't try to be original. Just try to be good. That sounds sort of naïve, but it's true."

—PAUL RAND

Most authors think the purpose of the introduction is to explain everything they will talk about in the book.

That is boring and wrong.

Just because someone is reading an introduction does not mean they are going to finish the book. The actual purpose of a good introduction is to ***engage the reader and get them to turn the page and start on the book.***

One thing to know about introductions: there is a formula to effective ones, and you should follow it. Even though it may not seem like there's a formula, there is one, and if you don't stick to it, then your readers will feel it and be upset, even if they don't know why.

You can be very creative within the boundaries of the formula, but follow the formula, and your introduction will work well.

WHAT AN INTRODUCTION SHOULD DO

- Get the reader immediately interested in the book
- Clearly layout the pain the reader is facing
- Paint a picture of a better future or a benefit the reader can get
- Outline briefly what the reader will learn in the book
- Explain why the author is the expert and authority on this subject
- Get the reader committed to reading the book

WHAT AN INTRODUCTION SHOULD NOT DO

- Be a summary of the book
- Try to tell the whole story of something that is already in the book
- Tell the author's whole life story
- Tediously explain exactly what is coming in the book
- Have a meandering story that the reader doesn't care about
- Have too much background

- Be too long
- Start at the beginning of the author's life
- Have too much autobiography
- Be entirely about the author and what they want to talk about

WHY TO WRITE YOUR INTRO LAST

Most authors find the introduction to be the hardest part of the book to write, and that's why we recommend authors outline it LAST.

WHY is it hardest and better when it's done last? I tell authors we outline the intro last because we want it to hit hard and entice, and it's easier to be more effective in that when we already have a specific understanding of the full scope and key messaging of the book.

You can't effectively tease something if you don't fully understand how it's going to play out in practice.

WHAT ARE THE PARTS OF AN INTRODUCTION?

A good introduction is like an interesting sales pitch, not a dry and boring informational piece. Introductions are built from these elements:

- Hook the reader
- Tell a story about the reader's current pain

- Tell a story about the reader's potential pleasure
- Tell them what they'll learn
- Describe the author's background/origin of book
- Set up the book with a call to action

INTRO PART 1: HOOK THE READER

An introduction has to hook the reader FAST. It should grab them by the lapels and force them to pay attention.

Here are examples of hooks. They start average and then get much better:

"Let's start with a question: why do certain groups perform better than other groups?"

"You've been told a lie."

"I got everything wrong for the first ten years of my professional career."

"I thought I was going to die."

"We shot dogs. Not by accident. We did it on purpose, and we called it Operation Scooby. I'm a dog person, so I thought a lot about that."

These all grab your attention. Even the ones that are not riveting, like the last one about dogs, are still engaging and make you take notice.

There is not a specific formula to figuring out your hook. These are the three questions we use to help determine what the hook is:

- What is the most interesting story or claim in the book?
- What sentence or fact makes people sit up and take notice?
- What is the intended audience going to care about the most or be most interested in or shocked by?

Some other things to think about when finding your hook:

- A great hook is counterintuitive, and it violates expectations or reverses them
- It's not going to be the first story you think of
- It's the story people always ask you about
- It is NEVER the story that makes you look the best

Often, the hook is an anecdote. One powerful way to write an anecdotal hook well is to use the "cinematic" technique: tell it as if you are describing a scene in a movie. At its core, the hook makes the reader sit up and take notice.

Though the first sentence must be effective, the rest of the page and initial story must do the same thing. Starting with an attention grabber—a short story, example, statistic, or historical context that introduces the subject in a way that is interesting and exciting—will engage the reader, compel them to read more, and lead them into the rest of the material.

INTRO PART 2: TELL STORIES ABOUT THE READER'S CURRENT PAIN

Once you have the reader's attention with the hook, the introduction next answers the implicit reader question: "Why do I care?"

Basically, what's the reason the reader went to the bookstore? What problem were they looking to solve?

This is NOT about giving the reader simple information. It's not enough to list nothing but boring facts and figures. No one pays attention to that.

People pay attention to stories, especially stories that resonate with their problems, pain, and conflicts. Once they are in touch with those pain points, then they want to hear about solutions that provide relief and pleasure, and maybe even take them somewhere new in their life.

This ties directly into the audience section you wrote in your positioning. You should know your reader's pain precisely because you've already told that story once, at least in the abstract. The story or stories in the introduction should dive deep and describe the massive pain the reader is suffering by not taking the advice or lessons in your book. Pain induces action.

INTRO PART 3: TELL STORIES ABOUT THE READER'S POTENTIAL PLEASURE

Once you've appealed to the reader's pain point, then you

should tell a story that describes the pleasure that comes from taking the action. Show them why the results are so amazing and that the goal is worth the pain.

Again, this ties into your positioning. You already have this story. You did it in your audience section. Dive deep into it and provide more specifics.

INTRO PART 4: TELL THEM WHAT THEY'LL LEARN

Once you've laid out the pain and pleasure stories, and the reader understands what's at stake for them by reading this book, then you need to explain exactly how you are going to help them solve their pain and get to their pleasure.

Make sure this is so clear and simple that even a seventh grader could understand. It should be as basic as, "I am going to show you precisely how to do this. I'll walk you through step by step until you have mastered everything necessary to get your results."

INTRO PART 5: DESCRIBE YOUR BACKGROUND/ORIGIN OF THE BOOK

Once you've hooked the reader, appealed to their pain, and shown them what they can have if they overcome it, now it's time to explain who you are, why you wrote the book, and why the reader should trust what you have to say. Essentially, you'll establish your authority and contextualize the book for them.

The best way to do this, again, is to tell a story. Why did you write this book? Why does this subject matter to you? How did you learn enough to be in a position to teach what you know to people? Why are you qualified, even uniquely qualified, to write this book? Why should the reader credit what you have to say?

This is where you can talk about your hero's journey story—what it took for you to get to this place—because this is where the reader is wondering why they should trust you. After all, if you are going to help them by teaching them so much, they need to know why they should listen to you.

But—and this is VERY important—remember that the reader doesn't care about you. They only care about you and your story insofar as it applies to the book and to your expertise. Do not give them an autobiography. Just enough about you to know that they should listen is all it takes.

INTRO PART 6: WHAT THE BOOK IS AND IS NOT

This is an optional part of the intro, but many authors like to put this in. By telling the reader what the book is and is not, it sets the right expectations in the beginning. You can do this very simply, mainly by stating what you will not be and the things they will not get out of it.

Underselling here, just a little, works great.

INTRO PART 7: SEGUE TO THE FIRST CHAPTER

Once you have done all of this, then all that is left is a simple transition to get the reader ready to dive in and start engaging the book.

I know this all seems like a lot, so here is an example intro to help you see how it ties together.

EXAMPLE INTRODUCTION OUTLINE

INTRODUCTION

1. Hook	"The doctors told me I was going to die. So did the nurses. In fact, everyone I talked to for the forty-one days I was in that hospital told me I would die. They were wrong. But it wasn't them or their care that saved me. It was an accident, caused when a tired janitor left his mop bucket in my room, that saved my life…and led to the breakthrough that has since saved millions of people."
2. The reader's problem	When the Cures Act was signed into law in 2016, pharmaceutical companies and healthcare product manufacturers were required to be more transparent so that more research outside of clinical trials was required. Suddenly, companies *had* to increase their understanding of patients. But these were only baby steps in understanding the depth of patients and their stories, and how their stories impact their healthcare. Healthcare products, devices, and drugs—healthcare solutions—impact patients and their families in a much more extensive way than healthcare professionals realize. They can make a difference in the quality of care for millions just by understanding how anthropology and design thinking work together to create patient centricity in healthcare.

3. The reader's solution	Author will explain how the tenets of anthropology and design thinking work together in a healthcare marketing environment to benefit patients, their loved ones, and the healthcare product manufacturers involved.
4. What they'll learn	Readers will learn how to design marketing messages and products that are grounded in patient education—solutions that support these patients in their daily lives as they tackle their healthcare challenges. Readers will become aware of the value of patient understanding and empowerment in healthcare marketing.
5. Author's background/ book origin	After a horrible hospital stay riddled with bad care, the author started his company to address this human angle of healthcare that he found lacking in the product marketing side of the system. He felt that no one else was using anthropology, then design thinking, in the manufacture of healthcare solutions. He wanted to start with the patient to first understand them and their situation before creating the educational or marketing tools that would benefit the type of care they receive.
6. What the book *is* and *isn't*	This book is presenting a new paradigm for healthcare marketers and product designers. However, it is not just a theoretical presentation. Readers will learn how they can improve their business and the quality of healthcare with a more ethical, successful, patient-driven (and patient-centered) approach.
7. Segue to first chapter	Getting to know people—the humans beneath the patient—is the first step in quality healthcare.

OUTLINE THE CONCLUSION

"Think like a wise man, but communicate in the language of the people."

—WILLIAM BUTLER YEATS

Your conclusion helps tie everything together, neatly summarizes your book, and then provides a specific call or calls to action.

WHAT A CONCLUSION SHOULD DO

1. A conclusion should clearly summarize the book. That's the best thing you can do, not only to deliver value to the reader, but also to make the book memorable (and recommendable).
2. A conclusion should address any lingering issues and close any open loops. The reader should feel like everything is wrapped up in a bow.

3. A conclusion should have a call to action of some sort. In essence, tell the reader what to do.
4. A conclusion should point them to any additional resources you have for them that could help them.

WHAT A CONCLUSION SHOULD NOT DO

1. A conclusion should NOT introduce any new content. This should only be summarization of what is in the book. You can have new stories or anecdotes, of course.
2. A conclusion should not be too long. The rule of thumb is that it should be the shortest chapter in your book.
3. A conclusion should not break faith with the reader. Don't tell them "operators are standing by" or try to sell them in a preposterous way that turns them off.

CONCLUSION TEMPLATE

We like to outline the conclusion with this template:

- Hook
  - An anecdote or story that wraps up the book should lead.
  - By this time, you've mentioned a lot of different topics. The easiest and most compelling way to begin the conclusion is by referring back to one of them.
  - Consider adding another dimension to a story you already told or tying up loose ends.

- The hook in a conclusion is one that looks to the future, whereas the hook in intro looks to the past, how we got here.
- Restate the book's mission/thesis
- Tie together each chapter's takeaway with the overarching theme of the book
  - Summarize the key points so succinctly and clearly that the reader can't help but understand your lessons the same way that you do.
  - You want the reader to think about and talk about your book to their friends the same way you do.
  - Specifically, this is about nailing what it is you want them to remember about your book.
- Call to action: What should the reader do when they finish the book?
  - When they finish the last word and put the book down, what is the first thing you want your reader to do?

NOTE ON THE CALL TO ACTION

A call to action (CTA) is not required in all conclusions, but most nonfiction books have them. It's usually the very last bit of the conclusion, the final word to readers, and it ensures they know what you want them to do.

Authors generally adopt a different tone with the CTA—one that's not just more explicitly inspirational but is also framed as an imperative. The underlying message of the call to action is straightforward and empowering: *now that you have all the tools, go out there and use them.*

Some authors feel uncomfortable including such a direct appeal to readers because they may feel it's unprofessional, and they can be right (sometimes).

Authors often want to pitch too much in the introduction and not enough in the conclusion. This is when you can really tell your reader what to do.

Yes, CTAs *can* be written in an unprofessional way, but they don't have to be. You can make your point without your CTA feeling like a pep rally.

What you ***do not want to do*** is write a glorified sales brochure.

Readers are smart. They're interested in your topic because they've picked up your book, and they've already read pages of your knowledge and expertise. They can form their own conclusions when it comes to contacting you.

If you want to ask them to contact you, though, do so authentically—from a place of trying to help them, not yourself. Tell them you want to hear from them or to assist them moving forward. If your website or the name of your firm is in your bio or "About the Author" page, that's sufficient. Give them your email in the conclusion if you like.

Ultimately, your goal is to provide so much value to them that they respect and admire you and your work, and choose to contact you because they have sold themselves, not because you sold them.

Some authors want a more explicit CTA, such as directing readers of the book to a specific landing page. This can work, as long as the page you are directing them to gives the reader something.

Bear in mind the first point: don't break faith with the reader, because that will cost you the reader's respect.

PART 4

WRITE YOUR BOOK

HOW TO CREATE YOUR BOOK WRITING PLAN

"If you want to get something done, decide when and where you're going to do it. Otherwise, take it off your list."

—PETER BREGMAN

It took me three years as a professional writer before I understood that I needed a writing plan for every book I wrote. Writing without a plan is like going cross country without a map. Yeah, you might get there, but it'll take you at least twice as long.

WHY SHOULD YOU HAVE A WRITING PLAN?

Shouldn't you just get inspired to write? If you wait until inspiration strikes and then use that as fuel to write, you'll be good, right?

No.

If you rely on inspiration to write your book, **you will fail.**

There is one single thing that creates success with writing, and every single writer will tell you this:

Discipline.

You must sit your ass in the chair and write, just about every day, until the book is done.

That is why you need a writing plan. Because it defines exactly what you will do to finish your book.

Inspiration might be how you decide to start the book—and that's fine—but discipline is how you'll finish.

WHAT IS A WRITING PLAN?

A writing plan is nothing more than a specific plan that lays out exactly when and where you're going to write each day, how much you will write, when everything is due, and what your accountability is.

HOW TO CREATE YOUR WRITING PLAN
STEP 1: SCHEDULE A TIME AND PLACE TO WRITE

You must start by picking the exact time and place you will write each day. For example, you could write every day from

8 a.m. to 10 a.m. in your home office. Or from 3 p.m. to 4:30 p.m. at Compass Coffee.

This is not negotiable. If you tell yourself that you'll "write when you have time," then the book won't ever get done. If you don't think about the environment where you will do your writing, you won't make effective use of that time you've set aside.

With both of these elements, you want to be as specific as possible. The more you plan now, the less you have to think later.

If the book matters, then you figure out precisely when and where you will write it.

How Much Time Should You Write Each Day?

We recommend writing for at least one hour per day. If you only have thirty minutes per day to write, then do that. The optimal amount of time is two hours, but very few people can set aside that much time.

Also, be realistic. Most authors cannot write (effectively) for more than three hours a day.

What Time of Day Should You Write?

The data is very clear: most people are the most creative

about an hour after they wake up, until about four hours after they wake up. That means you're probably most creative in the morning.

But outliers DO exist, and so do night owls. If you are one of those, honor it.

All that matters is consistency and action. Make writing a routine that works for you, and you'll do it.

How Consistently Should You Write?

If you can, write every day. Even if you only get through a half page per day, you're that much closer to a finished book.

If seven days a week is too much, then take one day off and write for six. God rested on the seventh day—so can you.

The key thing to remember with a book is that *you don't stay where you are with a book; you either move forward or you move backward.*

Momentum is a key element in seeing a book through from beginning to end. You will make that decision each and every day for the duration of the book-writing process. Your plan will help you stay accountable so you continue moving in the right direction.

How Do You Pick Your Writing Location?

It's very simple to pick where you should write: *where you get writing done.*

These are the general factors people consider when writing: ambient noise, temperature, view, comfort, and isolation. A universal "correct" place to write doesn't exist. If you write well in coffee shops, do that. If you write well at a desk in your basement, do that. Wherever you are most creative, most functional, and most confident, write there.

Don't waste time trying to find the "perfect place" to write or a perfect tool or the perfect desk. They don't exist.

People who get stuck on finding the perfect spot or the perfect inspiration to write are looking for a way to avoid the work. This unrecognized fear will cause them to wait for the perfect environment, but that perfect environment doesn't exist. Even when accounting for someone's personal preferences, if they think they've found the "perfect" writing place, that's just the place where they allow themselves to look past the distractions that exist everywhere (unless they write in a sensory deprivation tank).

Focusing on the distractions is resistance—a way for people to avoid the hard work of actual writing. Every minute you spend trying to find the perfect anything is a minute you are stealing from your writing.

Find the place and setting that works for you and then recreate that each day. If your initial location stops working for you after a while, acknowledge that, figure out what you need to change, and identify a new location.

STEP 2: SET SPECIFIC WRITING GOALS

In addition to scheduling the time and place of each writing session, also give yourself a specific writing goal for each session. We recommend a goal of 250 words per hour of writing.

Why 250 words? It's approximately the number of words per page in a printed book.

So if you're writing about 250 words a day, that's about a page a day.

Yes, this is a very low goal. But a low goal is good. A low goal is not intimidating, so it will help you get started. It will also make you feel good when you surpass it and entice you to keep writing.

This is a classic sales technique—lowering the quota to inspire action—that works wonderfully with writing.

The best part is that it adds up quickly:

> *By writing just 250 words a day, you can get a 120-page (30,000-word) first draft done in about four months.*

That is fast, and you'll do it with what feels like very little effort. As you can see, it's all about consistency.

STEP 3: BUILD DEADLINES

Deadlines force action and demand accountability. Below is a rough outline of how to pace yourself. You can adjust it to your schedule.

Book Writing

If you want to move fast, give yourself a deadline of about a chapter a week.

If you want to move at a reasonable speed, give yourself two weeks per chapter.

If you want to move slower, allow three weeks.

If you have a hectic life, do a chapter per month.

Book Editing

Once you finish your rough draft, schedule sixty days for editing. This gives you enough time to do your edits, but not so much time you will take forever.

Step 4: Announce the Book

To take accountability one step further: *announce that you are working on a book.*

Use whatever social media platform you prefer, but the point is to publicly claim your intention to people you care about.

You'll get a lot of positive feedback, which will help you start, and the fact that you have announced your intention will help you push through when you are wavering.

NOTE: If you're serious about writing this book, the platform you're most uncomfortable about putting it on is the one you should use. That means it's the one with the most people on it that you care about. If you are afraid of telling them, it's all the more reason to do it. Remember, we want to identify any and all resistance and push through it.

NOTE: FOCUS ON WHAT WORKS

What I just laid out for you is a tested, proven method. It will work.

That doesn't make it the "right" method. *There is no "right" method.*

The only "right" method of writing is the one that works for you.

For example, we have one author who can only write by sitting in his Tesla while it is charging in his garage, putting a specific playlist on his phone, plugging in earbuds, and turning up the volume. He knows he has forty-five minutes of charge time to get his work done, and he makes the most of that window.

There is only the method that WORKS for you. ALWAYS feel free to use what works. So, if any part of this feels off, substitute what makes more sense for you.

That being said—unless you KNOW you have a method that works better for you—assume what I'm telling you is the best way to do it. Our writing plan is based both on decades of experience with actual authors and on the best empirical data about how authors succeed.

"You can't wait for inspiration. You have to go after it with a club."

—JACK LONDON

HOW TO WRITE YOUR ROUGH DRAFT USING THE SCRIBE METHOD

"You must understand that there is more than one path to the top of the mountain."

—MIYAMOTO MUSASHI

For most people, writing is both intimidating and the most difficult method. I'll tell you everything, but this is hard, so I would not recommend this technique unless it really appeals to you.

THE SCRIBE METHOD

The idea behind the Scribe Method is very simple: instead of facing a blank page and typing your first draft, you get your first draft down by speaking it out loud. You record yourself, then get the recording transcribed. You then edit that transcript into the first draft.

This will not get you to a final draft, but it substantially accelerates the writing process.

This method is an updated version of the old way books used to be written: they were dictated to professional scribes.

If you know you want to do it this way, skip down to "How to Use the Scribe Method."

If you still aren't sure and need some convincing, read the next section.

WHY DO IT THIS WAY?

Writing is challenging for most people. Why?

It's not because they are stupid or lazy or unskilled. It's because writing requires deep, specialized skill. The writing skill is a totally different skill from having intelligence, wisdom, experience, or knowledge to share.

Think about it. How many intelligent and accomplished people do you know who have all kinds of things to say but hate writing?

Quite a few, I am sure (you might even be one).

The inverse is true, as well. How many skilled and experienced writers have you read who use lots of beautiful words to effectively say nothing? Sadly, that might describe the majority of professional writers.

Writing is a specific cognitive skill that is totally distinct from thinking and acquiring wisdom. Just like the ability to do math in your head is a skill distinct from being a good mathematician (Richard Feynman, the brilliant quantum physicist, often used calculators) or the ability to read sheet music is not a necessary skill to be a great musician (Jimi Hendrix, the legendary guitarist and performer, couldn't read sheet music), writing has nothing to do with anything other than the ability to write.

This begs the question: *is the skill of writing really a necessary part of sharing knowledge and ideas?*

After all, if the ultimate goal of a book is to share your knowledge and ideas with the world, is there another way to record this wisdom without having to physically write it down yourself?

Of course there's another way to share knowledge and wisdom: by talking.

Talking is the most natural way to communicate ideas and information between humans.

We've been talking for at least 150,000 years, but we've only been writing for about 10,000 of those.

Think about people with dyslexia. Some of the smartest, most accomplished people on earth—Richard Branson, for example—can barely write an email. Branson is not stupid, nor is anyone else just because they have dyslexia. Those with severe dyslexia are never able to efficiently develop writing and reading functions.

Simply put, some human brains are not optimized to read or write text, but we are all optimized to talk and listen. Richard Branson can't write, but he can absolutely talk.

In fact, most of human knowledge throughout antiquity was shared and recorded through oral history.

For most people, talking is easier than writing, but that still leaves the work of turning the talking into a book. Is there a way for a person to talk about their wisdom and ideas instead of writing them down and to use that talking as the basis for the book?

Yes, of course there is, and people have been leveraging this method throughout history. Here's a very short list of people whose words still move the world, yet they never wrote anything down:

- Socrates never wrote anything down; Plato recorded his words.
- Jesus Christ never wrote down a word; the Apostles (like Paul) did.
- Buddha never wrote any of his teachings; his disciples did.
- Marco Polo told his cellmate about his travels while they were in jail, and his cellmate (who was an actual scribe) wrote them down.
- Dostoyevsky dictated his novels to his wife, who wrote them down.
- Winston Churchill dictated most of his writing to his secretary.
- Malcolm X dictated his iconic autobiography to journalist Alex Haley.

For thousands of years, writing was a specific job, different from thinking. People who did the writing were called "scribes," and they were not themselves the esteemed thinkers and influencers of their era (what we would now call a "thought leader"). They were considered artisans with particular skills, like those of lawyers or mechanics.

Take one of the most prolific authors of the Roman age, the great Julius Caesar. He used scribes to record almost every single line in all of his letters and books.

Why did he use scribes instead of writing them himself?

For the obvious reason: his time was too valuable to be

spent mastering the skill of writing words so they read properly on the page.

Julius Caesar spent his time thinking and doing things, not writing.

Caesar had scribes record his thoughts as he spoke them out loud, and then he signed his name to them. His volumes of letters and correspondences are all rightly authored by him, yet he wrote none of the actual words down.

That's why we advocate the scribe process for some people: it works, it saves time, and it even generally makes for better writing. It is how many of history's most important figures recorded their wisdom for posterity.

In summary, the reasons you might want to use this method:

1. **Much easier:** It gets you a very rough draft to edit in about 30 percent of the time it will take you to write a first draft.
2. **Much faster:** Saves you the time and anxiety of contending with a blank page.
3. **Makes a better book:** It forces you to teach your knowledge in a way that is reader-centric.

WHO SHOULD NOT USE THE SCRIBE METHOD?

Here are the main reasons not to use the Scribe Method:

1. **You're used to, and like, writing:** If you like writing and are used to it—i.e., you "think through your fingers"—learning a new method would be counterproductive at this point. A number of professional writers are like this (myself included).

2. **You don't know the topic well:** If you can't teach your topic out loud yet, in essence, you have to figure out your book as you write it. This is also common for writers but less common for the authors we work with.

3. **You're afraid of a new method:** There is nothing wrong with being uncertain about a "new" method. If you feel more confident with the methods you know better, then use them.

Again, there is no right or wrong way to write a book. The right way is the way that works for you and that ultimately results in a published book.

HOW TO USE THE SCRIBE METHOD

The Scribe process is very simple: instead of writing down the first draft, you take the outline and record yourself speaking through it, as if you were teaching that information to someone or giving a lecture. Then you get it transcribed and use that transcription as your rough draft.

STEP 1: PREPARE TO RECORD YOUR AUDIO

Technology makes the logistics of recording your content

incredibly easy. There are an infinite number of ways to record yourself and a number of services you can use to get that recording transcribed.

Your computer or iPhone has a built-in recorder. You can use that easily.

We recommend one service specifically, simply because they make everything so simple: Rev.com. The cost is $1 per minute, which is standard in the industry.

There is also an app called Temi that uses AI to transcribe, and it's only $0.10 per minute. The quality is lower than human transcription, but considering it's 90 percent cheaper, that's a worthwhile option as well.

Because you are going to have your recording transcribed, be sure to create a quality audio file that will produce a clean and complete transcript. That means no background noise (like side conversations), and a good enough microphone, placed close to your mouth, to cleanly capture everything you say. You don't need anything fancy. iPhone earbud microphones are great.

This should be obvious, but only record one chapter at a time and one chapter per audio file. This makes the transcripts easy to manage.

For a final book of 30,000 words, you'll have around ten

to twelve chapters and should aim for six to eight hours of interview recording. This means about thirty to forty-five minutes per chapter.

Obviously, you won't be able to do this all in one sitting. It is important that you divvy out the length and make sure to get enough interview material for each chapter.

STEP 2: TIPS FOR RECORDING YOUR ROUGH DRAFT

Here are some tips and ideas to keep in mind while you are delivering your first draft—all strategies we've found to be true in the past.

A. Frame It as Teaching

Think about who the ideal audience is for this book and then pretend that you are talking to them. Go back to your avatar. If you can picture a real person you know who fits that mold, that will make this even easier.

Anticipate what this reader will be most interested in, what they will want to know next, and what questions they will have.

Be as thorough as humanly possible—even if it seems ridiculous—with the details of your instructions or inquiries. Make sure not to gloss over any steps or rungs in the ladder leading up to your conclusion, even if they seem trivial or self-evident, because the reader won't fully understand unless you explain everything.

B. Stay with the Outline

Your outline is sequential for a reason. Don't just move through it randomly from point to point. Stay with the outline and on the point you mean to make. Remember, this is the foundation of the first draft, so the more you stay with the outline and on track, the easier it will be for you to use the transcript to write the book. You may realize you want to add or subtract information at some point down the line. That is precisely what later drafts are for. For now, stick with the outline.

C. Explain Everything Completely

If you were lecturing simply to make your point, you could do it very quickly. But that's not the point of you speaking. You are teaching so the eventual reader will learn.

Your goal is to get a full, complete explanation out—far more than you probably need—so when you sit down to write out the book from your audio transcription, everything is there. The book needs to contain enough information to explain the concepts to uninformed, as well as informed, readers.

More is almost always better than less, so please say everything that comes to mind on the current point, especially anything you think is relevant. Don't worry about phrasing things eloquently, explaining everything perfectly on your first try, or not rambling. Substance matters more than style. You only need to worry about getting the substance right. It's much easier to cut words than to add words in places where you don't explain enough.

If you feel like you're being too obvious, always remember this quote by Nina Paley:

"Don't be original; be obvious. When you state the obvious, you actually seem original."

CREATING YOUR ROUGH DRAFT FROM THE TRANSCRIPT

Once you get the transcript of your audio recording from the transcription service, you will start the process of "translating" that audio transcript into book prose, which will be your first draft. Here's how you take the raw transcript and turn it into a rough draft:

STEP 1: ORGANIZE YOUR CHAPTERS

If you recorded each chapter as its own audio file, then you will get them back from the transcriptionist in their own separate Word files.

The easiest method we've found to edit them is this:

1. Create a new document (in Word or Google Docs).
2. Copy and paste the outline sections from each chapter at the top of the corresponding chapter transcript.
3. Paste the entire audio transcript for each chapter below the chapter outline.

This allows you to have the chapter structure up top and work on the audio transcript right below it.

STEP 2: "TRANSLATE" THE AUDIO TRANSCRIPT INTO BOOK PROSE

Once you have each chapter organized, you're going to "translate" your audio text into book prose. This is not as challenging as original writing since the words and ideas are there.

But this is important: this is not editing. You will need to rewrite the transcript in most cases.

There are a number of ways to do this, but there is one process that is most effective for us. It's counterintuitive, but the trick is to go slowly in order to finish more quickly. These are the exact steps we recommend going through for each chapter.

We use a two-document process. One open document that is the transcript in. The other is the manuscript draft. You should "read, digest, write," shifting attention from transcript to manuscript.

We recommend you go paragraph by paragraph, rewriting each transcription passage onto the manuscript.

The point is you need to physically type your new chapters, paragraph by paragraph. DO NOT just edit the existing chunks of raw transcription.

Why not just edit the transcription directly?

Because writing this way is MUCH easier than editing your transcription into writing that reads well on the page.

There's a tendency to want to turn off your brain and use exactly what you say in the transcription, verbatim. This leads to the need for a LOT of editing and ends up making the process pretty painful.

Once you get your transcript back, you'll see that transcribed audio is not written English. It's not even close. Attempting to edit it will drive you crazy. It's much better to read and absorb the spirit of what each paragraph of the transcript is trying to say, and then start fresh with sentences that make sense on the page.

This is essentially translating from one medium (audio) to another (writing).

Of course, there will be places where you can almost exactly use your words from the transcript. When that happens, it's great, and it makes your job easier. But for most people, this won't happen often.

Note: In some cases, this may include adding content that isn't in the transcript. Some ideas require some expansion to connect properly. You will need to add transitions or connections that aren't part of the transcript. This is totally fine, of course. They're your ideas, after all.

If this gets hard, and it will, just keep going. This is where it's easy to give up. You'll regret it if you do.

Again, don't worry about being perfect, as you're going to come back and do an edit later. This is just getting the first draft done.

You're getting something down that you can come back to and perfect later.

HOW TO WRITE YOUR ROUGH DRAFT USING THE REGULAR METHOD

"1. To begin, give yourself permission to write a bad book.

2. Revise until it's not a bad book."

—BARBARA KINGSOLVER

Do you really need me to teach you how to sit in a chair and type?

Of course not.

What we have found working with thousands of authors is that almost all of them know how to write out their ideas. What they need most is what we've already gone over: defined book positioning and a clear book plan. From there, the writing itself is easy.

Where problems arise is in the *mindset around writing*. Let's talk about that.

THE FIRST DRAFT IS ABOUT MOVING FORWARD

Once you are here, you should have your positioning and outline done. Next you write. This might be the most important advice in this book, so pay attention:

> *Write your first draft as quickly as possible. Don't stop. Don't edit. Move forward until your first draft is done.*

Let me repeat that and break it down to be very clear and be sure you've got it.

Write your first draft as quickly as possible.

DO NOT STOP.

DO NOT EDIT.

MOVE FORWARD UNTIL YOUR FIRST DRAFT IS DONE.

I cannot be more serious or literal about this.

In fact, I want you to say this out loud, right now:

> *"I will not edit my first draft until I am done writing it."*

The quickest way to derail a rough draft is to start editing before you finish. I don't care who you are. If you start editing your first draft, you WILL get stuck.

If you edit during the first draft stage, the best-case scenario is you double the amount of time it takes to write the book.

The worst-case, and more common, scenario is that it totally derails your book. The bully in your brain, the part of you that is ridiculously hard on yourself, will start to second guess you and shame you and will, at best, slow you down—if not kill your motivation altogether.

If you think something is terrible and you hate it, that's fine. Use the "comment" function to highlight it and say "edit this later" and then move on. You'll get to it later.

The thing to remember is that the first draft is for you.

NO ONE but you will ever read it.

Once you start editing (which I will explain how to do soon), then you can focus on what people will think. The parts of yourself that want to edit as you go will be useful down the line. The perfectionist, self-critical part of your brain is a great editor, but a terrible writer. Put it away until the first draft is done.

FINDING YOUR VOICE

For some reason, when it comes time to writing, lots of authors become obsessed with "finding their voice."

I'll often tease authors and ask them things like, "Hey, did you look behind your sofa? Your voice might be there."

The joke is silly, but the point is right. You don't "find" your voice outside of yourself. Your voice is already a part of who you are. Your job as an author is to get out of the way and let it out.

The second thing authors do wrong is try to mimic a voice. You can't be Malcolm Gladwell; you can only be you.

So how to do make sure it's your voice in your book? There are two frames we recommend authors take.

VOICE FRAME #1: CONVERSATION WITH A FRIEND

This is the most common mental frame that our authors use. When they sit down to write, they envision themselves talking to a friend.

This is literally the frame I used to write this section. I pretended to explain this to a friend of mine.

Getting in that state of mind does several things:

- It relieves any anxiety, because this is just a conversation with friends.
- It helps keep my focus on the listener because they're a friend and I want to be attentive to them.
- It helps me stay centered on providing value to the listener because, in a teaching-style conversation, I am only thinking about what the other person is learning and taking in.
- It helps me keep momentum and motivation because I want to make sure I am always helpful to my friend.

VOICE FRAME #2: HELP A STRANGER HEAL THE SAME PAIN YOU HAD

This is very similar to the "conversation with a friend" frame, but it is also different in a few ways. If you envision yourself helping a stranger solve a painful problem, you do these things:

- You make it much easier to be brave in your writing and get past any fear or anxiety because you are focused on their pain.
- You focus on specific and actionable information, which will make your book better and more meaningful to your readers.
- It helps you keep momentum and motivation because you are focused on alleviating their pain.

Uber cool trick: combine the two. If you envision yourself talking to a friend AND helping them through something difficult you've already done, that might be the best of both worlds.

Both of these methods allow you to get out of your own way and let your voice come through naturally.

Why?

Because you *aren't* actually thinking about voice. You are focused on the reader. Focusing on the reader, rather than on yourself, is a superpower technique you can use at every stage to create an effective, successful book.

USING JARGON

Make sure your voice is accessible and not full of needless jargon.

If you find yourself wanting to use jargon, go back to your ideal reader and ask yourself, "Will they understand this? Is this necessary to effectively communicate with them?"

Now, if your audience likes jargon and wants to hear that in a book addressed to them, then use it. Just make sure it's appropriate to your audience.

HOW DO YOU MAINTAIN ENERGY?

Most authors who ask about "energy" are really asking

about something else. This is generally fear or anxiety taking another form. Go look at the fear chapter for reminders on how to deal with that.

That being said, the most important aspect of energy is maintaining a baseline of self-care and then having a schedule and sticking to it. If you do those two things, you'll generate and protect at least 50 percent of your energy levels.

HOW TO BEAT PROCRASTINATION

Like almost everything that stops you from sitting down and writing, procrastination is a symptom of fear and anxiety in another form.

If you find yourself procrastinating, ask yourself if you believe in your plan and your outline. Sometimes procrastination is your subconscious telling you that something is wrong with your plan.

Look at your plan for your book again. Examine it and ask yourself if you believe in each section. If you don't, then fix wherever you see a problem, and you should be good.

Also, another great way to beat procrastination is to use public accountability. When you are lagging on your book, post about it, and that will help you get support and make sure you find the will to keep going.

SHOULD YOU WRITE SEQUENTIALLY?

For most authors, you're better off going sequentially unless you get stuck. If you get stuck, leave it, and go to the next place you can pick up. Fill in holes later.

PART 5

EDIT YOUR BOOK

HOW TO EDIT
YOUR BOOK

"When your story is ready for rewrite, cut it to the bone. Get rid of every ounce of excess fat. This is going to hurt; revising a story down to the bare essentials is always a little like murdering children, but it must be done."

—STEPHEN KING

Congratulations!

It feels amazing to get through the first draft. Reward yourself with some time to rest and relax. The hardest part is over. You now have a real book in your hands, even if it is rough.

When I say take some time to rest and relax, I'm very serious. Set the entire thing aside for *at least* a week, ideally two. This will give you a valuable, fresh perspective when you come back and begin editing.

It's possible to begin editing immediately, but the result won't be as good. This is part of why we tell you to schedule two months for your editing—to give you a buffer to rest your mind and come back to your manuscript fresh.

HOW TO APPROACH EDITING

As you start editing, there are two frames we recommend you use:

1. The book is not for you; it's for your reader
2. Edit for a twelve-year-old

Sound weird? Let me explain.

1. THE BOOK IS NOT FOR YOU; IT'S FOR YOUR READER

Yes of course the book is yours. Yes, it probably has a lot of your stories in it; in fact, it should. Yes, the book is going to create benefits for you.

But as we discussed in positioning, if you want the book to help you, then the book has to provide value to the reader. In essence, to get what you want, you must give them what they want.

That is much easier said than done. Here are some facts about readers. They are:

1. Impatient
2. Selfish
3. Ignorant (about your subject)

I don't mean that in a bad way. It's just how all readers are (including you and me).

The reality is that, in a book, you are buying the attention of the reader ONE PARAGRAPH AT A TIME.

You can write the book without worrying about that fact, but once you start editing, it becomes very important.

The point is that as you write, you can think of yourself, but as you edit, you need to be thinking about your reader.

How do you think about them? This leads directly to the next frame.

2. EDIT FOR A TWELVE-YEAR-OLD

What's the top bestselling book of the past three decades?

Fifty Shades of Grey.

Which is written at a teenage/young adult level.

What's the bestselling novel series of the past three decades?

Harry Potter.

Which is written at a teenage/young adult level.

Even though those books were written at the reading level of teenage audiences, 80 percent of the *Fifty Shades* audience was adults, and 60 percent of the *Harry Potter* audience was adults.

Why am I telling you this? What does fiction have to do with you? Because when you write for a smart, interested twelve-year-old, it forces you to be clear and direct—which in turn makes your book MORE appealing to older audiences.

I know this might seem far-fetched, but think about this.

On the list of the ten bestselling business books of the past thirty years, there are three NOVELS. I'm not kidding:

- *Who Moved My Cheese?*
- *The Five Dysfunctions of a Team*
- *The One Minute Manager*

What is the lesson for you here?

Telling simple and compelling stories to convey your point WORKS.

In my experience, the best frame to use to get in the mindset of telling a simple and compelling story is to assume you are editing your book so that it is interesting to a curious, smart twelve-year-old.

If you do that—without being condescending in tone—the book will probably be as clear and direct as you need it to be.

I'm not saying you should be simplistic. I'm not saying you should leave out any important information. I'm not even telling you to dumb anything down—far from it.

I am telling you to write your ideas in a digestible, direct way such that a smart and interested twelve-year-old could understand them.

To be clear, that doesn't mean your ideas *themselves* have to be simple. It just means your presentation of them is simple and direct.

The problem is that so many people think good writing is complicated and difficult to read. That is not true. There are some fields, like academia, where writing in a needlessly complex way is given high status.

But outside of those fields, the more direct and simple the writing is, the more accessible your actual ideas will be, and the better the book will do with readers—which is how you get everything you want as well.

THE THREE-STEP EDITING METHOD

We recommend a three-step editing process:

1. **Make-It-Right Edit:** Make sure everything is in there, in the right order, and it all makes sense.
2. **Piece-by-Piece Edit:** Go deep into the chapters, paragraphs, and sentences to make sure it says exactly what you want.
3. **Read-Aloud Edit:** Read the manuscript out loud—preferably to a person—and make sure it sounds right to the ear.

I'll explain both processes.

PART 1: MAKE-IT-RIGHT EDIT

This should be the easiest and simplest editing pass. There are three goals to the make-it-right edit. You want to ensure that:

1. All content is in the book
2. It's in the right order
3. The structure and positioning all make sense

This is basically just making sure the book has everything in it so you can actually begin the deep editing. All the writing and stories that need to be in are in, and they are in the right order, and it all makes sense.

That's pretty much it. Don't make this more complicated than it needs to be.

PART 2: PIECE-BY-PIECE EDIT

This is the framework we use for line-by-line editing. It's simple to understand but powerful if you do it right. It gives you the exact questions to ask yourself at each level of editing.

As you read every **chapter**, ask yourself these six questions:

1. What point am I making?
2. Is it necessary?
3. Is it clear?
4. Is it as simple as possible?
5. Is it as short as possible?
6. Did I leave anything necessary out?

We mean this literally. Ask yourself these questions, each time.

Yes, this is tedious. But if you do this exercise consistently, it becomes second nature. Once that happens, you'll find that you can not only cut the fluff out of your book, but you can also make your book sharper and more refined, and you'll be able to home in on what you are trying to say and nail it.

Do it for each paragraph, then do it for each sentence. If you do this, you'll have an excellent book.

(By the way, I adapted these instructions from George Orwell's essay "Politics and the English Language," which contains editing instructions from arguably the greatest writer of the twentieth century.)

PART 3: READ-ALOUD EDITING

This is an editing process that's not commonly taught but is a secret trick of numerous bestselling authors. Brené Brown, Neil Strauss, myself—we all do this.

When I was first writing *I Hope They Serve Beer in Hell*, I had teams of proofreaders working through the book. First, I proofread it, then I had the help of professional editor friends, and finally the publishing company had their people do their copyedits. I did not think that a single mistake would sneak by, and I happily locked in the manuscript.

A few months later, I recorded my audiobook, and as I read through the manuscript out loud, I was horrified.

There were 100 tiny little mistakes and changes I only heard once I said them out loud.

It drove me NUTS.

Don't make the mistake I made. Read your manuscript out loud and mark changes as you go.

If the words roll off your tongue, they'll also flow smoothly in readers' heads. Because I waited until so late in the process to read it out loud, it was too late to make edits to the book.

Learn from my mistake—read your manuscript out loud and make your changes before you start the publishing process.

If you find taking the time to sit and read out loud difficult (and a lot of authors do), we recommend having a friend help you out. If someone is sitting in the room with you, listening as you read through the manuscript, it'll create the social pressure you need to actually do it.

If it's something you would say out loud, then it reads clearly on the page. If it's something you would never say to another person, it won't read as clearly.

This sounds crazy, *but it works*. Paul Graham explains why:

> Ok, so written and spoken language are different. Does that make written language worse?

> If you want people to read and understand what you write, yes. Written language is more complex, which makes it more work to read. It's also more formal and distant, which gives the reader's attention permission to drift.

> You don't need complex sentences to express complex ideas.

When specialists in some abstruse topic talk to one another about ideas in their field, they don't use sentences any more complex than they do when talking about what to have for lunch. They use different words, certainly. But even those they use no more than necessary. And in my experience, the harder the subject, the more informally experts speak. Partly, I think, because they have less to prove, and partly because the harder the ideas you're talking about, the less you can afford to let language get in the way.

If you simply manage to write in spoken language, you'll be ahead of 95 percent of writers. And it's so easy to do: just don't let a sentence through unless it's the way you'd say it to a friend.

The reason reading your manuscript out loud works so well is because you will catch dozens of things you would have otherwise missed. Like Paul says, hearing yourself speak forces you to notice bad or strange phrasings. Even if you don't know *why* it's off, you know it's off.

Step 1: Read It Out Loud to a Person (or a Microphone)

If possible, read each chapter to a person. I know, that sounds awful and tedious, but reading to actual people forces you to really hear what is and is not working. It's an incredible forcing function.

If you can't do that, then set up a microphone and record yourself as you read aloud.

You can delete the recording afterwards. All that matters is that you are reading it OUT LOUD.

This is KEY to making this process work.

If you can't do this, then there is another solution: Google "Natural Reader." It's a site that translates your text to speech, so it's like someone else reading your manuscript to you.

Then you listen to what your words are saying. You'll hear the errors.

Step 2: Edit by Feel

As you read, you will naturally ask yourself:

> *"Does this sound the same way I'd say it to an actual person? Does it feel right to me?"*

You (and the other person) will inevitably hear errors, phrasings you want to change, and sentences that sound off that you want corrected. As you read it out loud, correct your mistakes.

If you "feel" something is off and aren't sure how to change it, that's fine. Just mark it the first time through. The first time reading it, you want to hear the problems so you can go back and fix them on the page later.

"In general, what is written must be easy to read and easy to speak; which is the same."

—ARISTOTLE

HOW MANY TIMES SHOULD I EDIT?

We recommend that authors do each phase one time. If you do them right, one time each is enough.

Now, it is important to note: we recommend this because the authors who work directly with us go from these three rounds of edits to then send their manuscript to us. Our scribes will do a full content edit, which would be a fourth round of edits, and then send it back to the author. The author then reviews all of those edits and makes changes based on them.

So for those authors, there are really five total rounds of edits. I did not list them here because many people can and do write their books by themselves without those editing rounds.

Just know that if you want another set of eyes on your book after you finish the first three rounds, you can do that as well.

WHEN TO STOP EDITING

You'll know you're close to being done editing when you hate your book.

I'm joking, but only a little.

I've written seven books, and I hated every single book in editing. It usually happens somewhere around the 70–80 percent mark. When I was close enough that I could see the end but far enough that it still felt like it would be forever to get there, I hated everything and wanted to quit.

Now when I write a book, I know it's coming, I can prepare for it and recognize it when it comes, and in a way, I actually welcome it. When I start hating my book, I know I'm close to being done, and I just need one more final push.

Here's what's funny about this: by about the three-month mark after your book is released, you will have totally forgotten about this.

I'm not joking at all. It reminds me of my wife and our children.

Her first childbirth went well, at least as far as first births go. We had midwives and did a home birth. It took about seven hours, and everything went smoothly.

But if you've had kids, you know smooth does not mean pleasant. She was in SERIOUS pain. It was seven hours of agony and suffering. She hated every minute of it.

Then, when our son was like nine months old, we were at

dinner with some friends and talking about kids. She said, "I can't wait to have our next one. The first birth was so pleasant and wonderful."

I went slack-jawed. "What? Were you not there? You were in screaming agony the whole time, you yelled curses at me and at God, and you swore like a sailor."

She kind of looked at me funny: "Yeah, I know you are right. I know that's all true. But I don't remember it that way at all."

That is what writing a book is like. You hate it at the end and love it once it's out.

A FINAL NOTE ON FINISHING YOUR EDITS

Most first-time authors fall into the "editing death spiral." This is when they keep editing the same thing over and over and cannot stop.

We see this all the time. They will do the first three rounds of edits fine, then we finish our edits on the book, give it back to the author, and they spend six months with it.

Not because they are making substantive changes. Instead, they get lost in details, fretting over small word choices, making tiny edits, and obsessing over obscure details. We almost have to pry the book out of their hands so we can finish it, even though they don't really have anything left to change.

This can be driven by many different forces, such as perfectionism, fear of publishing, fear of success, or fear of failure. There will always be more to work on, more to change, more to improve. That thinking will kill your book. There are two aphorisms we use to help get authors past this point:

"Perfect is the enemy of good; shipped is better than perfect."

—SETH GODIN

"[Books are] never finished, only abandoned."

—LEONARDO DA VINCI

Pick your aphorism. They all mean the same thing: stop editing, get your book in print, or it doesn't do anyone any good.

If you have reached this point and are editing too much, then you need to stop. We can write a whole different book about this subject, but we're going to simply say this:

> At least one person, and probably many more, want to learn what your book will teach them. You have an obligation to yourself and to your audience to stop editing and put the book out.

Give your knowledge to them, even if it's not perfect. They want and need it.

SHOULD YOU ASK PEOPLE FOR FEEDBACK?

"I try to leave out the parts that people skip."

—ELMORE LEONARD

If your car broke down, would you ask a chef to look at it and tell you what's wrong?

Unless it's the Oscar Meyer Weiner Mobile, what's a chef going to tell you?

At best, he'll scratch his head and say, "Yeah, looks like it's not working." Thanks. Super helpful.

At worst, he'll try to be helpful and end up sending you down some nonsense rabbit hole.

No, if you want your car fixed, you take it to a mechanic, because a mechanic has experience at fixing cars. It's literally what they get paid for.

I know this example is silly. Yet authors will do this exact thing.

I could tell you Halloween-style horror stories about authors who had great a manuscript and then sent it to random friends for feedback.

What happens is that the friends either feel like they have to say something, so they just make random comments, or even worse, they think they know how to write because they spend all day writing emails, but they don't know anything about books, and their nonsense comments will send the author into a tailspin.

If you want to get feedback, there is a right way to ask, and you should only ask specific people. Those specific people should generally be a person from one of these three groups:

1. People who are experienced writers/editors
2. People who are experts in your specific field
3. People who are in the exact audience you want your book to reach

Let's break down each category.

1. EXPERIENCED WRITERS OR EDITORS

This is obvious. Someone who has a lot of experience in writing and editing can almost certainly help you with your manuscript and give useful feedback.

Keep in mind that many people *vastly overestimate* their experience and ability in these areas. Many people think because they write emails all day, it qualifies them as skilled writers or editors, when in fact they are not that at all.

This is why, at Scribe, we have a rigorous testing process before we even begin to work with editors, outliners, and publishing managers—even if they are employed full time as writers or editors, we don't assume they're skilled. We want to see their work, and we judge their ability by the quality of their work.

What happens as a result of these tests? We reject about 98 percent of the people who apply to work with us, all of whom have legitimate writing or editing experience. That should tell you the general quality of the "experts" out there.

We bring this up only because we've seen many authors give their manuscript to a friend who claimed to be a "great" writer, only to see that friend give truly awful notes that left the author confused and hurt, and ended up creating lots of problems with the book.

Here's the hard reality of asking for feedback: *most people have NO IDEA what they are talking about,* especially with regards to books and writing, and getting feedback from those people is harmful.

2. SOMEONE IN YOUR FIELD OR NICHE

Asking someone who shares your field of expertise for feedback can be quite helpful. For example, if you are a financial advisor, and you give your book to two of your trusted financial advisor friends to read it, they can give you a perspective on the book that could be both helpful and unique.

The key to making this fruitful is to ask them to specifically focus on what they know well. When you give them the manuscript, ask them to read it as a financial advisor, checking to make sure that you haven't made any factual errors, that clients will understand it, and that your tone is appropriate for your profession—things like that.

Basically, you are asking them to apply their decades of expertise to your manuscript. That will work well.

3. SOMEONE IN YOUR AUDIENCE

If your book is about how to build an app business and you give it to two friends who are trying to build app businesses, that is perfect. They could tell you what helped them in the book, which parts they wished had more content, and where they got confused or lost. That sort of feedback tends to be valuable.

Just be very careful who you select and give them very specific instructions. If you pick someone in your primary audience, make sure to tell them what you want to know.

For example, say, "I'd love you to read my manuscript and tell me where it loses you or doesn't make sense or is hard to follow."

ALL FEEDBACK IS WRONG

Be careful with feedback. The best piece of advice I've ever heard about feedback on a book is this:

> "All feedback is wrong somehow. Your job is to figure out what's right about it and only pay attention to that."

What this means is that most people are giving you feedback based on how they feel, and they almost certainly don't know how to fix the issue. This quote from author Neil Gaiman sums it up:

> "When people tell you something's wrong or doesn't work for them, they are almost always right. When they tell you exactly what they think is wrong and how to fix it, they are almost always wrong."

His point is that the reader may know that your book isn't

working for them in some way, and you should listen to that critique.

However, their *ideas for solutions* are probably bad because they have no experience solving writing problems.

If someone in your audience says something isn't working for them, listen to their comments, but use your own ideas and knowledge to fix the problem. No one knows your book and your subject matter better than you do.

THE WORST THINGS TO DO (AND HOW TO FIX THEM)

There are few things you should never do in terms of feedback.

DO NOT put some pages out on Facebook/Twitter for feedback: This is a disaster. You will deeply regret it. In my fifteen-plus years as a writer, I have never seen this work for anyone. There are so many reasons this goes wrong it is hard to list them all. Just think of it this way.

If you wanted advice on your clothes, would you stand in the middle of an amusement park and randomly ask people who walked by?

Of course not.

Asking for an opinion of your writing on social media is

the same thing. I cannot stress enough that you should not do this.

DO pick specific people to ask for help: There is nothing wrong with asking specific people for specific forms of feedback, as discussed above. The keyword there is "specific people." Experts at writing or experts in your field or people in your audience. That is the key.

DO NOT give your manuscript to someone without asking for specific feedback: Do not throw your manuscript to someone and say, "Hey, take a look at this and tell me what you think." That is a recipe for all kinds of wasted time and effort.

DO be specific in your ask. There are definitely situations where asking for feedback is both appropriate and helpful, but always say something like, "Hey, can you tell me if you think my voice in the book comes off as too unprofessional for an accountant?"

SHOULD YOU LET FRIENDS AND FAMILY GIVE FEEDBACK ON YOUR MANUSCRIPT?

Be very careful with asking friends and family give you feedback. I've seen a lot of manuscripts ruined by friends and family trying to be nice.

What happens is they feel like they are supposed to give

feedback, so they just mention things that occur to them. While they are well-intentioned, most of their advice is not only wrong, but it's also counterproductive and toxic—a dynamic that can send authors into spirals.

The bottom line? Unless your friends and family fit into the above categories, or you are okay with ignoring them, don't let them give you feedback.

PART 6

FINISH YOUR MANUSCRIPT

PICKING THE PERFECT BOOK TITLE

"All that is clever eschew. Do not do."

—ANNE HERBERT

Shockingly, there's little useful guidance out there about book titling. What advice exists is usually of little help:

- Trite ("Go with your gut!")
- Superficial ("Browse bookstores for ideas!")
- Or worst of all, actively harmful ("Don't spend too much time on it.")

They're all wrong.

Just like companies that spend millions on naming new products and media companies that spend time testing different titles for posts, *you should spend substantial time and energy finding the right book title.*

This is a very important decision—one you need to think about and get right to ensure your book has the best possible chance of success.

In this comprehensive guide to picking the perfect book title, I will walk you through how to think about book titles, then tell you how to pick yours and how to test it.

WHY DO BOOK TITLES MATTER?

Your book title is the most important marketing decision you'll make. Period.

The title is the first piece of information someone gets about your book and informs the reader's judgment about your book.

Empirical evidence and decades of experience in the book business gives us a clear picture of what happens in the mind of a potential reader when evaluating a book. They consider these pieces of information about a book, in this order (assuming they come across it randomly in a bookstore or browsing on the internet):

1. The title of the book
2. The cover of the book
3. The back cover copy (the book description copy, if it's online)
4. The blurbs/flap copy (or the reviews, if it's online)

5. The author bio (depending on where it is)
6. The book text itself (or they use the "see inside" function to read a few paragraphs)
7. The price

The title is the first thing the reader sees or hears about your book—even before the cover in most cases—and getting it right is the single most important book marketing decision you'll make (even though most people don't think about it as marketing).

Let's be clear: A good title *won't* make your book do well. But a bad title will almost certainly *prevent* it from doing well.

The iconic example of the importance of a book title is the title change that led to an obscure book becoming a number one bestseller. In 1982, Naura Hayden released a book called *Astro-Logical Love*. It bombed.

She then took the exact same book, changed a small amount of the content, and reissued it with a different title: *How to Satisfy a Woman Every Time...and Have Her Beg for More!*

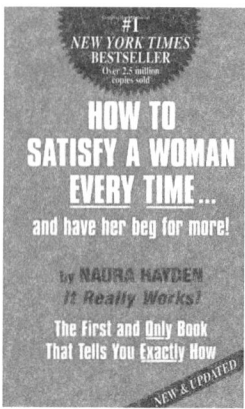

That book became a massive cultural phenomenon and a number one bestseller. Same book, same content, just a different title.

The takeaway for you is simple and clear: *Spend time figuring out the best possible title for your book, because it will largely determine what people think about your book and, thus, your book's success.*

THE SIX ATTRIBUTES OF A GOOD BOOK TITLE

A good title should have all of these attributes:

1. Attention-grabbing
2. Memorable and searchable

3. Informative (gives an idea of what the book is about)
4. Easy to say
5. Not embarrassing or problematic to say
6. Keep it short

1. ATTENTION-GRABBING

This should be pretty obvious. There are a million things pulling on people's attention, and you need a title that stands out. A bad title is boring.

There are many ways to grab attention: you can be provocative, controversial, exciting, make a promise, etc. The point is your title should make people stop and pay attention to it. Here is what number-one bestselling author Tim Ferriss says about titles:

> *The 4-Hour Workweek* also bothered some people and was ridiculed by others, which I took as a positive indicator. It's not accidental that Jay Leno parodied the book on-air—the title lends itself to it, and that was by design. You can't have strong positive responses without strong negative responses, and beware—above all—the lukewarm reception from all. "Oh, that's nice. I think it's pretty good," is a death sentence.

2. MEMORABLE AND SEARCHABLE

This is not the same thing as grabbing attention (even though many people think it is). It's much easier to get a reaction out of someone and then be forgotten than it is to get a reaction *and be memorable.*

Remember, a book title is not only the first thing a reader hears about your book; it's the one piece of information that a reader has that leads them back to the book itself.

If your book is recommended to them by a friend, and they can't remember the title, then they can't go find it in a bookstore or on Amazon. Bestselling author Scott Berkun says it well:

> Often [the title] is all a potential buyer ever gets to see, and if they can draw interest the book crosses its first of many hurdles in the improbable struggle of getting noticed. But titles only help so much. Most people hear about books the same way they hear about new bands. Or new people to meet. A friend or trusted source tells them it was good and it was called <NAME HERE>. The title at that point serves as a moniker. It's the thing you need to remember to get the thing you want to get and little more.

This also means you want the book title to be easily searchable. In the world we live in, search is how people find things now. If your title does not lend itself to easy memorization and searchability on Google and Amazon, that is very bad.

3. INFORMATIVE (GIVES AN IDEA OF WHAT THE BOOK IS ABOUT)

This is the least crucial aspect for fiction books but very important for nonfiction. The title, including the subtitle, should give the reader some sort of idea of what the book is about.

People aren't going to do your work for you. The easier you make it for them to understand the subject, the more likely you are to draw in the people who would find your book interesting.

A good test is to ask yourself this: *if you were to tell someone the title of your book at a party, would they have to ask what it's about?*

If so, that's probably a bad title.

Don't out-think yourself on your title. A title that is overly clever or somewhat unclear signals that the book is for people who immediately understand the word or phrase— which makes people who don't get it right away feel unintelligent and, thus, less likely to buy the book.

By using a word or phrase that is either not immediately understandable by your desired audience or doesn't convey the point of the book, you are putting a huge obstacle in front of your success.

Though your book title should be informative and easily

understood, it does not need to spell out the whole book idea. Take Malcolm Gladwell's *Outliers* for example: this title does a great job of cuing the content of the book without describing it outright.

4. EASY TO SAY

This is closely tied to being understandable, but not the exact same thing. Obscure or difficult to pronounce words are killers for titles. Tongue twisters and hard-to-say phrases reduce the likelihood that people will engage with the book or say it out loud to other people.

It is a concept called cognitive fluency, and to make it simple, it means that people are more likely to remember and respond favorably to words and phrases they can immediately understand and pronounce. We don't want to go too far into the psychological literature here, but the point is this: don't try to be too sophisticated at the risk of becoming obscure. It will only hurt your book.

5. NOT EMBARRASSING OR PROBLEMATIC TO SAY

It's a basic fact of human psychology. People don't like to feel stupid or socially awkward. If a book title is hard to pronounce or, more importantly, if it's a phrase that sounds stupid when said out loud, it makes them far less likely to buy it, and chances are they won't talk about it to other people.

One of the most important things to think about when picking your book title is word of mouth. Think about *how people will feel* about saying this book title out loud to their friends. Does it make them look smart or stupid?

The worst possible title is one that makes someone feel silly saying it out loud. For example, if the book title is something like *Why Racism Is Great*, no one is ever going to tell their friends about it, no matter how good the book is, because they have to then face the scrutiny of why they bought that book in the first place. Social context doesn't just matter some; it matters a lot.

6. KEEP IT SHORT

Generally speaking, shorter titles are best. A short title is not only more memorable and easier to say, but it also gives more space and flexibility for better cover design.

People get lured into crafting titles that are exacting and long-winded in an effort to make the title signal the book idea and audience. In the title, stick to the core idea. Readers have the whole book to learn the details.

It's a balancing act because, as you can see, the title is accomplishing a lot. It needs to hook the reader and help the reader see they need the book. Crafting a title is like flirting. It's not meant to convey the whole context or every benefit. Instead, it should make the reader eager to see more.

If you can, aim to keep the main title around five words or less. The subtitle can offer context or tell a bit more about what the reader will learn. Cameron Herold's book *Meetings Suck* has a pithy title, with a subtitle that helps the reader see why they need the book: *Turning One of the Most Loathed Elements of Business into One of the Most Valuable.*

All this being said, I wrote a book that had a seven-word title and was very successful (though it did not have a subtitle). Long titles can work.

But if you are picking a long title, do it for a very good reason—one that is so compelling that it overcomes the natural disadvantage that longer word strings create.

SPECIFIC STEPS TO FIND THE PERFECT BOOK TITLE
STEP 1: GET CLEAR ON YOUR BOOK OBJECTIVES

Your book objectives (building authority, raising your visibility, etc.) determine what type of title you pick. If you want to build a brand out of your nonfiction book, your title options are quite different than if you want to publish a memoir with a whimsical feel.

Let's examine all the functions your book title can serve, and the places for potential use before we walk you through the precise process of thinking up title ideas.

How a Book Title Can Be Used

- To sell the book to readers
- To establish the author's authority in a subject
- As a hook for the author to get media visibility
- As branding for a company, author, conference, or course materials
- To advertise/market the book
- In speeches, slides, or other in-person activities
- In reviews, blog posts, articles, etc.
- As something the author has to say in all their press appearances
- To become a defining part of an author's future bio
- To decorate the cover
- To identify the Amazon/B&N listing
- To start a line of books
- On T-shirts, flyers, or other promotional material

The point of this whole list is simple. *Know which of these objectives apply to your book, and make sure your title can serve those objectives.*

For example, if your goal is to build a brand, make sure your book title is your brand. Dave Asprey's first diet book is called *The Bulletproof Diet* because that's his brand: Bulletproof. The book is about selling everything around the book, not just the book itself.

If your goal is authority in your field, make sure the book title sounds authoritative to whom you are trying to speak.

Whimsical doesn't work in serious academic fields, whereas serious doesn't work in comedic fields.

If your goal is to get media attention and raise your visibility, make sure the book title appeals to media and makes them want to cover you.

STEP 2: BRAINSTORM SEVERAL POTENTIAL TITLES

You'll want to see brainstorming for titles not as a specific thing you do for an hour, but rather, as a long-term process. It may take you months to finalize a title.

But you start by simply brainstorming titles. Literally start a file and write down every book title you can think of for your book.

I know that telling someone to brainstorm is like telling someone to "be creative," so what I'll do is list every possible way we know of to find a good book title, complete with examples (remember, these techniques are not just for your main title—they will be the basis for your subtitles as well). Feel free to use any of these as inspiration for your brainstorming.

Also, do not be afraid to put bad titles on your brainstorm list. Bad titles actually help you, because they will get you to a good title.

Here are some best practices.

1. Use clever or noteworthy phrases from the book: This is very common in fiction and can work well with novels. It also works well with nonfiction books when the concept of the book can be summed up quickly or with one phrase.

Examples:

- *The Black Swan*
- *Lecturing Birds on Flying*
- *I Hope They Serve Beer in Hell*

2. Use both short and long phrases: We usually start with a really long title and work our way down to much shorter phrases. The goal is to have the main title be as short as possible—no more than five words—and have the subtitle offer the context and put in important keywords.

3. Use relevant keywords: For nonfiction especially, search matters. You want to make sure that, when someone searches for the subject or topic of your book, it will come up on Google and Amazon. But it's a balancing act, because you don't want to sacrifice the authenticity of the work for what looks and feels like a search string query.

If you are unsure of this, go look on Amazon and see how often subtitles and titles use additional keywords to attract more search-engine traffic.

Examples:

- *The 7 Habits of Highly Effective People: Powerful Lessons in Personal Change*
- *Mindset: The New Psychology of Success*
- *Predictable Revenue: Turn Your Business into a Sales Machine with the $100 Million Best Practices of Salesforce. com*

4. Make a promise of a benefit: Some of the best titles promise to help readers achieve a desired goal or get some wanted benefit. They specifically call out an end result that people want:

Examples:

- *How to Win Friends and Influence People*
- *Getting Things Done*
- *Think And Grow Rich*

5. Be simple and direct: Some of the very best titles are just basic statements about what the book is. There is nothing wrong with this. It can work well, especially for strictly instructional books.

Examples:

- *Getting Past No*
- *Steve Jobs*
- *The Power of Habit*

6. Target an audience: As we said, people use titles to judge if the book is for them. Part of helping people understand this can be targeting them in your title. You can target specific audiences by naming them or by describing their characteristics. This works especially well if you have a series of books and then do versions targeted to specific niches.

Examples:

- *What to Expect When You're Expecting*
- *Physics for Future Presidents*

7. Offer a specific solution to a problem: This is very popular in the self-help and diet spaces. You tell the reader exactly what problem your book solves in the title. This is similar to the promise of a benefit but not the exact same thing. A benefit is something additive, like being sexy. A solution to a problem takes away something negative, like losing weight.

Examples:

- *Man's Search for Meaning*
- *6 Ways to Lose Belly Fat Without Exercise!*
- *Secrets of Closing the Sale*

8. Use numbers to add credibility: Specifics, like numbers, add credibility and urgency to your titles. They can provide structure for your information, or they can make hard things seem easier. Specificity enables people to engage the idea in a more concrete way, and gives bounded limits and certainty on time frames as well.

Examples:

- *The 48 Laws of Power*
- *The 5 Love Languages: The Secret to Love that Lasts*
- *The 21 Irrefutable Laws of Leadership*

9. Pique the reader's curiosity (but withhold the answer): Using statements that seem to be impossible, unusual contrasts, or paradoxes can make readers curious about what is in the book. The idea is to make a claim or statement that seems a little far-fetched or fantastical but promises delivery. This is very popular now with headline writing on sites like Upworthy and ViralNova.

The iconic recent example of this with books is one we already mentioned, *The 4-Hour Workweek.* Everyone wants to know how to work four hours a week, except it seems impossible, so you pick up the book to see what that guy is talking about.

Examples:

- *Networking Is Not Working*
- *10% Happier*

- *Who Moved My Cheese?*

10. Use metaphors or symbols associated with the themes in your book: Humans think in symbol and metaphor. Using these powerful devices can help you create a title that really resonates.

The iconic metaphor-based series is *Chicken Soup for the Soul.* The title signals the warm, nurturing feeling that our culture associates with chicken soup and connects it to something else—stories that nurture your soul.

Examples:

- *Lean In*
- *The Untethered Soul*

11. Use alliteration: Alliteration is the use of the same letter at the beginning of all or most of the words in your title. This makes things easier for humans to remember.

Examples:

- *The Mighty Miss Malone*
- *A Storm of Swords*
- *The Pop-Up Paradigm*

12. Alter a popular phrase: This is common in book titles and tends to work well—taking a famous phrase and altering it in a way that makes sense for you book. This works because it's close to something people know but not exactly the same thing.

Examples:

- *The War of Art*
- *Assholes Finish First*

13. Use slang: Slang can work really well, especially if it's used in a way that is nonintuitive but also novel.

Examples:

- *Ain't Too Proud to Beg*
- *No Mopes Allowed: A Small Town Police Chief Rants and Babbles about Hugs and High Fives, Meth Busts, Internet Celebrity, and Other Adventures*

14. Try cliché formats (or reversing them): There are a ton of book-naming tropes that can work well if used correctly:

- The Art of [TOPIC]
- The Myth of [TOPIC]
- Confessions of [TOPIC]
- How to [TOPIC]
- The Joy of [TOPIC]
- The End of [TOPIC]

Examples:

- *The Art of Racing in the Rain*
- *The Myth of Male Power*
- *Confessions of an Economic Hitman*
- *How to Train Your Dragon*
- *The Joy of Sex*
- *The End of Science*

Done poorly, these kinds of titles can seem clichéd and cloying instead of fresh. This technique is best used when it offers a twist but isn't so far out that it confuses the reader.

15. Consider coining a phrase or new word: This is very helpful, especially if you want to create a brand or company or extended product line out of your book. The problem with this is that it's not an easy thing to do. Many authors try to create new words. Few succeed, so try this sparingly. The most important element of this technique is that the word is easy to say and understand.

Examples:

- *Babbitt*
- *Denialism*
- *Essentialism*

First off, let me very clear about this: **you cannot copyright titles.**

Technically, you can call your book *To Kill a Mockingbird* or *Lord of the Rings* or even *The Holy Bible*.

That being said, copying a popular book makes it VERY hard for your book to stand out and pretty much guarantees a lot of negative reviews from people who are not getting the book they expected.

That being said, you can trademark a title, if it is part of a larger brand. For example, the term "Bulletproof" is trademarked in the health and fitness space by Dave Asprey. You (probably) can't title a book *The Bulletproof Diet* because it infringes on a trademark (not the copyright).

If this is confusing, and you have a book title you think might be a trademark infringement, then talk to an IP attorney.

Also, make sure you check that the title and subtitle have the right keywords you want to address your market, and aligns with any domain and brand issues you have.

STEP 4: PICK YOUR FAVORITES

At this point, you should have a long list of title ideas. Once that's done, you can move on to the next step: picking your titles.

I cannot emphasize how important this next step is:

Everyone has opinions on book titles. Most of those opinions are stupid and wrong.

Even people who get PAID to come up with book titles (editors, publishers, etc.) are usually bad at it.

Test #1: Imagine People Saying the Title

Here's a great test as to whether or not you have a good book title: imagine one of your readers talking about your book at a party to other people.

If you can see them confidently saying the book title aloud, and the people listening nodding and immediately either understanding what the book is about based on that (and perhaps a sentence or two of explanation), or asking for further explanation because it sounds interesting, then you've got a good title.

If you imagine *any other reaction than this one*, you need to rethink your title and probably change it.

Remember, so much of book marketing boils down to word of mouth, and word of mouth is all about people signaling things to other people. You want your book title to inspire and motivate the right people to talk about it because it lets them signal the right things to their friends.

Test #2: (Optional) Test Actual Clicks

Here's one of the keys to testing your titles: test both the main title and subtitle, and test them in many different iterations. Usually what you'll find is most things test about the same, while there will be one thing that clearly tests better as a title and another that clearly tests best as a subtitle.

HOW NOT TO TEST YOUR TITLE

Most of the things authors do to test their title are very, very bad.

For example, posting on social media is NOT TESTING YOUR TITLE. In fact, posting on social media is about the worst possible way to test a title.

Why is this?

Well, your Facebook/Instagram/Twitter friends are probably not your audience, so asking them about the title won't help you. And even worse, everyone on your social media have an agenda relative to you, the author, that will often put you off kilter.

Friends and family don't work. Generally speaking, they want to make you happy. They don't want to give you an objective answer. Or they want to make sure you look good, but they don't know what will actually make you look good.

Furthermore, oftentimes colleagues will be critical because they are jealous. It happens a lot, and they will give you bad advice, even if only subconsciously.

And some authors will go to their marketing teams for title advice, which can often lead you way off kilter. You know the saying that a camel is a horse designed by committee? When you start getting opinions from lots of different sources, you get the "camel effect" hard core.

DOES YOUR BOOK NEED A SUBTITLE?

If you're doing a nonfiction book, yes, probably so.

The way we like to frame it is that the title is the hook, and the subtitle is the explanation. The subtitle is the promise of the book.

Books need a subtitle if it's necessary to contextualize the subject alluded to in the main title. Typically, the subtitle tells the reader some combination of what the book's central premise is, who the book is for, and what promise the book delivers on or need it meets.

Some examples where subtitles help contextualize the title and deliver the promise of the implied title:

1. *The 4-Hour Workweek: Escape 9–5, Live Anywhere, and Join the New Rich*

See how the title hooks you by being interesting and the subtitle explains the premise? Very well done.

2. *Daring Greatly: How the Courage to Be Vulnerable Transforms the Way We Live, Love, Parent, and Lead*

It's a bit long, but the same thing is going on here: the subtitle contextualizes and frames the title, which is clear, easy to understand, and say.

3. *Kitchen Confidential*

This originally had a subtitle, *Adventures in the Culinary Underbelly*, but it was later dropped. No subtitle was needed on this work of nonfiction because the meaning is clear, especially when paired with a picture of a chef on the front (and because it became very famous, which helps).

4. *The Looming Tower: Al-Qaeda and the Road to 9/11*

This is an example of a book where the subtitle is very important. That title could mean many things, but the subtitle quickly signals what the book is about and who it's for.

HOW TO WRITE YOUR BOOK DEDICATION

"We are the stories we tell ourselves."

—JOAN DIDION

WHAT IS A BOOK DEDICATION?

A book dedication is a device that some authors use to bestow a very high honor on a person (or small group of people) they want to praise or otherwise spotlight. It is not fundamentally different than dedicating anything else, like a ship or a monument.

This proclamation usually goes on the dedication page, which is in the very front of the book, after the title page.

WHO CAN AN AUTHOR DEDICATE THEIR BOOK TO?

Anyone they would like. A dedication section is short and

usually focused on one person (or specific group of people). It is usually personal rather than professional. These are categories of people that are common focuses of a book dedication:

1. Family members (spouse, children, siblings, parents)
2. Close friends
3. People impacted by the book or featured in it
4. The readers of the book
5. Inspirational or supportive figures in one's life
6. People the author believes should be highlighted in some way

DO YOU NEED TO DEDICATE YOUR BOOK?

No. Most authors *do* dedicate their books, but it is not required or mandatory.

HOW TO DEDICATE YOUR BOOK

1. DECIDE WHO WILL BE THE FOCUS

Think about the people to whom you want to dedicate this work. Who was the most important person? The seminal influence? The people you care the most about?

Many people write their book dedication to a child or dedicate their book to a friend who has impacted their creative process. There's no magic formula, and you don't have to get everyone in there. This should be short and sweet, and there are no wrong answers. You are expressing a personal sentiment, so only you can decide.

The worst thing you can do is get stuck on it. Either do it or don't, and if you do decide to have one, don't fret over it. Go with your gut. Anyone you leave out can be thanked in the acknowledgments.

2. REMEMBER, EVERYONE WHO READS THE BOOK WILL SEE THIS

Because the dedication is at the beginning of a book, many of the readers will read it and be influenced by it. Think not just about the person or people named in the book dedication but also about all of the readers who will pass by this page and be impacted. Make a conscious choice about what you want that impact to be (if any).

3. MAKE IT SHORT; IT IS NOT AN ACKNOWLEDGMENTS

In contrast to an acknowledgments section, the dedication should be short and to the point. You should not mention everyone who contributed to the book's creation. You can thank everyone you've ever met in the acknowledgements if you want.

4. REVIEW BOOK DEDICATION EXAMPLES (IF NECESSARY)

The easiest way to get some examples of a dedication is to pick up any book on your shelf and look. Almost every book has a dedication, so you can find endless examples. Most of them are very basic and simple, something like this:

For my wife, Megan, and children, Ava, Jaxon, and Elle.

George R. R. Martin, who wrote the *Song of Ice and Fire* series, has a unique dedication in *A Game of Thrones*:

For Phyllis, who made me put the dragons in.

This concise line holds enormous depth for both the readers and the person mentioned. If you've read the books or seen *Game of Thrones*, you'd know that dragons and the fantasy world they represent were a big part of the appeal. To imagine the book without them would be nearly impossible. Phyllis clearly played a big role in the creation of this piece (it's also an inside joke for fans).

Here's the dedication that C. S. Lewis wrote to his god-daughter in *The Lion, the Witch, and the Wardrobe*:

My dear Lucy,

I wrote this story for you, but when I began it I had not realized that girls grow quicker than books. As a result you are already too old for fairy tales, and by the time it is printed and bound you will be older still. But some day you will be old enough to start reading fairy tales again. You can then take it down from some upper shelf, dust it, and tell me what you think of it. I shall

probably be too deaf to hear, and too old to understand a word
you say, but I shall still be

your affectionate Godfather,

C. S. LEWIS

This book was listed as one of *Time* magazine's top 100
novels ever written, and yet he wrote it for his goddaughter.
This dedication gives real substance to the book and to the
author before you even dive in.

This next example is a short-and-sweet dedication from a
book I cowrote with Dr. Geoffrey Miller:

To our 17-year-old former selves, and to Bishop, Atalanta, and
all the sons and daughters who deserve the great relationships
we want for them.

5. WRITE YOUR BOOK DEDICATION

The number one thing to keep in mind is that there is NO
specific formula for this. The dedication is one of the most
personal sections in the book, and it's up to you to decide
how you want to use it.

What's inside of your book is more important, and getting
it out into the world is the MOST important thing.

HOW TO WRITE YOUR BOOK ACKNOWLEDGMENTS

"The only two things that can satisfy the soul are a person and a story; and even a story must be about a person."

—G. K. CHESTERTON

WHAT IS THE ACKNOWLEDGMENTS?

The acknowledgements section is where you recognize and thank everyone who helped you with your book. It's a way to display your appreciation to them in a public and permanent forum.

WHO SHOULD YOU THANK IN THE ACKNOWLEDGMENTS?

This is entirely up to you. Recognize whoever you feel contributed enough to your book that you feel they deserve it.

For example, common groups of people that authors thank include:

1. Family members (spouse, children, parents)
2. Friends
3. Editors/people who worked on the book production
4. Publishers
5. Coworkers/assistants
6. Agents/managers
7. Contributors/advisors/sources of information
8. Teachers/mentors/bosses
9. Inspirations

DO YOU NEED ONE?

No. Most books do have them, but by no means are they required or mandatory.

HOW TO WRITE YOUR ACKNOWLEDGMENTS SECTION

1. REMEMBER, PEOPLE WILL READ THIS

People will read the acknowledgments section, and it will impact them—especially the people who are in them. This section is about those people you are naming, not about you, so approach this as you should your entire book: make it good for the people you are naming, who will read it.

2. START WITH A LIST OF WHO WILL GO IN (BY FULL NAME)

This method has worked well in many situations: write out all the people you want to thank BEFORE you start writing this section. Doing this allows you to see them all together in a list and helps ensure that everyone is on the list who should be there.

Note: A great way to make sure you are not missing anyone is to group people by category so that you are more likely to remember them. When you put your family members together, you are less likely to leave any out.

3. BE SPECIFIC FOR THE IMPORTANT PEOPLE

For the most important people, the more specific you can be in your thanks, the better.

For example, this is not specific:

I want to thank my wife, Veronica. Thank you.

This is specific:

I have to start by thanking my awesome wife, Veronica. From reading early drafts to giving me advice on the cover to keeping the munchkins out of my hair so I could edit, she was as important to this book getting done as I was. Thank you so much, dear.

Being specific in thanks is all about making them feel special. The more detailed you can be in your thanks, the more you're showing that you recognized and appreciated their help. It is rewarding when someone thanks you for a particular thing you did, as opposed to just thanking you overall.

As you go further into your list, you can group people. But again, be specific in your thanks, even to groups. For example, this is not specific:

> Thanks to everyone on my publishing team.

This is specific:

> Thanks to everyone on the Scribe team who helped me so much. Special thanks to Ellie, the ever patient publishing manager, and Meghan, my amazing Scribe, and Erin, the greatest cover designer I could ever imagine.

4. BE SINCERE IN YOUR THANKS

The worst thing you can do in an acknowledgments section is say things you don't believe. If you aren't willing to be sincere, then you are better off not doing one at all.

Sincerity means honestly and deeply thanking the people who helped you (mentioning the specific ways they helped, as noted above) and remembering the way that they sacrificed for you.

At the same time, don't feel the need to go overboard. You're not accepting an Oscar, so don't go on and on or say things just to make yourself look good. Make it meaningful and sincere.

5. DON'T WORRY ABOUT LENGTH

You might see some people recommend the acknowledgments section be only one page. Ignore that.

This is the only section I will tell you that you can go long if you want. You may only write one book in your life, and if that is the case, then take all the time and space you need to thank everyone who helped you. Readers can skip this section if they are bored, but you can never go back and re-thank the people you left out because of some arbitrary "rule."

EXAMPLES OF ACKNOWLEDGMENTS SECTIONS

You can pull almost any book off your shelf and read the acknowledgements section for examples. Here are some examples of different acknowledgments sections for books we have done.

This is from *I Got There*:

> Writing a book is harder than I thought and more rewarding than I could have ever imagined. None of this would have

been possible without my best friend, Bishop. He was the first friend I made when I moved to San Antonio. He stood by me during every struggle and all my successes. That is true friendship.

I'm eternally grateful to my uncle Bobby, who took in an extra mouth to feed when he didn't have to. He taught me discipline, tough love, manners, respect, and so much more that has helped me succeed in life. I truly have no idea where I'd be if he hadn't given me a roof over my head or become the father figure whom I desperately needed at that age.

To Mr. Gentry, who took a chance on a twenty-three-year-old kid and let him run his offices in Portland, Oregon. He never saw my age, my race, or my lack of formal education. He just saw a kid hungry to learn, hungry to grow, and hungry to succeed in business. He never stopped me; he only encouraged me.

Although this period of my life was filled with many ups and downs, my time in the mortgage industry was worth it. My time in the industry wouldn't have been made possible without Guy Stidham, who taught me the honest mortgage game.

A very special thanks to Dustin Wells, who brought me on as the lowest-paid employee at Headspring and then allowed me to rise through the ranks to become president of the company. Thank you for introducing me to company culture.

Writing a book about the story of your life is a surreal process. I'm forever indebted to Tucker Max, Mark Chait, and Amanda Ibey for their editorial help, keen insight, and ongoing support in bringing my stories to life. It is because of their efforts and encouragement that I have a legacy to pass on to my family where one didn't exist before.

To everyone at the Scribe Tribe who enable me to be the CEO of a company that I'm honored to be a part of, thank you for letting me serve, for being a part of our amazing company, and for showing up every day and helping more authors turn their ideas into stories.

To my family. To Aunt Jean: for always being the person I could turn to during those dark and desperate years. She sustained me in ways that I never knew that I needed. To my little brother, Mario, and sisters, Rachel and Kristin: thank you for letting me know that you had nothing but great memories of me. So thankful to have you back in my life.

Finally, to all those who have been a part of my getting there: Jennifer Jackson, Kay Oder, Sharon Slonaker, Julie Fisher, Kathy Chesner, and Brother Smith (RIP). To the original Headspring team: Kevin Hurwitz, Jimmy Bogard, Mahendra Mavani, Pedro Reyes, Eric Sollenberger, Glenn Burnside, Justin Pope, Sharon Cechelli, Anne Epstein.

JT McCormick names people that made his book possible in relative order from most to least impactful. Note how he writes it directly "to" the people who made an impact rather than to the reader "about" those people. He rounds it out with a series of names at the end to make sure people do not feel forgotten, even if he does not have the space to devote a full paragraph to each person.

Bill Hicks, in *The Leadership Manifesto*, starts his acknowledgments off with a blanket acknowledgment of leaders everywhere before naming a handful of them by name. He then thanks his book publishing team and closes with a paragraph acknowledging his CEO. This is a good example of an acknowledgment from a business executive:

> The world is a better place thanks to people who want to develop and lead others. What makes it even better are people who share the gift of their time to mentor future leaders. Thank you to everyone who strives to grow and help others grow. It is the business version of *The Lion King* song "Circle of Life."
>
> To all the individuals I have had the opportunity to lead, be led by, or watch their leadership from afar, I want to say thank you for being the inspiration and foundation for *The Leadership Manifesto*.
>
> Without the experiences and support from my peers and team at Ultimate Software, this book would not exist. You have given me the opportunity to lead a great group of individuals—to be a leader of great leaders is a blessed place to be. Thank you to Chad, Dan, Dave, Gretchen, JC, Laura, Patrick, Scott, and Susan.

Having an idea and turning it into a book is as hard as it sounds. The experience is both internally challenging and rewarding. I especially want to thank the individuals that helped make this happen. Complete thanks to Joanie, Randy Walton, Patrick O'Neill, Barbara Boyd, Carol Raphael, and Dan Bernitt.

Scott Scherr, thank you for being a leader I trust, honor, and respect. I will always welcome the chance to represent you. "Au Au Au!"

Tiffany Haddish, a well-known comedian, continues her "simple yet emotionally powerful" style from her book *The Last Black Unicorn* into the acknowledgments. She thanks her close family and then closes with a joke in line with the subject matter of the book and a blanket acknowledgment to the untold masses who have encouraged her.

I want to thank:

My Grandma.

My Mama.

My Aunties.

My Daddy for donating the sperm that made me.

All my brothers and sisters.

My best friends Selena, Shermona, Aiko, Shana, Richea.

My old agent, my current agents and managers, and Tucker Max.

Department of Children Services and the court system for taking care of me when no one else would.

I want to thank EVERYONE who ever said anything positive to me or taught me something. I heard it all, and it meant something.

All the dudes I ever slept with, I appreciate the experiences, but I ain't naming none of you!

I want to thank God most of all, because without God, I wouldn't be able to do any of this.

SCRIBE GUIDE TO BOOK FOREWORDS

Before you read this, let me really emphasize this point:

Most books do not need a foreword.

If you are unsure if your book needs a foreword, then it probably does not.

However, if you think it might, this guide is designed to help you think through whether it does, and if so, how to get one written.

WHAT IS A BOOK FOREWORD?

A foreword is basically an introduction that's written by someone other than the author. The reasons for it are twofold.

1. CONFER STATUS AND CREDIBILITY ON THE AUTHOR

A foreword is often written by someone who is a credible authority or expert. Having this person write a foreword is a great way to show that a first-time author should be taken seriously.

For example, when James Altucher released *Choose Yourself,* he asked Dick Costolo, CEO of Twitter from 2010 to 2015, to write the foreword. Many readers did not know who James Altucher was at the time, but they knew that the CEO of one of the largest tech companies in the world was willing to vouch for him and his book, which was a strong signal of credibility.

2. PROVIDE CONTEXT AND BACKGROUND FOR THE READER

For some nonfiction books, a foreword explains why readers need this book, and says things about the book that the author cannot.

This context could also say nice things about the author that the author cannot say about themselves. It's much more powerful when someone else calls you a "thought leader," but (like blurbs) it has to be the *right* someone.

For example, we did a book with a man who was well known in real estate but not known outside that space. He was friends with Kevin Harrington, who wrote the foreword. Kevin is well known in many business areas and not only conferred status on the author but also said some great things about him that he could not say about himself, or they would have come off as bragging.

Note again that great forewords do both—they confer status and provide context. If the foreword won't accomplish one of these two things, then it shouldn't be written. As long as it's doing at least one, then the foreword is doing its job.

WHO WRITES THE FOREWORD?

If you want a foreword for your book, the first question is, *"Who do you know that could write one?"*

If you have a good relationship with someone who makes sense, great. Move down to the "how" section.

If you do not know someone that makes sense, then you have two options:

1. Reach out to people you don't know and ask them to write a foreword
2. Do not have a foreword

For many reasons, #2 is the best option.

While it may be possible to get a foreword from someone you don't know, it will be *very* hard. It's easier to get a blurb than a foreword, and the best people to ask are those who you have a personal connection to.

The best way to ask someone to write a foreword is to call them on the phone. If you're not comfortable picking up the phone and dialing their number, then they are probably the wrong person to ask. If you don't know them to call them, why would they ever write a foreword for you?

A foreword tends to be a "personal vouch," and that sort of thing is much easier to get from someone with whom you already have a relationship.

It's also a lot of work. Unlike a blurb that is only a few sentences, this person has to be willing to write a substantial piece of work for you. Also, their name in your book reflects on them, either positively or negatively. If you reach out to someone you don't know, it is hard to ask for both of those things.

If you are unsure about asking someone to do a foreword, you are better off asking for a blurb instead.

Another rule of thumb we like to use is that if we won't put the "Foreword by [NAME]" on the cover of the book, then you are better off asking the person for a blurb.

HOW DO THEY WRITE THE FOREWORD?

Writing a foreword seems pretty obvious: ask someone to write a foreword, and they do it, right?

Some people do exactly that. And in a perfect world, they would all do that, but they don't, for two reasons:

1. People don't have time to sit down and write
2. They're not a good writer, so they get intimidated

For these reasons, we recommend that authors give their foreword writers two options if they do not have the time or desire to sit down and write it the conventional way.

LETTER TO READER OPTION

This is a really simple framework that helps someone get started. You can send these exact instructions to your foreword author:

> "Thank you so much for agreeing to do this. Here is all I need:
>
> - A very short piece, 500 words or so.
> - It can be framed as a 'letter to the reader,' where you tell them why they should read the book.
> - If you want to say nice things about me, I won't be upset."

For this option, make sure that if you need to make any edits to the foreword (aside from obvious misspellings), you get the approval of the author.

You can also "record" their foreword and then have that written (we do this for our authors if they ask).

The process works like this:

1. The author (or someone they hire) interviews the foreword author via phone.
2. The author transcribes the interview. (We use Rev.)
3. The author (or the person they hire) writes the foreword based off that call.
4. The foreword is then sent to the author who makes any changes and then approves it.

This is the basic list of questions we use for a foreword interview:

1. Who is the author? Tell me about them.
2. What is remarkable about the author, especially as it relates to the book topic?
3. What is important about the subject matter of the book?
4. What does the reader need to know about the subject matter of the book?
5. Why should the reader care about this book's subject matter?

HOW LONG SHOULD THE FOREWORD BE?

Only rarely should a foreword exceed 500 words. If it's over that, it needs to be *exceptionally* good.

The mention of the foreword author on the cover is enough to confer status and credibility, and any more than 500 words may detract or distract from the book itself.

The foreword is like a movie trailer. Tell the audience what they need to know in a short amount of time, then get out of the way for the main event.

DOES THE FOREWORD AUTHOR NEED TO READ THE BOOK FIRST?

Not necessarily.

The two reasons for a foreword (confer credibility or provide context) don't necessarily require any commentary on the content.

The foreword should really be focused on the author: who are they, what is their work, and what are they aiming to do with this book?

They don't always need to have read the book to understand the background and context of what's going on in the industry or space that the author is writing about. They can, but it's not crucial.

Now, of course, if the foreword author wants to read it, then let them, obviously. But generally speaking, you should know them so well and have such a good relationship with them that they have plenty to say about you without knowing the specific contents of the book.

START THIS PROCESS EARLY

Understand that most people take forever to write their foreword, so start this process early. If you do not, if you try to do this last minute, it will cause a delay with your book.

HOW TO GET INCREDIBLE BLURBS FOR YOUR BOOK

"The most powerful person in the world is the storyteller."

—STEVE JOBS

WHAT PURPOSE DO BLURBS SERVE?

There are more than 500,000 books published each year in the US alone. How is a potential reader supposed to know that yours is actually good? How are they supposed to know that you and your book are worth their time and money?

There are several ways to signal that your book is serious and professional. The book cover, book title, and book description are three we have covered.

Once you have those locked in, a way to add credibility to your book is through the use of blurbs.

A "book blurb" is a quote from someone that says something positive about you or your book. Here are some blurbs from Mona Patel's book, *Reframe*:

"Why not? What if? If those questions give you pause, it might be because you've been carrying around the wrong frame. In this personal book, Mona Patel wants to outfit you with a new way of seeing and working."

—SETH GODIN, MARKETING GURU AND MULTIPLE TIME *NEW YORK TIMES* BESTSELLING AUTHOR

"Part business, part personal development, Reframe is full of practical ways to jumpstart innovation."

—ADAM GRANT, WHARTON PROFESSOR AND *NEW YORK TIMES* BESTSELLING AUTHOR OF *GIVE AND TAKE*

"This book, like its author, is innovative, clear, and able to open pathways to new ideas."

—NIR EYAL, AUTHOR OF *HOOKED: HOW TO BUILD HABIT-FORMING PRODUCTS*

Done properly, a good blurb will:

1. Signal that the book is important
2. Provide social proof that the author is important
3. Help readers see the book is relevant to them

4. Most importantly, convince a potential reader to buy the book

Blurbs are a great way to "credential" a book (and more importantly, in many cases, an author as well) and help it stand out from the field.

ARE BLURBS NECESSARY?

Absolutely not.

Blurbs fall into the "nice to have" category and not the "must have" category.

They do impact the book but don't move the needle anywhere near as much as reviews. Actual reviews on Amazon or BarnesandNoble.com are much more powerful in terms of selling copies.

It is generally better not to include blurbs than to have bad ones or ones from unknown sources.

Do not get obsessed with them. Again, blurbs are not a necessity, and many famous books have launched and succeeded without them.

For example, name your favorite three books. Who blurbed those books?

WHERE DO BLURBS GO?

Blurbs are multipurpose and can go several places. For example:

1. **Front of book cover:** Usually only one can go on the cover, and that would generally be from someone of very high status to your audience.
2. **Back of book cover:** You can usually put up to three of them here without crowding the back.
3. **Inside flap cover:** This is for hardcovers usually, and they can go on the inside front or back, depending on various decisions.
4. **Before the title page:** If you have a lot of blurbs, you can put them on their own pages, usually right at the beginning of the book. This is usually called the "Advance Praise" section.
5. **On the Amazon/Barnes and Noble book page:** Putting blurbs in the book description or the "About the Book" section can add a lot of social proof to the book.
6. **On your website:** Another place to put them, though only one or possibly two tend to work here.
7. **In your press materials:** This is definitely a place to put them as well, as they will help land you press.

WHAT IS A GOOD BLURB?

A good blurb generally has these attributes:

1. COMES FROM A RELEVANT, HIGH-STATUS, OR CREDIBLE PERSON

This is key. You want your source to be one that sends the right signals to the audience of the book and conveys the authority you want to achieve with your book. There are a lot of subtleties to this we will explain later in this section.

2. HELPS THE READER UNDERSTAND WHY THE BOOK MATTERS TO THEM

It's not easy to frame or explain your book to a reader, and a blurb can help them understand why they need to buy and read your book.

3. IS NOT PITCHY OR OVER THE TOP

The worst thing you can do is get a great person to leave a gushing blurb that sounds paid for or ridiculous. Realistic is better than explosively optimistic. People tend to discount things that seem too good to be true.

WHERE CAN BLURBS COME FROM?

There are three basic types of blurbs, and we'll walk through each one in detail.

1. Quotes from credible, high-status people
2. Press mentions
3. Reader and customer testimonials

1. QUOTES FROM CREDIBLE OR HIGH-STATUS PEOPLE

Most people do not pay much attention to what blurbs actually say, since almost all blurbs are uniformly positive. Instead, people pay attention to *who* gave the blurb and judge your book based on the person endorsing it.

The more credibility and social status the endorser holds, the more powerful the blurb. You are using some of the credibility and status of the person giving the blurb and reflecting it back on your book.

An excellent example is, *Give and Take*. When it was published, Adam Grant was a fairly obscure professor, not well known outside of academic circles. But his work had been influential on many famous authors, and he asked them to provide blurbs for his book. Look at the list of people who blurbed him:

- Susan Cain
- Dan Pink
- Tony Hsieh
- Seth Godin
- Dan Ariely
- Gretchen Rubin
- David Allen
- Dan Gilbert
- Robert Cialdini

Those people are all famous authors (at least to the type of reader to whom Adam wanted to sell). That list forced his audience to not only give it a chance but made the media take it seriously as well.

You're trying to borrow the credibility and authority of a person, and sometimes that can be conveyed by their position, even if they aren't famous themselves.

Not all people know famous authors, and not all blurbs should come from famous authors. You can also get blurbs from people who have high-status positions.

For example, look at the blurbs for *Chasing Excellence* (a book about fitness and athletic training). Do you know who any of these people are?

- Javier Vazquez
- Chris Hinshaw
- Bethany Hart-Gerry

Probably not. They're not widely famous by name. Now, let's look at how they are listed on the *Chasing Excellence* Amazon page:

- Javier Vazquez, Major League Baseball All-Star
- Chris Hinshaw, Professional Triathlete, winner of Ironman Brazil
- Bethany Hart-Gerry, US Olympic Bobsled Team

You don't know the names, but given their titles and accomplishments, you now take their comments on a book about fitness and training VERY seriously.

2. PRESS MENTIONS

Most of your blurbs will come from people that you ask. However, another good place to find blurbs is in press or media attention you may have gotten from a media source. For example:

"Hilariously entertaining and thoroughly reprehensible."

—*NEW YORK TIMES*

The above example was a quote about my first book *I Hope They Serve Beer in Hell*. The article itself was not resoundingly positive, but this was a positive mention, so I took it and put it on my book. Having the *New York Times* even mention my book was significant social proof to a potential reader.

Press from anywhere can make a difference—even from a relatively unknown media source. Any third-party press adds credibility to you and your book regardless of whether the praise was directly for your book or not.

3. READER AND CUSTOMER TESTIMONIALS

You can also use customer reviews as testimonials. If you've written a book before, your old reviews may be a good place to search for an extra blurb or two. Early reviews can be moved up on the Amazon page, to round out the blurbs.

The book *Predictable Revenue* does this. The authors received feedback from people who read the book and used them as blurbs (and made sure to list their job titles to gain more social proof):

"I couldn't put it down. It's saved me so much time, and now revenue is ramping up. After reading the book, we closed major deals immediately with the strategies."

—KURT DARADICS, CEO, FREEDOM SPEAKS/CITYSOURCED.COM

"I just finished reading your book. Unbelievable! I now know what's wrong with our sales process."

—PAT SHAH, CEO, SURCHSQUAD

"I have read Predictable Revenue and it's entrepreneurial crack!"

—DAMIEN STEVENS, CEO, SERVOSITY

You can even solicit testimonials from actual clients (depending on what you do and how it relates to your book). The authors of *Predictable Revenue* did this as well:

"Working with Aaron Ross has been nothing short of amazing! His methods applied to our sales organization helped us produce a profitable and scalable new stream of predictable

revenue. We saw at least 40+% new business growth. The best part is, we had a blast while doing it!"

—MICHAEL STONE, VP SALES AND STRATEGY, WPROMOTE (#1 RANKED SEARCH MARKETING FIRM ON THE INC. 500)

This works because the *Predictable Revenue* audience is entrepreneurs and CEOs, and that is who is giving the blurbs.

WHO SHOULD YOU ASK FOR BLURBS?

Blurbs are ideal to request from people in your network who are well known, important, or have important jobs.

The key consideration here is to focus on asking people who fit two criteria:

1. They are known to the audience you're trying to reach (or have jobs or titles that sound credible to that audience)
2. You already know them

To decide who to reach out to, start with a big list—the more names, the more likely you are to get a yes.

These should be specific people, not a list of famous people you've never met.

If you do not have some connection to them in your network, do not put them on your list. If you don't know the person or have a credible connection that is already established, then you aren't getting a blurb.

Ask someone who has a strong connection with **both** your audience and the material. It's much better to get a quote from a person that your audience knows well but is anonymous outside that niche than someone who is very famous but has nothing to do with your book.

For example, if you write a book about pop-up retail, and you happen to be friends with a famous politician who has nothing to do with retail or any connection, a blurb from her won't resonate with your audience.

Whereas if you can get the VP of Macy's to blurb your book—even though no one outside of retail has any idea who she is—that quote will be a powerful signal to the audience for your book (people who care about retail).

HOW SHOULD YOU ASK SOMEONE FOR A BLURB?

The process of asking for blurbs can be a bit uncomfortable for most authors. The best thing you can do when asking for a blurb is to make it as easy as possible for people to give you one.

In that vein, we're going to let you in on a dirty little secret: *most people who give blurbs don't actually read the book.*

In fact, most of them *don't even write the blurb*...they just approve it.

Here is the email template we recommend using when asking someone for a blurb. Of course, you need to modify this with details relevant to the person you're asking:

[INSERT NAME],

Hey, I'm writing to ask if you'd provide a blurb for my upcoming book, [INSERT TITLE].

It would mean a great deal to me if you gave an endorsement. [INSERT SPECIFIC REASON WHY BASED ON YOUR RELATIONSHIP].

I've attached a PDF to this email with the manuscript so you can read it if you'd like.

Obviously, I'd love it if you read the full book, but I value your time highly, so I am providing 2–3 example blurbs for you. Feel free to approve any of these or edit them in any way you'd like that reflects your feelings:

[INSERT EXAMPLE BLURB #1]

[INSERT EXAMPLE BLURB #2]

[INSERT EXAMPLE BLURB #3]

KEY TO BLURBS: BLURB THE PERSON, NOT THE BOOK

Most people don't have the time to read your book and carefully consider a blurb, but they don't feel comfortable blurbing something they haven't read. That's okay.

There is a very simple solution: **have them blurb you as a person.**

This is more than acceptable and a very easy give for most people.

For example, I helped Kamal Ravikant do this for his second book *Live Your Truth*. He is friends with Tim Ferriss, but Tim was too busy to read the book (at that time—he has since read and loved the book), so I got Tim to give Kamal this blurb:

"Kamal is one of those people whose words are as powerful as his presence. When Kamal speaks, I listen."

—TIM FERRISS, AUTHOR OF #1 *NEW YORK TIMES* BESTSELLER *THE 4-HOUR WORKWEEK*

That quote is now on his Amazon page and the book, and is a powerful piece of social proof for Kamal and his book.

ANOTHER BLURB TRICK

Speaking of Tim, he uses a great trick to get blurbs, and I helped him do this on two books.

While the book is still in process, he would print the most relevant chapter to the person he was asking for the blurb, personally highlight relevant sections and passages (with a highlighter and pen), and mail THAT to the person, with the offer of sending the whole book if they want.

That's a smart, strategic, and generous move, and it worked almost every time.

HOW TO WRITE BLURBS FOR APPROVAL

There is not a formula to write blurbs, but there are a few rules:

- They cannot be too long, or no one will read them.
- They can't be too pitchy or over the top, or they lose credibility.
- The most important thing is that the blurb focuses on the benefit for the reader—why should the reader care about the book?

For this, the best advice is for you to go find the five to ten books on Amazon that you think are good comparisons to your book (or in similar niches), read the blurbs for them, and imitate their style. Different niches have different blurb styles, and the best thing you can do with a blurb is not violate any norms the readers are expecting.

EXAMPLE OF A GREAT, DIRECTED BLURB LIST

Remember, the more focused the blurb list is on your audience, the better it will be for you. Here is an excellent example of the appropriate use of blurbs from the book *Common Financial Sense*, by Harris Nydick and Greg Makowski:

"This guide delivers the most practical and straightforward tutorial I have ever read."

—HAZEL O'LEARY, FORMER UNITED
STATES SECRETARY OF ENERGY

"I wish I had access to this book earlier in my career! I promise to pay it forward by sending a copy of Common Financial Sense to each of my three twenty-something kids."

—SKIP SCHWEISS, PRESIDENT, TD
AMERITRADE TRUST COMPANY

"Common Financial Sense is an insightful new guide that simplifies and demystifies retirement plan investing. Read this book! It will help you make smart decisions to successfully pursue your financial goals."

—JOSHUA PACE, PRESIDENT AND CEO, E*TRADE

"Common Financial Sense is a breath of fresh air and should be required reading for everyone entering or in the workforce."

—DEAN DURLING, PRESIDENT AND
CEO, QUICKCHEK CORPORATION

Unless you're in the financial industry, few of these names mean anything to you.

But it's still a great list because the people have high-status job titles, and they are extremely important *to the audience to whom this book is trying to appeal.*

This list of blurbs signals exactly who this book is for and converts those specific people at a very high rate from browsers into readers.

LOCK IN YOUR MANUSCRIPT: COPYEDITING

"Remember, Grammar Nazis: it's YOU'RE going to die alone."

—DAMIEN FAHEY

To be perfectly clear, when we say you need "a finished manuscript" to start the publishing process, we don't just mean a document that's pretty close to your finished book. We don't mean a file with only a few typos left.

We mean a *finished manuscript.*

It's crucial that you get as much of that work out of the way as possible before starting the publishing process. Adding a paragraph now rather than after the interior layout is finished means the difference between a few minutes and *a few hours* of work.

This is NOT hyperbole. Getting your manuscript locked prior to publishing often translates to thousands of dollars of savings. It's worth taking the time to lock everything in thoroughly.

STEP 1: HIRE A PROFESSIONAL COPY EDITOR

I can't be any clearer about it than this: hire at least one professional copy editor to review your book.

Don't rely on spellcheck. Don't ask your friends. Don't get your neighbor to look it over.

I don't care how confident you are that there are no mistakes. You're wrong. They are there, and if you don't hire professionals to find them, you'll miss them, and then readers will think you are stupid.

There is a lot of data on this, but average people only detect about 60 percent of errors, and even professionals usually only catch about 85 percent. (That is why we have two different people review every manuscript we do for authors at Scribe.)

While your out-loud editing will catch a lot of the small, sloppy mistakes and wording issues, there are a whole other set of issues that professional proofreaders are looking for: small grammatical rules that native English speakers often don't even realize exist.

For example:

- Do you know the difference between an en dash and an em dash?
- Do you end sentences in prepositions?
- Do you start too many sentences with conjunctions?

These kinds of mistakes are not life threatening, but they make the difference between a professional book and one that comes across as amateur. And beyond that, if Amazon gets too many reports about typos in your book, they will pull the book down.

There are two distinct types of copyediting services: those that allow you to submit the manuscript and they manage their team internally, and marketplaces that allow you to find your own freelancer. The first is simpler, but the second (marketplaces) tends to be more effective.

EDITING SERVICES

If you choose to go with editing services, you'll likely be charged a flat fee. You can ballpark that these options will cost about $250–$750 depending in various factors. You'll submit the manuscript, and within a week, you'll get back a finished product. Simple.

Here are a few services we've tested and recommend:

- PostScripting (https://postscripting.net/)
- Kibin (https://www.kibin.com/)
- Scribendi (http://www.scribendi.com/)

MARKETPLACES

The other alternative is to use a marketplace. Most of these options will allow you to list a job for free, and the marketplace will take a percentage of the cost. The copy editors will usually work on a per-hour or per-word basis ($20–$30 per hour and 0.75–1 cent per word are normal), but some will be open to charging a flat fee as well. The total cost should be similar to the prices above.

Here are a few marketplaces we've tested and recommend:

- Upwork (https://www.upwork.com/)
- People Per Hour (http://www.peopleperhour.com/)
- MediaBistro (http://mediabistro.com/)

The real benefit of using a marketplace instead of a service is the direct engagement you get with the copyeditor. Not only will you be able to choose someone who seems best suited for your project (and who has been rated well by past clients), but you'll also be able to convey extra information to them that might be useful in their proofreading work.

STEP 2: WORKING WITH YOUR COPY EDITOR

Once you've found the right copy editor, you'll need to assign them the job and work with them. We spoke to our team of professionals to gather feedback on what they need out of a job assignment. Here is there advice:

1) Define the role: As one of our editors said, "Copyediting is rarely just copyediting, no matter what the client calls it." There's a lot of responsibility that can be put on a copy editor, and it's important to be clear about what that responsibility is.

Traditionally, a copy editor's task is to find any mistakes, inconsistencies and errors, like typos and grammatical and spelling mistakes. However, it's not uncommon (because they're the last line of defense against a faulty manuscript being released) for them to take on more responsibility.

2) Explain the audience: Not every book is written in the Queen's English, nor should they be. For a proofreader to accurately distinguish between what to edit and what's an intentional style choice, it's important for them to understand the audience for the book and the message it's trying to convey.

This can be as high level as whether or not profanity is okay, or as specific as the country of origin to make sure that the sayings and spellings are correct.

3) Point out what needs work: You can often (although not always) anticipate issues. For example, we recently worked on a book that was written in such a way that it jumped back and forth between past and present tense. We fixed this problem in the manuscript, but it was worth explaining the situation to the proofreader so that she, too, could be on the lookout for similar mistakes. You can apply this strategy too. If you know you have a tendency to make sloppy typos or misuse a certain type of punctuation, for example, tell your editor. The more clues you can give them as to what they might be looking for, the better your book will be.

STEP 3: FINISH THE PROCESS

Once the copy editor is done, they should send you back a Word document with all their changes made in Track Changes. This is the industry standard, and it's worth confirming with them **before** hiring them that they'll be tracking the changes for you.

When you receive the document, you should expect to find a lot of small tracked changes. Most of these will be obvious mistakes that you're happy to accept, but some may be phrasing recommendations or questions about pieces that are unclear.

Some may be spelling or punctuation corrections that are *technically* accurate but not commonly used. Remember, a proofreader's job is to follow rules, not make editorial choices.

Sometimes you may want to purposely break rules to stay current or create your unique tone and voice. Be sure to go through all of these changes and make your own decisions about what should be implemented and what shouldn't.

STEP 4: READY TO PUBLISH?

At this point, you should have a manuscript that you're confident enough to lock in and publish.

We should note that you'll probably never be 100 percent confident that your manuscript is ready to go. No writer is.

But at some point—generally after all of these steps—there is nothing else left for you to do other than lock it in and put it out. Don't waste weeks or months trying to get it from 99.9 percent perfect to 100 percent. It's impossible. Recognize when diminishing marginal returns have set in and move on.

Once your manuscript is locked, it's time to get started with the publishing process.

PART 7

DESIGN AND MARKET YOUR BOOK

HOW TO WRITE A BOOK DESCRIPTION THAT SELLS

"Anyone who tries to make a distinction between education and entertainment doesn't know the first thing about either."

—MARSHALL MCLUHAN

After the title and the cover, the most important marketing material for your book is the description.

The book description goes multiple places, most prominently on the back cover and right below the price (on Amazon). It's crucial for this short description to be right.

In this chapter, we will walk you through how to write and create your book description and include some examples of authors who did it well and those who didn't.

WHY YOUR BOOK DESCRIPTION MATTERS

The book description is the pitch to the reader about why they should buy your book. It is sales copy to get them to see that the book is for them (or not), and then make the purchase.

There are so many examples of how book descriptions lead to huge changes in sales. One of my favorite stories is for JT McCormick's book, *I Got There*.

Despite having a nice cover and receiving good reviews, it wasn't selling as many copies as it should have. So we dove into the book description, figured out the flaws, and completely revamped it.

Sales doubled—*within an hour*.

This isn't uncommon. In many cases, the description is the factor that solidifies in the reader's mind whether the book is for them or not. If you get it right, the purchase is almost automatic. If you get it wrong, very little else can really save you (except a recommendation from the right source).

Remember, people are looking for a reason to not buy your book, so having a good book description is key to keeping them on the purchasing track.

HOW TO WRITE YOUR BOOK DESCRIPTION

At Scribe, our copywriters use the *Hook, Pain, Pleasure, Legitimacy, Open Loop* format.

1. HOOK

The first sentence should be something that will grab your desired reader and make them take notice. If that isn't right—or worse, if it's *wrong*—you can lose the reader immediately, and then it doesn't matter what the rest of the description says.

People are always looking for a reason to move on to the next thing. Don't give it to them. Make the first sentence something that forces them to read the rest of the description. Every good book description you see is interesting from the first sentence.

Generally speaking, this means focusing on the boldest claim in the book, the most sensational fact, or the most compelling idea.

2. PAIN

Once you have their attention, clearly describe the current pain they are in. If you can accurately and realistically describe the pain of the reader, you will have them fully engaged in the description and seriously entertaining the idea of buying the book.

You don't need to be gratuitous here, all you need to do is be accurate: What pain is in their life? What unsolved problems do they have? Or, perhaps, what unachieved aspirations or goals do they have? Clearly and directly articulate these in plain and simple language.

3. PLEASURE

Then tell them what the book does to help them solve for this pain. Done right, this creates an emotional connection by describing how the book will make the potential reader feel after reading it. Or even better, what the reader will get out of reading the book.

Will it make them happy or rich? Will it help them lose weight or have more friends? What do they get once they read this book?

Be clear about the benefits—don't insinuate them. You are selling a result to the reader, not a process (even though your book is the process). Explain exactly what the book is about in clear, obvious terms.

4. LEGITIMACY

This is simply about letting the reader know why they should listen to you, why you are the authority and the expert that they need to hear from. This can be very short and should not be a focus of the book description.

You want just enough social proof to make them keep reading.

This can also go in the hook. If there is an impressive fact to mention (e.g., *New York Times* bestseller), that should be bolded in the first sentence. Or if there is one salient and amazing thing about you or the book, that can go in the book description, something like, "From the author of [INSERT WELL KNOWN BESTSELLING BOOK]." Or perhaps, "From the world's most highly decorated Marine sniper, this is the definitive book on shooting."

5. OPEN LOOP

You state the problem or question your book addresses, you show that you solve or answer it, but you also leave a small key piece out. This piques the interest of the reader and leaves them wanting more.

You do want to be very explicit about what they will learn, but you don't have to go deep into the "how." This is to create an "open loop," so to speak. You are keeping back the secret sauce that is actually in the book.

This being said, do not make the reader struggle to understand what your point is or how to get the reader there. This is especially true for prescriptive books (how-to, self-help, motivational, etc.). People like to understand the basics of the "how" (as well as the "what"), especially if it's something new or novel. This is a balance that our examples will show you how to hit.

EXAMPLES OF GOOD BOOK DESCRIPTIONS
CAMERON HEROLD'S *VIVID VISION*

Many corporations have slick, flashy mission statements that ultimately do little to motivate employees and less to impress customers, investors, and partners.

But there is a way to share your excitement for the future of your company in a clear, compelling, and powerful way, and entrepreneur and business growth expert Cameron Herold can show you how.

Vivid Vision is a revolutionary tool that will help owners, CEOs, and senior managers create inspirational, detailed, and actionable three-year mission statements for their companies. In this easy-to-follow guide, Herold walks organization leaders through the simple steps to creating their own *Vivid Vision*, from brainstorming to sharing the ideas to using the document to drive progress in the years to come.

By focusing on mapping out how you see your company looking and feeling in every category of business, without getting bogged down by data and numbers, *Vivid Vision* creates a holistic road map to success that will get all of your teammates passionate about the big picture.

Your company is your dream—one that you want to share with your staff, clients, and stakeholders. *Vivid Vision* is the tool you need to make that dream a reality.

What Makes It Good?

Three things make this good:

1. **Engaging hook:** Everyone knows that mission statements are BS, but how many people say this out loud? By doing so, it takes a stand and engages the potential reader immediately.

2. **Important key words:** We tend to advocate staying away from buzzwords in your book description, but in some cases—especially business books—the right use of them can work. This is an example of where they work. Words and phrases like "easy-to-follow" and "simple steps" and "drive progress" actually work.

3. **Clear pain and benefit:** This book is not appealing to everyone, but to the perfect reader, it's very appealing because it clearly articulates a real problem (*"slick, flashy mission statements that ultimately do little"*) and then tells you the result it delivers (*"detailed, actionable three-year mission statements for their companies"*) and basically how it gets you there (*"mapping out how you see your company looking and feeling in every category of business"*).

Forget the old concept of retirement and the rest of the deferred-life plan—there is no need to wait and every reason not to, especially in unpredictable economic times.

Whether your dream is escaping the rat race, experiencing high-end world travel, earning a monthly five-figure income with zero management, or just living more and working less, *The 4-Hour Workweek* is the blueprint.

This step-by-step guide to luxury lifestyle design teaches:

· How Tim went from $40K per year and 80 hours per week to $40K per month and four hours per week
· How to outsource your life to overseas virtual assistants for $5 per hour and do whatever you want
· How blue-chip escape artists travel the world without quitting their jobs
· How to eliminate 50% of your work in 48 hours using the principles of a forgotten Italian economist
· How to trade a long-haul career for short work bursts and frequent "mini-retirements"

What Makes It Good?

There are three things that make this good.

1. **It has a great hook:** Tim immediately tells you why this book matters to YOU—because you can stop waiting for

retirement. Who doesn't want to retire now? Okay, I'm interested, tell me more.

2. **It has bulleted, specific info about pain and pleasure:** A vague promise is no good if it doesn't deliver. Tim then makes specific promises about the information in the book, both about things that have happened and things it will teach you.

3. **It makes you want to read more:** After the contrast of the big broad goal and the specific information, at the very least, any reader is going to keep going into the reviews and other information. You're hooked. You want to know HOW he teaches this.

TYLER COWEN'S *AVERAGE IS OVER*

Widely acclaimed as one of the world's most influential economists, Tyler Cowen returns with his groundbreaking follow-up to the *New York Times* bestseller *The Great Stagnation.*

The widening gap between rich and poor means dealing with one big, uncomfortable truth: If you're not at the top, you're at the bottom.

The global labor market is changing radically thanks to growth at the high end—and the low. About three quarters of the jobs created in the United States since the great recession pay only a bit more than minimum wage. Still, the United States has more millionaires and billionaires than any country ever, and we continue to mint them.

In this eye-opening book, renowned economist and bestselling author Tyler Cowen explains that phenomenon: High earners are taking ever more advantage of machine intelligence in data analysis and achieving ever-better results. Meanwhile, low earners who haven't committed to learning, to making the most of new technologies, have poor prospects. Nearly every business sector relies less and less on manual labor, and this fact is forever changing the world of work and wages. A steady, secure life somewhere in the middle—average—is over.

With *The Great Stagnation*, Cowen explained why median wages stagnated over the last four decades; in *Average Is Over*, he reveals the essential nature of the new economy, identifies the best path forward for workers and entrepreneurs, and provides readers with actionable advice to make the most of the new economic landscape. It is a challenging and sober must-read but ultimately exciting, good news. In debates about our nation's economic future, it will be impossible to ignore.

What Makes It Good?

This book description does almost everything right. It quickly establishes the author credentials, it immediately states the huge social question it addresses, and it does so in a way that creates an emotional reaction from the reader. Questions of equality are highly emotionally charged.

It then spends two short paragraphs laying out the context

of the debate over economic equality and then tells you exactly what the book will tell you without giving its thesis away. This description almost forces you to read this book.

EXAMPLES OF BAD BOOK DESCRIPTIONS

BEN HOROWITZ'S *THE HARD THING ABOUT HARD THINGS*

Ben Horowitz, cofounder of Andreessen Horowitz and one of Silicon Valley's most respected and experienced entrepreneurs, offers essential advice on building and running a startup—practical wisdom for managing the toughest problems business school doesn't cover, based on his popular Ben's blog.

While many people talk about how great it is to start a business, very few are honest about how difficult it is to run one. Ben Horowitz analyzes the problems that confront leaders every day, sharing the insights he's gained developing, managing, selling, buying, investing in, and supervising technology companies. A lifelong rap fanatic, he amplifies business lessons with lyrics from his favorite songs, telling it straight about everything from firing friends to poaching competitors, cultivating and sustaining a CEO mentality, to knowing the right time to cash in.

Filled with his trademark humor and straight talk, *The Hard Thing About Hard Things* is invaluable for veteran entrepreneurs as well as those aspiring to their own new ventures, drawing from Horowitz's personal and often humbling experiences.

What's Wrong with It?

This description is bad because—based just on this description—the book seems somewhat bland and boring. If I don't know anything about Horowitz before I read that description, what in there makes me want to know more? Nor does it really tell me anything about the substance of what he says in the book, and it substantially undersells both Horowitz's prominence and the resonance and importance of the book's message. And who cares that he likes rap? What does that matter to me, the reader?

Compare this with the description for Tyler Cowen's book above. It explains who Cowen is and why I should care, it tells me what he says, applies the book to my life, and shows me exactly why I need to care about what he wrote.

The irony is that having read both books, I can tell you that Horowitz's is just as good if not *better* than Cowen's. But you would never know this from comparing the descriptions.

DOUGLAS RUSHKOFF'S *COERCION: WHY WE LISTEN TO WHAT "THEY" SAY*

Noted media pundit and author of *Playing the Future* Douglas Rushkoff gives a devastating critique of the influence techniques behind our culture of rampant consumerism. With a skilled analysis of how experts in the fields of marketing, advertising, retail atmospherics, and hand-selling attempt to take away our ability to make rational decisions, Rushkoff delivers a bracing account of media ecology today, consumerism in America, and why we buy what we buy, helping us recognize when we're being treated like consumers instead of human beings.

What's Wrong with It?

Short descriptions are great, but this is too short to even tell me what the book says. This is an example of overselling, without doing it right. Look at the descriptions: "devastating," "skilled analysis," and "bracing account." This description sounds like he's doing what he says he's warning us about: selling without substance. In no place does this description connect the reader to the issues in the book in a way that is engaging or compelling.

MORE BOOK DESCRIPTION BEST PRACTICES

1. MINDSET SHIFT: IT'S AN AD, NOT A SUMMARY

Don't think of the book description as a synopsis. It is not meant to summarize your book. So many authors want to put everything about their book in this section. Resist that urge.

It is an advertisement. Think of it like a trailer for your book. It is designed to make people *want to read* your book. You want them to take action and buy it.

2. USE COMPELLING KEYWORDS

It's not enough to be accurate—you need to use high traffic

keywords that increase the likelihood your book will get picked up in search. For example, if *Sports Illustrated* does a book, you'd want to not only say *Sports Illustrated* magazine but also mention the names of the A-list athletes in the book. Even better, use words that evoke an emotional response on the part of the reader. Don't use "jerk" when "asshole" will work.

3. KEEP IT SHORT

On average, Amazon bestsellers have descriptions that are about 200 words long. Most descriptions are broken up into two paragraphs, but some are kept at one, and some run to three.

4. SIMPLE WRITING

Keep the writing simple. Use short, clear sentences. You don't want anyone to struggle to comprehend what you're trying to convey because you've strung too many ideas together in one long run-on sentence.

5. WRITE AS THE PUBLISHER, NOT THE AUTHOR

This will probably be obvious to you, but the book description should always be in a third-person objective voice, and never your author voice. It is always written as someone else describing your book.

6. NO INSECURITY

Don't compare your book to other books. I see this all the time, and all it does is make the book (and the author) immediately look inferior. Plus, a reader may hate the book you are comparing yourself to, and you'll lose them.

The only place a comparison makes sense is if you are quoting a very reputable source that makes the comparison itself.

7. DON'T INSIST ON DOING IT YOURSELF

I can't tell you how many amazing authors I've had come to me utterly befuddled because they couldn't write their own book description. This is normal.

The reality is that the author is often the worst person to write their own book description. They're too close to the material and too emotionally invested. If this is the case, we recommend either asking a friend to help or going to a professional editor or—even better—a professional copywriter for assistance.

HOW TO WRITE YOUR AUTHOR BIO (AND WHY IT MATTERS)

Unless you're one of the household name authors (Steven King, J. K. Rowling, Malcolm Gladwell), you have to assume people thinking about buying your book will not know who you are.

So how will they learn about you? And why is this even important?

That's what this chapter will explain: how to properly write your author bio and why it's so important.

WHY YOUR AUTHOR BIO IS SO IMPORTANT

Even though very few authors think about it and even fewer writing or publishing guides talk about it, the "Author Bio" section will impact sales and reputation and will often determine what media you get.

The author bio impacts sales directly. "Author reputation" is consistently cited as one of the main factors that influence book buying. If you can establish yourself as an authority on your book topic, readers will be much more inclined to buy your book, read it, and regard you the way you want them to. People are considering spending their disposable income on your book, and they are looking for a reason to do it or not do it. A great bio helps them do it (while a bad bio will often stop them).

Furthermore, if you want your book to help create a business for you or establish your credibility or authority in a subject, often the author bio is more important than what's actually in the book. The sad but true reality is that more people will read your author bio than your actual book. It takes a long time to read a book, but it's very easy to make a snap judgment based on a short paragraph, and most people do that.

This is doubly true for media. Most people in media work very hard under tight deadlines and don't have time to read long books or even long, meandering pitch emails. But a good author bio cuts right to the point by saying: *this is a person who is important, and I need to pay attention to them.*

HOW TO WRITE YOUR AUTHOR BIO

Writing about yourself is typically a task that most writers shy away from, but writing an effective author bio doesn't have to be painful. A few simple steps can get you to an effective bio that will not only impress interested readers and media but also help sell your book.

1. DEMONSTRATE YOUR AUTHORITY AND CREDENTIALS ON YOUR BOOK SUBJECT (BUT DON'T OVERSTATE THEM)

Whatever your book is about, it's important to establish your credentials in that area. For example, if you're writing a diet book, mention professional degrees or training or accomplishments, or other things that clearly signal your authority and credibility in that space.

If you struggle with what to say about yourself, remember that the idea is to make it clear why you're credible and professional (as opposed to an unknown, untrusted source), i.e., why the reader should listen to you.

For some types of books and authors, this is harder to do. If there's no clear way to signal direct authority or credentials—for example, a novel or a book about your life stories—then don't make up things or try to "invent" authority. Focus on the other parts of the author bio.

2. INCLUDE ACHIEVEMENTS THAT BUILD CREDIBILITY OR ARE INTERESTING TO THE READER (WITHOUT GOING OVERBOARD)

In your author bio, you'll want to include some things you've accomplished in your life, especially if you don't have direct credentials and authority in the book subject matter. This will help your audience understand why they should spend their time and money reading what you've got to say.

If you have something about you or your life that is unusual, even if it's not totally relevant, you should still consider putting it in your bio.

For example, if you were a Rhodes Scholar or you started a major national organization or you won a national championship in ping-pong—whatever—the point is to show the reader that you have done things that matter, even if they don't matter to the book.

If you are lacking on credentials or exciting things, you can always put in your passions and interests. Anything that you enjoy doing, writing about, or consider a hobby, especially if they are relevant to the book topic.

That being said, do NOT ramble on and on about things that reader doesn't care about. Put yourself in your readers' shoes and ask yourself, "Does this fact really matter to anyone but me?"

3. MENTION ANY BOOKS YOU'VE WRITTEN, AND YOUR WEBSITE (BUT DON'T OVERSELL THEM)

If you've written other books, especially on that subject, make sure to mention them. If they're bestsellers or won awards, even better. If you've won multiple awards and you are finding that listing them all is becoming tedious, aim for brevity instead. Simply writing *"John Smith is an award-winning author whose works include..."* is more than enough to show your readers you know what you're doing.

If you have a website, a longer bio page, or anything else that helps promote your brand, then you should make sure you include it at the bottom of your bio (assuming this meets your goals). Again, you don't want to brag here, so just be humble and simply put something like *"Find out more about John at JohnSmithWriter.com."* It's simple and has a clear call to action.

4. DROP SOME RELEVANT NAMES, IF THEY'RE APPROPRIATE (WITHOUT BEING CRASS)

Yes, name-dropping can put off readers if it's done wrong. But there is a right way to do it.

For example, if you are relatively unknown, you can say something like, "The woman that Seth Godin called 'the most important writer of our time' reveals to you the secrets of..." This way, you are trading on Seth Godin's reputation and establishing your credentials at the same time (assuming he said this).

Also, if you've worked for or with very well-known people, name-dropping is not seen as bad; it's seen as an effective signal to the reader of your importance and ability. What matters is that there is a reason that you are using someone else's name that makes sense and is not just a gratuitous name-drop.

5. KEEP IT SHORT AND INTERESTING (WITHOUT LEAVING ANYTHING IMPORTANT OUT)

While your readers are interested in finding out more about you, they don't want to get bored or listen to arrogant braggadocio about how great you are. If your bio is too long or too full of overstated accomplishments and awards, it will turn your readers off and actually make you look less credible.

Typically, if you keep your bio under 200 words, you're going to be okay. Anything longer than that means you've gone on too long about your accomplishments, your personal life, or both. Also, it will make your back cover look cluttered and amateurish. Cut it down to the most important things.

TEMPLATE FOR AUTHOR BIO INFO

This is a template you can use to write your author bio. I'm not saying it's the very best way to write an author bio; in fact, many of the best ones above do NOT fit this template.

But many people asked for an easy-to-follow template, and this is the template we use with our authors.

1. **First sentence:** "[Author] is [statement to establish credibility on this subject and/or authorship of previous books]"
2. **Second sentence(s):** Statement(s) further establishing credibility or qualifications of author to write the book.
3. **Third sentence (optional):** Historical "before that" information that is at least tangentially relevant to the book or very compelling in another way.
4. **Fourth sentence:** Endorsement of author's credibility by others, awards, or some other social proof, if available.
5. **Fifth sentence:** Tidbit of personal information.
6. **Sixth sentence:** Link to website or other resource (if relevant).

Here is how that looks in practice:

Will Leach is the founder of TriggerPoint Design, a leading behavior research and design consultancy specializing in using behavior economics and decision design to drive consumer decision-making. He is a behavior design instructor at the Cox School of Business at Southern Methodist University and has more than twenty years of behavior insights experience working with Fortune 50 companies to solve their most important behavior challenges. Will is the only two-time winner of the EXPLOR Award for his work in behavior design and is known as America's foremost authority in applying behavior science to marketing. Will lives in Dallas with his wife and family.

IF YOU CAN'T WRITE ABOUT YOURSELF, HAVE FRIENDS HELP YOU

People, especially writers, have a hard time writing about themselves. Often the author bio is the most difficult part of the marketing process for an author to write effectively.

If you are unsure about whether your author bio seems either incomplete or too arrogant, run it by a few friends for feedback. For example, when I was doing my first bio, I made all the mistakes I outlined above. I eventually had to have my friend Nils Parker write my bio for me. It's always easier for your friends to praise you and see the amazing things you do.

EXAMPLES OF DIFFERENT AUTHOR BIOS

I'm going to show you a lot of different bios to give you an idea of how many different authors did them.

HIGH STATUS AND SHORT: LYNN VINCENT

This bio is the perfect "less is more" for an author with a lot of credentials. When you have done what Lynn has done, you can just say it quickly and succinctly.

Lynn Vincent is the *New York Times* bestselling writer of

Heaven Is for Real and *Same Kind of Different As Me*. The author or coauthor of ten books, Lynn has sold 12 million copies since 2006. She worked for eleven years as a writer and editor at the national news biweekly *WORLD* magazine and is a U.S. Navy veteran.

HIGH STATUS BUT UNDERSELLS: MICHAEL LEWIS

Contrast this to Michael Lewis, who is a very well-known author but still leaves quite a bit out of his bio that would help many readers understand who he is and why they should care. (Even Michael Lewis is not famous enough to assume people know him.)

Michael Lewis, the author of *Boomerang*, *Liar's Poker*, *The New New Thing*, *Moneyball*, *The Blind Side*, *Panic*, *Home Game*, and *The Big Short*, among other works, lives in Berkeley, California, with his wife, Tabitha Soren, and their three children.

BAD BIO: AMANDA RIPLEY

Many authors have different bios on different books (because they leave the bio writing to their publisher, which is a huge mistake). You can see the difference in the bio for author Amanda Ripley. Her bad bio is strangely both boring and overselling:

Amanda Ripley is a literary journalist whose stories on human behavior and public policy have appeared in *Time*,

The Atlantic, and *Slate* and helped *Time* win two National Magazine Awards. To discuss her work, she has appeared on ABC, NBC, CNN, Fox, and NPR. Ripley's first book *The Unthinkable* was published in fifteen countries and turned into a PBS documentary.

GOOD BIO: AMANDA RIPLEY

Contrast that to this good bio, where she comes off as much more of an authority, mainly because her other books are mentioned, as were her awards.

Amanda Ripley is an investigative journalist for *Time*, *The Atlantic*, and other magazines. She is the author, most recently, of *The Smartest Kids in the World—and How They Got That Way*. Her first book, *The Unthinkable: Who Survives when Disaster Strikes—and Why*, was published in 15 countries and turned into a PBS documentary. Her work has helped *Time* win two National Magazine Awards.

BAD BIO: DR. DAVID PERLMUTTER

This is a long, uninterrupted string of hard to process things. Dr. Perlmutter is very qualified but mentions everything (including medical school awards) which detracts from the overall effect.

David Perlmutter, MD, FACN, ABIHM, is a Board-Certified Neurologist and Fellow of the American College of Nutrition who received his M.D. degree from the University of Miami School of Medicine where he won the research award. Dr. Perlmutter is a frequent lecturer at symposia sponsored by such medical institutions as Columbia University, the University of Arizona, Scripps Institute, and Harvard University. He has contributed extensively to the world medical literature with publications appearing in the *Journal of Neurosurgery*, the *Southern Medical Journal*, the *Journal of Applied Nutrition*, and *Archives of Neurology*. He is the author of *The Better Brain Book* and the #1 New York Times bestseller *Grain Brain*. He is recognized internationally as a leader in the field of nutritional influences in neurological disorders. Dr. Perlmutter has been interviewed on many nationally syndicated radio and television programs including *20/20*, *Larry King Live*, CNN, Fox News, *Fox and Friends*, *The Today Show*, *Oprah*, *Dr. Oz*, and *The CBS Early Show*. In 2002 Dr. Perlmutter was the recipient of the Linus Pauling Award for his innovative approaches to neurological disorders and in addition was awarded the Denham Harmon Award for his pioneering work in the application of free radical science to clinical medicine. He is the recipient of the 2006 National Nutritional Foods Association Clinician of the Year Award. Dr. Perlmutter serves as Medical Advisor for *The Dr. Oz Show*.

GOOD BIO: DR. BENJAMIN CARSON

Contrast this to Dr. Carson, who focuses only on the credentials and status signifiers that the reader would care about and understand, like his specialties and companies he works for.

Dr. Benjamin Carson is a Professor of Neurosurgery, Plastic Surgery, Oncology, and Pediatrics, and the Director of Pediatric Neurosurgery at Johns Hopkins Medical Institutions. He is also the author of four bestselling books—*Gifted Hands*, *Think Big*, *The Big Picture*, and *Take the Risk*. He serves on the boards of the Kellogg Company, Costco, and the Academy of Achievement, among others, and is an Emeritus Fellow of the Yale Corporation.

He and his wife, Candy, cofounded the Carson Scholars Fund (www.carsonscholars.org), a 501(c)3 established to counteract America's crisis in education by identifying and rewarding academic role models in the fourth through eleventh grades, regardless of race, creed, religion and socio-economic status, who also demonstrate humanitarian qualities. There are over 4,800 scholars in forty-five states. Ben and Candy are the parents of three grown sons and reside in Baltimore County, Maryland.

GOOD BALANCE: TIM FERRISS

Tim does lean aggressively into the idea of listing all the cool things he's done and noteworthy outlets that have talked about him, but he still makes his bio interesting and relevant to the reader of his books:

Timothy Ferriss is a serial entrepreneur, #1 New York Times bestselling author, and angel investor/advisor (Facebook, Twitter, Evernote, Uber, and 20+ more). Best known for his rapid-learning techniques, Tim's books—*The 4-Hour Workweek*, *The 4-Hour Body*, and *The 4-Hour Chef*—have been published in 30+ languages. The *4-Hour Workweek* has spent seven years on the *New York Times* bestseller list.

Tim has been featured by more than 100 media outlets, including the *New York Times*, *The Economist*, *TIME*, *Forbes*, *Fortune*, *Outside*, NBC, CBS, ABC, Fox, and CNN. He has guest-lectured in entrepreneurship at Princeton University since 2003. His popular blog www.fourhourblog.com has 1M+ monthly readers, and his Twitter account @tferriss was selected by Mashable as one of only five "Must-Follow" accounts for entrepreneurs. Tim's primetime TV show *The Tim Ferriss Experiment* (www.upwave.com/tfx) teaches rapid-learning techniques for helping viewers to produce seemingly superhuman results in minimum time.

OUT OF BALANCE (CONFUSING AND OVERSELLING): CHERYL STRAYED

Cheryl is similar to Tim but runs several unrelated things together in a confusing way, and mentions things that no reader would ever care about (e.g., the director of a movie based on her book). This same bio could be 25 percent shorter and much stronger.

Cheryl Strayed is the author of #1 *New York Times* bestseller *Wild*, the *New York Times* bestseller *Tiny Beautiful Things*, and the novel *Torch*. *Wild* was chosen by Oprah Winfrey as her first selection for Oprah's Book Club 2.0. *Wild* won a Barnes & Noble Discover Award, an Indie Choice Award, an Oregon Book Award, a Pacific Northwest Booksellers Award, and a Midwest Booksellers Choice Award, among others. The movie adaptation of *Wild* will be released by Fox Searchlight in December 2014. The film is directed by Jean-Marc Vallée and stars Reese Witherspoon, with a screenplay by Nick Hornby. Strayed's writing has appeared in The Best American Essays, the *New York Times Magazine*, the *Washington Post Magazine*, *Vogue*, *Salon*, *The Missouri Review*, *The Sun*, *Tin House*, *The Rumpus*—where she wrote the popular Dear Sugar advice column—and elsewhere. Strayed was the guest editor of *Best American Essays 2013* and has contributed to many anthologies. Her books have been translated into more than thirty languages around the world. She holds an MFA in fiction writing from Syracuse University and a bachelor's degree from the University of Minnesota. She lives in Portland, Oregon, with her husband and their two children.

OVERSELLING: REBECCA SKLOOT

Below is an example of unnecessary overselling. Rebecca Skloot wrote a major bestseller (*Immortal Life of Henrietta Lacks*), but she mentions all sorts of nonsense in this bio that no reader will care about. You get the "doth protest too much" vibe from this. Compare this to Tim Ferriss, who also lists a lot but does so quickly and gets out of the way.

Rebecca Skloot is an award-winning science writer whose articles have appeared in the *New York Times Magazine*; *O, the Oprah Magazine*; *Discover*; and others. She has worked as a correspondent for NPR's *Radiolab* and PBS's *NOVA scienceNOW*, and is a contributing editor at *Popular Science* magazine and guest editor of *The Best American Science Writing 2011*. She is a former Vice President of the National Book Critics Circle and has taught creative nonfiction and science journalism at the University of Memphis, the University of Pittsburgh, and New York University. Her debut book *The Immortal Life of Henrietta Lacks* took more than ten years to research and write, and became an instant *New York Times* bestseller. She has been featured on numerous television shows, including *CBS Sunday Morning* and *The Colbert Report*. Her book has received widespread critical acclaim, with reviews appearing in *The New Yorker*, the *Washington Post*, *Science*, *Entertainment Weekly*, *People*, and many others. It won the *Chicago Tribune* Heartland Prize and the Wellcome Trust Book Prize, and was named the Best Book of 2010 by Amazon.com, and a Best Book of the Year by *Entertainment Weekly*; *O, The Oprah Magazine*; the *New York Times*; the *Washington Post*; *US News & World Report*; and numerous others.

RIDICULOUS OVERSELLING: DINESH D'SOUZA

I'll end with one of the worst bios I've ever seen. This is a real bio, pulled off the Amazon page of his recent book. It is over 500 WORDS of preposterously insecure and arrogant crap. I can't imagine reading this bio and not respecting the author LESS afterwards:

> Dinesh D'Souza has had a 25-year career as a writer, scholar, and public intellectual. A former policy analyst in the Reagan White House, D'Souza also served as John M. Olin Fellow at the American Enterprise Institute, and the Robert and Karen Rishwain Fellow at the Hoover Institution at Stanford University. He served as the president of The King's College in New York City from 2010 to 2012.
>
> Called one of the "top young public-policy makers in the country" by *Investor's Business Daily*, D'Souza quickly became known as a major influencer on public policy through his writings. His first book, *Illiberal Education* (1991), publicized the phenomenon of political correctness in America's colleges and universities and became a *New York Times* bestseller for 15 weeks. It has been listed as one of the most influential books of the 1990s.
>
> In 1995, D'Souza published *The End of Racism*, which became one of the most controversial books of the time and another national bestseller. His 1997 book, *Ronald Reagan: How an Ordinary Man Became an Extraordinary Leader*, was the first book to make the case for Reagan's intellectual and political importance. D'Souza's *The Virtue of Prosperity* (2000) explored the social and moral implications of wealth.

In 2002, D'Souza published his *New York Times* bestseller *What's So Great About America,* which was critically acclaimed for its thoughtful patriotism. His 2003 book, *Letters to a Young Conservative,* has become a handbook for a new generation of young conservatives inspired by D'Souza's style and ideas. *The Enemy at Home,* published in 2006, stirred up a furious debate both on the left and the right. It became a national bestseller and was published in paperback in 2008, with a new afterword by the author responding to his critics.

Just as in his early years D'Souza was one of the nation's most articulate spokesmen for a reasoned and thoughtful conservatism, in recent years he has been an equally brilliant and forceful defender of Christianity. *What's So Great about Christianity* not only intelligently explained the core doctrines of the Christian faith, it also explained how the freedom and prosperity associated with Western Civilization rest upon the foundation of biblical Christianity. *Life after Death: The Evidence* shows why the atheist critique of immortality is irrational and draws the striking conclusion that it is reasonable to believe in life after death.

In 2010, D'Souza wrote *The Roots of Obama's Rage (Regnery),* which was described as the most influential political book of the year and proved to be yet another bestseller.

In 2012, D'Souza published two books, *Godforsaken* and *Obama's America: Unmaking the American Dream,* the latter climbing to #1 on the *New York Times* bestseller list and inspiring a documentary on the same topic. The film, called *2016: Obama's America*, has risen to the second-highest all-time political documentary, passing Michael Moore's *Sicko* and Al Gore's *An Inconvenient Truth*. In addition, *2016* has risen to #4 on the bestselling list of all documentaries.

These endeavors—not to mention a razor-sharp wit and entertaining style—have allowed D'Souza to participate in highly-publicized debates about Christianity with some of the most famous atheists and skeptics of our time.

Born in Mumbai, India, D'Souza came to the U.S. as an exchange student and graduated Phi Beta Kappa from Dartmouth College in 1983.

D'Souza has been named one of America's most influential conservative thinkers by the *New York Times Magazine*. The World Affairs Council lists him as one of the nation's 500 leading authorities on international issues, and *Newsweek* cited him as one of the country's most prominent Asian-Americans.

D'Souza's articles have appeared in virtually every major magazine and newspaper, including the *New York Times*, *Wall Street Journal*, *The Atlantic Monthly*, *Vanity Fair*, *New Republic*, and *National Review*. He has appeared on numerous television programs, including the *The Today Show*, *Nightline*, *The News Hour* on PBS, *The O'Reilly Factor*, *Moneyline*, *Hannity*, *Bill Maher*, NPR's *All Things Considered*, CNBC's *Kudlow Report*, *Lou Dobbs Tonight*, and *Real Time with Bill Maher*.

REMEMBER, YOUR BIO GROWS AS YOU GROW

Treat your bio as a living document. Just because you've written it once, does not mean it's finished. As you grow and change as a writer, so too should your bio, and the best part is that they are easy to change online.

Also, remember that, if you are writing for different genres or different topics, some of your accomplishments and past works will be more relevant to your readers than others. It's not a bad idea to tweak your author bio for each new work you release.

CONCLUSION: TAKE THIS SERIOUSLY

Getting your author bio right is an important task. In fact, this small section is usually the ONLY source of information potential readers have about you (the author), and that's why it is one of the most important pieces of marketing material you write for your book. Take it seriously, get it right, and it will help you sell books.

HOW TO TAKE THE RIGHT AUTHOR PHOTO

This is an important and hard truth that most authors avoid:

Readers will judge you AND your book based on your author photo.

Is that fair? Maybe, maybe not.

Is it reality? Absolutely (and you probably do it, as well).

Why do people do this?

Because biologically, humans are visual creatures. It's mostly unconscious, but snap judgments of other humans based solely on physical characteristics and facial expressions evolved as a way for humans to quickly assess threats and opportunities and to determine relative social status of a new person to know how to deal interact with them. A deep discussion of this topic is far beyond the scope of this piece, but basically, it evolved because it worked (there is a ton of research and science on this, and most of it falls under what is called "signaling theory").

This might seem bad, but it is actually a good thing. Now that you understand the importance of your author photo, it means that you can ensure you take a great one and use this tool as a powerful advantage.

In this chapter, I'll go through some examples of author photos, both good and bad, so you can see what this looks like in practice, and then walk you through exactly how to ensure you get a great author photo for your book.

THE AUTHOR PHOTO RULE THAT RULES THEM ALL

There are many different ways to take an effective author photo, and one overarching rule is that when it comes to author photos (or any profile photo):

> *Know what you want to signal to which audience, and then signal it properly.*

This is the key to everything with photos. The author photo for a CEO of a Fortune 500 company should be totally different from the author photo for an up-and-coming comedian.

Why? Because they are signaling different things to different groups.

Generally speaking, the CEO's author photo should signal professionalism, effectiveness, reliability, and trust.

The comedian's photo could be wacky, goofy, or even pensively serious, all depending on the comedic style they want to signal.

To make sure you're taking the right author photo, you need to ask yourself two questions.

1. WHAT AM I TRYING TO SIGNAL WITH MY PHOTO?

You say just as much with your appearance as you do with your words. Clearly your words are the more important part of your book, but again, people are visual creatures, and they will judge your book (to some extent) by what you look like.

The good news is that, within reason, it's much easier to construct the image you want in a still photo. You can emphasize whatever traits or aspect of your appearance you want, and you can also minimize any physical limitations that would be difficult to minimize in person: height, for example.

You can signal seriousness or silliness, professionalism or pretention, positivity or pessimism. It's really up to you.

The important thing to remember is that you cannot have them all at once.

A well-calculated author photo is one of the best ways to build a connection of trust between you and the right reader.

2. WHO AM I TRYING TO SIGNAL IT TO?

It's not just what you are signaling—it's also who you want to signal it to that determines your author photo.

Why is that?

Because so much of signaling is about telling a specific group of people that you are one of them or that you speak their in-group language.

For example, if you are trying to signal to corporations that you are a competent and reliable professional that they should trust and listen to, then you must understand that they see the conventional Western business suit as a key signal not just of competence but as membership in their tribe. Suits tell them that *you are one of them*.

Whereas, if you want to signal trust to the tech and startup community, then wearing a suit sends the opposite signal. They see suits as a sign of being out of touch in their community. If you want them to see you as competent and tech-minded, you want to wear more casual clothes.

The importance of understanding this cannot be overstated. Remember, signaling is not just about what you are signaling, it's also about what other people are seeing, and what other people see depends almost entirely on what group they are part of and identify with.

Having a cutting-edge look in one field means you may be excluded in others, so knowing who you are trying to signal to and what signals they respond to is key for you.

This is all abstract. We'll show several you examples of author photos, both good and bad, and break them down for you.

EXAMPLE AUTHOR PHOTOS
GENERIC WRITER PHOTOS
Good: Joanna Penn

This is a classic author photo. This signals warmth and openness. Joanna has a broad, authentic smile in her face. You can almost see her enthusiasm and joy.

By making the photo black and white, and with a close crop that frames her face, she narrows your focus onto the things she wants you to know about her. She's positive, optimistic, and encouraging.

This makes sense for her. Joanna writes a lot of books for authors about writing, publishing, and marketing. She is a teacher and a writer, and this photo signals both trust and warmth.

Not as Good: Lisa Cartwright

 This is not a good author photo at all. First, it's tilted to the side in a weird angle that looks like an indie poster from the '90s. Second, it's a collection of technical no-nos—blurry, poorly lit, overly saturated, etc. This could have been taken by a buddy on a night out with a disposable camera. Third, her smile seems forced and less than genuine.

What is she signaling here? My first unconscious thought is something along the lines of, "Why is it not centered?" Whether intentional or not, this picture signals unprofessionalism, amateurishness, and lack of emotional connection.

TECH AUDIENCE AUTHOR PHOTOS
Eric Ries

Eric is a big author in the tech space and wants to signal that he is in the tech space but is very forward thinking and high status.

 Look at how he does this: Eric has a simple hairstyle, his glasses are contemporary, his smile is authentic. The photographer has shot him head-on, not from below. The lighting brings out the best in his face and skin tone. He's not slumping or accentuating any negative physical aspects of his appearance. His shirt is stylish without being ostentatious, and perhaps most important, look at the background. It is bottom lit and color shifting, which gives it a modern feel that is reminiscent of technology and the future.

This photo displays a very sophisticated understanding of how he is trying to position himself: a serious technical insider but not the stereotype of the socially awkward tech nerd. He wants nontech people to see him in a good light as well.

Giff Constable

 Giff is obviously sending very different signals to his audience. This photo is basically the generic "LinkedIn tech person photo." He has a parted, flat hairstyle. The inexperienced photographer shot him from below, capturing his smile at the most awkward angle. His shirt is distracting and visually unappealing. The hyper

white background makes him seem very pale and is jarring to the eye. An overly lit background can ruin a photo.

This photo sends very clear signals—not all of which are positive. If he is writing a book for a specific tribe that approves of these signals—for example, "nerdy" engineers—and he wants to signal to them that he is part of their tribe, this author photo actually does that. If that is the only audience we want to talk to, then this photo accomplishes that.

The problem is that this photo will repel most people who do not identify directly with that audience. Compare this photo with the one above. It's the complete opposite. Eric and Giff are in the same field—tech—and physically are very similar. But the photos feel totally different, don't they?

BUSINESS AUTHOR PHOTOS
Patrick Lencioni

 This is a very traditional business professional author photo. Everything about this photo says that this man is an American business executive: he's signaling solid, stable, trustworthy, and part of the establishment.

The suit is tailored, dark, expensive, and tasteful, and he has a conservative tie on. His wedding ring is clearly showing. His hair is graying, combed but not stiff, and his smile is there, but not forced. He's sitting in front of a whiteboard, signaling that he is a holder of knowledge and a fount of ideas.

This makes sense. Patrick's entire market is traditional corporate America, and this photo speaks directly to them, telling them that even though he has some new ideas (the whiteboard), he is still one of them.

Jay Papasan

Jay has a different version of the business professional author photo. He is signaling that he's a legitimate businessman, but younger and more modern and hip.

He is wearing a suit that is dark and tasteful, but he has no tie, and his top button is undone. The background is green and environmental, another code for openness and modernity.

Andrii Sedniev

If the author is trying to signal to business community, there are a lot of problems with this photo. The tie appears to be from the Salvation Army bargain bin. It has poorly matched colors, is off center, and it's clearly cheap. The shirt collar is not even tucked into his jacket. Both the jacket and shirt are

droopy and not tailored, and further-more, the material for both shirt and jacket are shiny, which is generally a signal for cheapness in suits.

His haircut is a slightly grown-out buzz cut, which not only signals youth and inexperience, but it also signals sloppiness. He didn't even bother to get his hair cut for his professional photo.

His smile is forced, as if he is trying to hide his teeth and is unsure of himself. Everything about this photo says "amateur." Just by looking at the photos, you can tell that Patrick and Jay are serious, established professionals, and that Andrii is not.

Mona Patel

This is an example of a great business author photo. All the signals are saying the same basic things, telling a coherent story about her taste and her warmth and her ability:

1. She is sitting in a very design-forward chair, and this signals great aesthetic taste.
2. The shot is in an empty warehouse-style loft, which signals a specific design sensibility—one that is con-temporary and minimalist.
3. The symmetry of the corridor draws the eye to her face. The off-center crop signals originality and uniqueness.

It says there's going to be something special in this book you can't find elsewhere.

4. She is dressed in a classic and perfectly tailored outfit, with stylish leather boots. This signals both excellent personal style and business professionalism, all at once.

5. She's looking away from the camera and smiling warmly, as if she's casually talking to someone in the background, signaling warmth and approachability.

6. She downplays her physical attractiveness with a masculine outfit and simple hair and makeup. She dresses in a traditionally male outfit (button-down shirt and black pants), but she accentuates it by tailoring the outfit to make it feminine and leaving an extra button open.

7. The photo is black and white, which signals high design and artistic sensibilities.

If all this feels a little artsy to you, just think about how this photo makes you feel. You're attracted to her and drawn in by her warmth and smile (though not in a sexual way). You know she's fashionable and has great taste, and you can see her design style. But the photo still makes you take her seriously as an intelligent, professional CEO.

Professional photos can be much more challenging for serious female CEOs than for men (for many reasons), and Mona walked that line perfectly.

TWO PHOTOS OF THE SAME AUTHOR

Patrick Vlaskovits

Here is a perfect example of how easy it is to create an air of competence and trust with an author photo. In this case, the same author has two different photos. The left is too dark, there is no smile, and it is poorly cropped. The right is well cropped, he has a good smile, and he is dressed in professional but casual clothes.

Like I said before, part of the "bad" versus "good" decision is about what signals you are trying to send to whom. If Patrick were an essayist and social commentator, perhaps the first photo would work.

But that's not what his books are about, nor the audience he is trying to signal to. His books are about entrepreneurship, branding, and startups. To speak to that audience, you are better off being optimistic, positive, and warm—which the second picture signals.

James Altucher

The first photo makes James look less like a genius and more like a crazy person. His glasses are off center, his hair is disheveled, he is wearing a ratty, white T-shirt, and he doesn't even appear to be looking into the camera.

Compare this to the second photo. He's dressed in dark and fashionable clothes and is set against a pleasant background, all of which signal competence and professionalism. He's also signaling quirkiness and humor: sitting cross-legged, retaining his trademark curly fro, and smiling mischievously. It reflects who James is, while still signaling that he's serious and professional and has taste.

Same person sending totally different signals and creating totally different emotional reactions in the viewer.

HOW TO TAKE YOUR AUTHOR PHOTO
STEP 1: DECIDE WHAT SIGNALS YOU WANT TO CONVEY

Before you even pick a photographer, you need to decide exactly what it is you want your author photo to signal and to what audience. If you have already done the positioning in this book, then this should be relatively easy. There are really only two questions to answer:

- Who is my audience?

- What do I want them to think about me?

Once you have a good idea of that, then you are ready to pick out your photographer.

STEP 2: PICK A GREAT PHOTOGRAPHER

Do not shoot your own author photo. Period. I don't care how good your Instagram account is, there is no substitute for the skills of a professional photographer.

How do you pick a great photographer? There is no substitute for looking at their portfolios. Go to their sites and look at the headshots they have done and see who has a style that represents what you are looking for. For example, if you want a headshot out of yourself in a forest, then find the photographer that does that really well.

Once you find a photographer who has already done headshots like you want, you have your person.

Some places to hire a pro:

Thumbtack

This is a good way to find an affordable pro right in your neighborhood. Enter your zip code and some details about the job. You'll receive bids from photographers in your area with links to their portfolios.

Model Mayhem

Obviously, a database of models is a magnet for photographers, and Model Mayhem has a directory specifically for finding photographers. The best part: there's a Time-for-Print option where newer photographers will photograph you for free.

GigSalad

GigSalad is like Craigslist for booking services for events or productions. If you search "Headshot Photography," you'll get a list of dozens of photographers in your city who specialize in the exact kind of pictures you need.

Yelp

Yelp is often a very good resource to find great photographers in your area and will have extensive reviews by people.

Price: Expect to pay anywhere from $150–$500+ for a great photographer, depending on where you live.

STEP 3: COMMUNICATE EXACTLY WHAT YOU WANT

Don't be shy about telling your photographer the look you're trying to pull off, and point to the shots in their portfolio to help you explain what you are looking for. If you need to, bring in other photos that help explain what you are looking for. The more clear and explicit you can be, with visual examples, the better the result will be.

Also, you need to make sure to get the proper assets from your photographer. You want all of these:

- Some photographers will sell you all the shots they take for one fee; some want to charge a per-photo fee. Make sure you are clear ahead of time how they are charging and what you will get.
- You want to get color and black-and-white versions of the photo you select. Let the photographer do the conversion, it usually works better.
- You want to get the raw files from the photographer as well as the online-ready versions.
- You want to make sure you own the raw files and do not have to pay any license fees.
- If your primary photo is going to be a full-body shot (like James or Mona), you may want to also get some headshots rather than you trying to edit/crop them yourself.

STEP 4: TEST YOUR AUTHOR PHOTO (OPTIONAL)

If you are unsure whether or not your author photo is conveying the signals you want, there is a way to test this: use a service called Photo Feeler. You can upload your photo and get ratings on multiple dimensions that tell you exactly what people think about it.

HOW TO GET A GREAT BOOK COVER

I could write an entire book just on book covers. It's a deeply interesting subject with a wealth of both art and data behind it, but I won't do that to you because you probably don't care.

Instead, I'm going to make this as simple as possible for you to get your book cover right.

This chapter will walk you through what you need to know about book covers, why you need a book cover designer, how to find a good one, how to work with them to ensure they create the cover you want, and how to make sure you have the right cover when the process is done.

WHAT YOU NEED TO KNOW ABOUT BOOK COVERS

There are three big principles you need to know.

1. YOUR BOOK WILL BE JUDGED BY ITS COVER (AND THAT'S GOOD)

We all know the saying "Don't judge a book by its cover." But that's not the reality of life, is it?

Everyone judges books by their covers.

In fact, we almost cannot biologically stop ourselves. Humans are visual creatures. We see our way through the world, and vision is our defining sense. Humans can be immediately reached, engaged, and moved by color and shape because these images enter the brain literally at light speed. This is the power of design.

Here's the thing: *it's good news that people judge your book by the cover.* Otherwise, they might not make any judgment at all, and no judgment means they aren't buying or reading it.

Can you imagine walking through a bookstore that had covers with no information on it other than the title? Or browsing Amazon and looking only at book titles? That would make book-buying decisions much more difficult.

People will judge your book cover and use that judgement to evaluate whether they want to buy it. This is a chance to win a reader and to reach the exact person who needs to read your book.

2. YOU SHOULD NOT DESIGN YOUR OWN BOOK COVER

When you want a bottle of beer, do you brew it yourself?

When you want a new coat, do you sew it yourself?

When you need a new bar of soap, do you make it yourself?

No. You buy those things from people who are experts at making them.

Book covers are no different. You should not design your book cover yourself. You should have your book cover designed by a professional to get a professional cover.

This is for the same reason that most people don't make home-brewed beer, even though it's not terribly complicated, and why no one wears homemade clothes, even though they're easy to make. They're awful when compared to the professional alternatives.

The only real difference between beer and coats and book covers is that some people *think* they can design their own book covers, even if they really can't.

For some reason I can't understand, many authors think

they are also designers. I don't know if it's that design software is fun to use or that great design has a simplicity to it that belies its difficulty, but let me be very clear about something:

Unless you are a multiyear publication designer with twenty-plus titles in your portfolio, you should not be designing your cover.

3. THERE ARE OBJECTIVELY GOOD AND BAD BOOK COVERS

Book cover design is not completely subjective. There are good and bad book covers, and a good designer can clearly tell you the difference between them.

This is because a book cover is a piece of art with a specific purpose:

Book covers exist to give visual form to written content.

A great cover makes someone in your intended audience say, "I need to read that," by *showing* them why the book matters to them in a way they can immediately grasp (or at least raising their interest enough to want to learn more). It should help your audience realize that they should be reading your book.

Another way to think about it is framed by Chip Kidd, a famous book cover designer, who said that *"a book cover is a distillation of the content, almost like what your book would look like as a haiku."*

That being said, a good book cover is not just an expression of the idea behind a book, it's the way the audience first engages that idea.

It's marketing. And that is how you measure an objectively good book cover:

> *A good book shows what's in the book and makes the audience interested in reading it.*

WHAT TO DO BEFORE YOU HIRE A BOOK COVER DESIGNER

Now that you understand what purpose a cover serves and why a professional book cover is important, you're ready to find a good book cover designer and hire them, right?

Not so fast.

The main problem book designers have with authors is poor communication. The author has no idea what they want or has vague, ambiguous cover ideas, and the two never get on the same page.

You can avoid this problem by doing some work prior to finding a book cover designer. Not only will this result in a better cover, but it can save you a lot of money.

1. LOOK AT LOTS OF BOOK COVERS, BOTH IN YOUR FIELD AND OUT

The first thing to do is get an idea of what other books in your field are like and maybe get some ideas from them.

Go to Amazon books and search in the category your book falls into. Search Pinterest for artsier titles if you'd like. If you want a classic, look to Bookcoverarchive.com for the best, most avant-garde titles.

Once you spend some time looking at a lot of book covers in your genre, you'll be shocked at how repetitive they are. That's common.

Don't feel bad about using some of these tropes. They exist for a reason, and they will help you, actually. It is a good thing for people to be able to identify your book as being in the genre you want to be in.

It's also important to look at books in lots of other fields to get ideas as well. Just because your book is about psychology doesn't mean you have to use the same tropes as all psychology books. You can use some ideas from business or self-help books or even novels.

Also, don't feel bad about taking inspiration from your favorite books. Great art and design don't magically appear in a vacuum. They have to be born of some inspiration point.

2. NARROW DOWN TO A FEW COVERS THAT HAVE ELEMENTS OF WHAT YOU WANT

As you look through the hundreds of covers, save a few examples of the ones you really like or ones that have elements that you really like. The reason you're doing this should be obvious: you need to *show* your designer what you like (not just try to describe it).

Save the links or images and send them to your designer. A picture is worth a thousand words, which is worth a massive savings in your time and money. Designers see the world visually, and the best way to get a point across to them is to show them.

At Scribe, we have a document with ten very different covers that we walk authors through to get a sense for their taste. Doing this is common practice.

3. PICK SOME BRANDS OR OTHER PIECES OF ART THAT CAPTURE YOUR AESTHETIC

Don't just look at covers. Pull in logos, websites, art, photos, or pretty much any image you can find that's in some way similar to what you want on your book cover.

Remember that design is everywhere. Do you love the clean, light simplicity of the Apple logo? Or are your more into the zany black and green playfulness of Android?

You are essentially creating a collage (some people call this a mood board) of visual inspiration and ideas that can help your designer understand how to best get your book's message across to your audience.

HOW DO YOU FIND A BOOK COVER DESIGNER?

There are many places to hire book cover designers. We're going to break them down by price point, and as always, priciest is best. You get what you pay for. Designers who are able to charge $2K and up for their services do so because their books SELL.

1. INDEPENDENT DESIGNER ($750–$2K+)

The highest quality option is always to hire an independent book cover designer. Many of the best book cover designers in the world, who work regularly with major publishing houses, are available to hire on a freelance basis.

There are a few ways to find these people. One of the best options is Reedsy, a freelance marketplace designed specifically for authors. The other option is to go to more general design sites, like Behance or Dribbble, and search for book designers there. They can be a bit slow to respond and difficult to get in touch with, but the quality there is outstanding as well.

But the best method is to look inside your favorite books

and see who designed the cover. Then Google their name. More than half the time, you'll find their design site, and can contact them directly.

2. 99DESIGNS ($300–$600+)

99Designs (and similar sites, like Crowdspring) can work sometimes, at least to get decent designs.

On 99Designs, you post a detailed brief with all the technical parameters and visual examples you pulled, and then their designers read this information and post their work. Dozens of designers take your brief, design a cover, and post it for your approval. You then have the option to choose the winning designer to take the cover from or, if you don't like any of the designs, get a full refund with no hassle.

99Designs is great as a first option to test if a great cover would be worth the money to you. That way you can see the designs, get some ideas, and hopefully find a great cover. But, if not, no harm, and you can go back to the drawing board with the other options.

We'd recommend doing the Silver contest (which costs $499). The lower end contests really repel the better designers on the site, and the higher-end ones don't seem to garner much higher quality (and actually tend to get fewer submissions).

3. UPWORK ($50-$500+)

The next step down the quality ladder would be a freelance network like Upwork. The overall quality on Upwork is not high, but there are some quality designers hidden on there. Expect to take your time to find the right person on one of these sites, but you will be able to find them. Job ads typically get dozens if not hundreds of responses, and designers typically link to a portfolio of past work.

Screen out anyone with more than a few negative reviews, and then focus 100 percent of your screening time on judging their portfolios. Do a side-by-side comparison of the covers you liked when you did your research on Amazon. Do they appear to be of similar quality? If you can't tell, ask a friend who understands the basics of design.

Portfolios are the only thing that can give you a real picture into the quality of their work. If you like their past work, you'll probably like their future work. Everything else is just marketing.

4. FIVERR ($5-$50)

Fiverr is a marketplace of services available for $5 or so. There are a ton of book cover designers on Fiverr, but almost all of them are absolute garbage.

I've never used Fiverr for cover design, but friends have been able to find a couple designers who are good.

What happens is that a new designer will do a great job, get a ton of 5-star reviews, and then disappear to another site where they can charge more than $5 for their work. Think of it this way: if someone has any design talent, why would they work for $5 a cover?

5. DIY ($0)

If you do this, you are a fool, and you will get precisely what you pay for.

HOW DO YOU WORK WITH YOUR BOOK COVER DESIGNER?

Once you've picked a designer and negotiated price, then comes discussion of your cover idea. Here is where all that work you did before comes into play.

1. SCHEDULE THE FIRST CALL FOR PHONE OR VIDEO

Schedule your first call to be phone or video. Email is very hard to effectively communicate with strangers, especially about abstract concepts like design.

2. BEFORE THE CALL, SEND THEM THE COVERS AND LOGOS YOU LIKED

Prior to the call, send them a cover design brief. This should include all the book covers you like, all the logos and other pictures you like, and everything else you assembled. Do this at least a day ahead of time. Designers like to have time to digest images and ideas.

3. EXPLAIN YOUR THINKING

Once on the call, walk them through your thinking:

- Start with explaining who your target reader is.
- Then, explain what you like and dislike about each cover.
- Talk about what you want your cover to feel like.
- Discuss the signals you are trying to send to your audience.
- If you can, discuss the emotions you want your reader to feel when they see the cover.

The more you explain all of your thinking to the cover designer, the better they will do.

4. ASK FOR AT LEAST THREE MOCK-UPS

This should be standard for good book cover designers. They will come up with an array of ideas and show you at least three different ones.

5. GIVE CONSTRUCTIVE NOTES ON THE MOCK-UPS

Once you get the mock-ups back, if one jumps out at you, great. Give specific notes and feedback to get it where you want, and then you're done.

If you aren't happy with any of the covers, that's okay too. Get back on the phone with the designer, and—while being polite—be as specific as possible about what you would like different.

This is not about getting angry or frustrated with the cover designer. They aren't in your head, and if their mock-ups did not fit your vision, that's okay. Just be clearer and more methodical in your description, and you'll get there.

Remember this: your cover designer is a human who has feelings but also a professional that wants to do a great job. You are both on the same team. You can be firm, but also polite and understanding.

HOW CAN YOU CHECK IF YOU HAVE A GOOD BOOK COVER?

Once you have a cover, or you think you have one, here are the questions to ask to check if it's working for you.

1. DOES IT STAND OUT?

This is crucial. Look at it from all angles, print it out, and put it across the room. Think of every possible way someone will look at it—on a screen, in a bookstore, etc.—and make sure it stands out that way. Can you read the title? Is the image clear?

Check it as a thumbnail too. Does your cover look good

when you shrink it down to a tiny thumbnail? That's how most of your readers will see it, as a small image on Amazon.

2. DOES IT HAVE A CLEAR FOCUS?

Establish a principal focus for the cover. Nothing is more important than this one thing. Your book is about something, and the cover ought to reflect that one idea clearly. You must have one element that takes control, that commands the overwhelming majority of attention, of space, and of emphasis on the cover.

Don't fall into the trap of loading up your cover with too many elements: three or four photos, illustrations, maps, "floating" ticket stubs. This just confuses people, and confused people become repelled.

And don't fall into the trap of believing your cover is a billboard and every inch of space on it is real estate that needs to be filled up with the biggest possible words. Type needs to sit within the appropriate amount of emptiness in order to be readable. What is NOT on your cover is just as important as what IS on it. A quality designer will intimately know the appropriate font sizing for subtitles, blurbs, and author titles. Asking for them to be bigger is merely going to drain the impact from your design.

3. DOES IT INDICATE WHAT THE BOOK IS AND WHO THE BOOK IS FOR?

Not only does your book stand out, but at a glance, your audience ought to know:

- The general genre of your book
- The general subject matter or focus
- Some idea of the tone or position of the book

A truly great book is one that captures the book inside in some fundamental and perhaps unforeseen way.

At the same time, don't fall into the trap of feeling it has to show the content of the book or show an element or scene from the book. (No one will know that is correct until after reading the book anyway.)

4. DID YOU EXPLORE TOO MANY OPTIONS?

Some authors spend far too much too time trying to find the perfect cover. Usually, this is because it's a way to work out their anxieties about publishing during the cover design process.

It's a major creative part of the publishing journey, and many people are nervous about what will happen when it ends. They force the hand of their designer through round after round of revisions, thinking they are bettering their cover.

In actuality, they are both running from their fears and

ruining their cover design. Ask your cover designer when they believe your cover is done, because they are the only impartial source for this knowledge.

5. DID YOU MAKE THE BRAVE CHOICE?

We see this happen all the time: we'll give an author three mock-ups, and there will almost always be a suboptimal choice, a solid choice, and a great choice.

The great choice will almost always require the author to be brave in selecting it. It will have some angle or position that is novel in your field or make a statement that is controversial or just be different in a way that will make you just a little uncomfortable.

I'd say that only about 25 percent of authors pick the brave choice.

You don't have to make the brave choice, but it's almost always the best one (if there is a brave choice available). Be aware if this happens to you.

The solid choice is not bad, but it means your book won't stand out or get the attention it deserves. The brave choice means it will.

If you are unsure how to define brave, here is a way to think about it:

The brave choice says what everyone is thinking but not saying out loud. The brave cover is the one that people will remember. You've worked too hard on writing your book to cover it in mediocrity because some stranger on Facebook doesn't like blue.

Be proud of your achievement. Be bold. Make your mark.

6. DO NOT POST ON SOCIAL MEDIA TO GET FEEDBACK

The best way to ensure you choose the mediocre (or even bad) cover is to poll people on social media.

Your average potential reader—when asked which cover they like—is going to channel their inner mob mentality and respond to the title that is most like what already saturates your market. They pick the most common design because, to them, common means fitting in. True, fitting in is better than looking a mess, but the cover game, first and foremost, is about BEING MEMORABLE.

Beyond that, a good book cover is not designed to appeal to everyone. It's designed to appeal to the target audience of the book. Your 2,500 Facebook friends include people you knew in high school and in-laws and that guy you met at conference three years ago. They are not the target audience for your book.

DESIGN YOUR BOOK LAYOUT

Have you ever started to read a book, and on the first page—before you've engaged the actual content—you immediately get a bad feeling and can't take the book seriously? And sometimes you can't even explain why?

This is the impact of the book's layout (sometimes called typesetting or interior design).

Book layout is one of those things that most people never notice...unless it's wrong.

Despite how simple it seems (or perhaps because of it), book layout is one of the major factors that separates amateurish books from professional ones.

I will describe how to design both print and e-book because they are very different formats and must be done differently.

Some people refer to PDFs that you download and view on a screen as "e-books." That is not what we're talking about. An e-book in this case is a unique format—typically an EPUB or MOBI—that is downloaded and read with a specialized device or software, such as a Kindle.

INTERIOR DESIGN IS HARD

Interior layout is easy to dismiss. It's just the formatting of words on a page. Google Docs does that automatically. What's the big deal, right?

Just like covers, what seems easy is actually very difficult. In fact, working with type is considered the most difficult thing to do in design. The first thing to realize is that there's a lot more that goes into designing the interior of a book than you might expect. These are just some of the decisions that must be made:

- trim size (as explained above)
- color vs. black and white
- other physical considerations (paperback vs. hardcover, paper stock, etc.)
- font selection
- page margins
- spacing decisions

- artistic direction and design elements
- sidebars (if any)
- if/how you want to incorporate illustrations, photography, or other graphics

There are also the more nerdy publishing details that your proofreader should have caught but likely didn't, like making sure you're using the right dashes in the right places (hyphens, em and en dashes all have distinct uses). The same goes for quotation marks (straight vs. curly vs. foot/inch marks—all different things), mathematical symbols (× vs. x) and nearly every other symbol you can (but won't) think of.

For example: Did you know that certain fonts and justification styles can give your readers headaches? Your interior designer does.

Did you know that breaking a paragraph improperly, leaving just a partial line on the next page can interrupt the mental engagement readers have with your material? These lonely fragments are called "widows," and your interior designer knows how to correct them.

But, truthfully, that's only a small part of the problem. The main reason that it's so complicated and expensive is that *nobody wants to do it.*

Interior layout is hard, tiring work and requires a lot of

hours from someone with at least a strong baseline of design skills. Most designers went into the field because they love working on beautiful, creative projects. Interior print layout has those elements, sure, but it also demands a lot of precision and "boring" practical considerations that designers don't always like to be constrained by (not unlike, say, industrial design).

SHOULD I SKIP A PRINT VERSION ENTIRELY?

Print books are a lot of work. So why should you even do them?

The reason is actually that you should do them precisely *because* they're a lot of work. The book market is flooded with thousands of new authors every day. As you know, it can be difficult to stand out.

Because of how challenging doing a good print book is and how embarrassingly ugly it can be when done wrong, a lot of new authors are veering away from the challenge and are publishing in e-book format only. In many circles, this has started to be a dividing line between books that should be taken seriously and books that shouldn't.

Many people see e-books as "not real books" and dismiss them as less impressive than paperbacks. If you are doing a business book, then this is crucial. You can't really hand out (or sell) an e-book at a conference or speaking engagement.

Creating a high-quality paperback or hardcover version is one of the most powerful ways to make sure your book is taken seriously and seen as a "real" book. We wouldn't skip this step if credibility is a key goal of yours.

DESIGNING THE PRINT INTERIOR
WHAT SHOULD A GOOD INTERIOR LAYOUT LOOK LIKE?

This is not an easy question to answer. Like we said earlier, very few people notice the interior layout unless it's wrong, and then it's a huge problem.

Below is an image with major elements of interior design, and then an explanation of some of them. I'm putting in a picture and explaining them, not because I expect you to learn them, but for two other reasons:

1. So when you hire a professional interior designer to layout your book for you (which we highly recommend), you have a list of things you can discuss with them.
2. So you know what good versus bad looks like.

BAD DESIGN

HERE IS AN EXAMPLE of **bad** page design. Painful right? You probably don't even want to read it. Power through it for a moment and right off the bat you'll notice a few things:

BAD TYPOGRAPHY

-**Poor font choices** (Cambria and Arial). Cambria (one of Word's default fonts) actually isn't that bad for the screen, but suffers in print. Arial is ubiquitous because it was a system font in Windows for so long, but is effectively just worse Helvetica.

-**Sloppy hyphenation/justification.** Professional layout software like Adobe InDesign uses powerful, customizable algorithms to help produce a natural text flow. Others, not so much.

-**The little things.** ALL CAPS, underlined text, "dumb quotes" and double dashes--there are hundreds of nuances that add up to text looking either professional, or like it came straight out of Word (and in this case it did--that's how this page was created).

BAD USE OF SPACE

Pretty much everywhere--the margins are too small, the space between lines is too tight, and space after each sentence is too big. It's a subtle thing but makes a huge difference in readability.

BAD STRUCTURE

Most writing apps include a defined hierarchy for organizing information--**Heading 1**, **Heading 2**, etc.--and most writers completely ignore it right out of the gate. Instead they opt for arbitrary or inconsistent headings that make it difficult for the reader to skim text quickly or understand how it is prioritized ("is this a new topic, or just a subsection?"). For example, although the three headings on this page all reference the same "level" of information, they are each styled differently.

18 - BAD DESIGN

······· **GOOD DESIGN** ·······

HERE IS AN EXAMPLE of *good* page design. Right off the bat you'll notice some important differences:

GOOD TYPOGRAPHY

- *Professional Typefaces* (Adobe Caslon Pro and Brandon Text) Caslon is considered a very "safe" pick and a popular choice among book designers for good reason: it reads very comfortably and suits a wide variety of content.

- *Natural-looking Justification & Careful Hyphenation* There aren't any huge gaps between words or "ladders" of hyphens running down the side of a paragraph.

- *The Little Things Make a Big Difference* SMALL CAPS, "curly quotes," em dashes—and no underlines. That last one is news to most people, but apart from links, underlining is mostly a relic of the manual typewriter. Today we can show **emphasis** in *better*, more PROFESSIONAL ways.

GOOD USE OF SPACE

The text on this page has room to breathe, is set on a baseline grid, and has single spaces after punctuation (double-spacing is wrong, forget what your English teacher said). Nice, isn't it?

GOOD STRUCTURE

The information is clearly and consistently organized. Much easier for the reader to follow, absorb, reference and skim.

Page Margins

One of the main elements in all design is what's called "negative space." That is the space with nothing in it. For your book interior, that is the margins between the words and the edge of the page.

Look at the "Bad Design" use of margins versus the "Good Design" use. You see how, without even knowing why, each of these margins are important, and serve a purpose?

The outside margins give room for the reader to hold the book without covering the words.

The inside margin makes sure the text doesn't slip into the binding area and become hard to read.

The top margin is for the name of the book and author's name, as well as the page number.

The bottom margin provides a pillow of white space that balances the rest of the page.

Traditionally, the four margins are close in size and around a half inch, though the inside margin is usually 25–50 percent larger than the other three.

Typography

Now, look at the typography and font choices. Font and type are incredibly complex fields and very important to books. Professional books are traditionally set in fonts like Adobe Caslon Pro and Brandon Text.

The font you choose must be clearly legible and have italics, semi-bold, bold, and small caps all included and well done. A comfortable size for most books is eleven-point font.

This is clearly visible in the diagram. The bad design font hurts to read, whereas the good design font feels calm and relaxing.

Titles and Headers

It is very important that the headers lead to an easy-to-read flow of words on the page. You can see the difference again in the bad design versus the good design page. The bad design headings on the page feel crowded and confused. The good design feels spaced and structured.

Head and Feet

Look at the bottom of the page, where the page number is next to the chapter title. Which looks better? Very clearly, the good design does. It's smaller, the dot looks better than a dash, and the font choices make better sense.

Trim Size

There aren't any hard and fast rules around trim size, but there are general trends. Trim sizes are always measured in inches, with the horizontal measurement first, then the vertical.

The most common book size is 6"×9". It works for books of almost any style and is generally the industry standard.

At Scribe Media, we typically use 5.5"×8.5". This slightly smaller size tends to be more common with business books. There are a lot of books that are 5"×8" as well, but I'd consider that the lower limit before the book starts looking awkwardly small.

HOW TO CREATE YOUR PRINT LAYOUT

Like most steps in this process, you have two options: you can do it yourself, or you can hire someone more talented than you who does it professionally.

DIY

As we've already discussed, doing a cheap interior can completely change the perception of your book. But if it's the only option that works for you financially, there are some ways to do it yourself. If you *really* want to go all out, you need to learn Adobe InDesign, alongside the fundamentals of professional typography and design. To be clear: *Don't* do that if you value your time at greater than $0.

Instead, we recommend a far more user-friendly application called Vellum. Vellum isn't free, and it's Mac-only, but it's the best tool available for do-it-yourselfers and allows you to generate both print and e-book files.

The print layout design quality is only so-so, but still better than you'd be able to do on your own or by hiring a bottom-tier designer. It's like the difference between editing a photo in Instagram versus Photoshop. A beginner will be able to get an okay result from Instagram quickly. Photoshop is far more powerful, and a professional will be able to get a much *better* result from it, but they had to invest a lot of time (and money) to get to that level.

If you're going to hire a designer—which you should—there are basically three options:

CHEAP

There are people offering layout services on Fiverr. Bookalope is another. Upwork is another.

As we described earlier, the quality of these designs is really low. It's easy to delude yourself when you're looking at a computer screen to think that the PDF looks good, but we've tested this path enough times to know better.

Only use the cheap options if you're okay with the book not looking entirely professional. We'd honestly recommend going the DIY route as a better alternative to hiring this quality of designer. That's how bad it usually turns out.

MIDDLE ROUTE

There are some decent layout people on Reedsy and similar websites. This bracket often contains graphic designers who are "moonlighting" with layout work and don't necessarily have a lot of specialized experience in book design, but you can find some people who will do a solid enough job. Careful though: do not assume you'll also get a quality e-book conversion out of the deal, as many graphic designers simply lack the expertise.

EXPENSIVE ROUTE

The other alternative is to hire a real pro. More than any other part of the book creation process, except maybe editing, there's a huge gap between good interior layout designers and mediocre ones. If you hire a bad editor, they're worse than useless. If you hire a great editor, they can completely transform your book. Same goes with interior layout.

The problem with the expensive freelancers in this space isn't their quality. The quality is good. The problem is the price and the turnaround time.

Because they're in an industry with so little competition, they're able to move slowly and charge a lot. But if you just care about someone doing a great job, the few freelancers you can find here do excellent work.

DESIGNING THE E-BOOK

Compared to the horror of designing your print interior, designing an e-book is actually pretty straightforward. Unlike the manual work and design aesthetic that need to go into a print book, creating e-books is mostly coding work, and a lot of it is automated. The cost is lower, and the results are more consistent.

UNDERSTANDING E-BOOK FILE FORMATS

There are two standard e-book file formats that you'll see. EPUB (book.epub) is the universal standard and is used by Apple iBook, Nook, Kobo, and most other e-book retailers. These files are a little more customizable, have a little more flexibility for design, and are frankly just easier to use.

MOBI files (book.mobi) are for Amazon Kindle. Because Amazon is the big player in the space, they are able to set their own standards that are different from anyone else's. MOBI files can be a little more complicated to edit, but they're crucial, as Amazon will be where the vast majority of your books are sold.

HOW TO CREATE YOUR E-BOOK LAYOUT

Like most steps in this process, you have two options: you can do it yourself, or you can hire someone.

We're just going to be blunt about this: unless you decided to go the Vellum route described earlier, *don't do it yourself.*

Steer clear of any "automated" e-book conversions that involve uploading a PDF or Word file. Ironically, Amazon accepts these formats and will attempt to create a Kindle file from them, but the results are never good.

Unlike with print books, the cheap e-book designers do a better job than you will, so it's not worth messing with. As with some of the other design elements, there are three places we'd turn for varying qualities of e-book.

FIVERR

As we discussed, Fiverr is a marketplace of services that are all available for $5. Obviously, no matter what you're getting, it isn't going to be of the highest quality, but with e-books, they're actually passable.

I wouldn't recommend them to an author doing a professional business book or for a book with a lot of hierarchy and headers (you should go through in Word and tag the headers properly in advance because a Fiverr designer won't get them right), but for authors with a seriously tight budget, it's an option.

UPWORK

Upwork is a good middle option. You can find pretty cheap talent and, if you look hard enough, pretty high-quality people. Especially for something like e-book design—which isn't overly complicated—finding someone with a lot of experience, great reviews, and some good examples of past work is usually enough to ensure success.

PROFESSIONALS

The final option is to work with a firm that's really professional. The challenge here is that a lot of the companies that look professional are really just fancy middlemen between you and cheaper, overseas labor. Don't mistake a high price tag for professionalism.

If you don't want to mess around or waste any time and you just want it done right without the back-and-forth, this is probably your best option.

THE SCRIBE GUIDE TO PRICING BOOKS

Book pricing can be both very simple and incredibly complex. It all depends how deep in the details you dive.

Most of the complex advice is pricing for fiction books or pricing for professional writers and is not really that useful for authors writing business or personal development books.

This guide is as simple as it gets (in fact, you can even skip to the "How to Price Your Book" section right now if you want) and will give you only the relevant information for you so you can confidently decide how to price your e-book, paperback, and hardcover.

E-BOOK PRICING

The largest e-book market—by far—is Amazon, and they set the standard for e-book pricing. They have a pretty simple set of rules for how they let authors price e-books:

- Between $0.99 and $2.98, they pay the author a 35 percent royalty
- Between $2.99 and $9.99, they pay the author a 70 percent royalty
- $10 and over, they pay the author a 35 percent royalty

Now, look at this chart that compares book sales to price. This data isn't perfect (it's gathered by Smashwords), but our experience and our data watching hundreds of authors in business and personal development maps very closely to this chart.

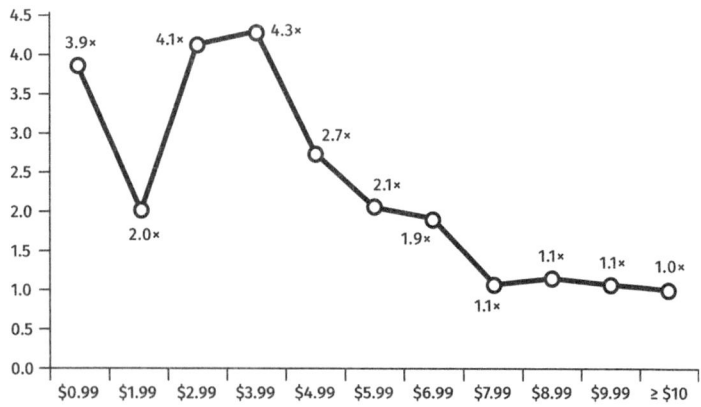

HOW DOES EBOOK PRICE IMPACT UNIT SALES VOLUME?
Data shown as multiple of unit volume at $10+

As you can see, there are basically three tiers:

- Maximize copies: $0.99–$3.99
- Middle ground: $4.99–$6.99
- Maximize perceived value: $7.99–$9.99

There are some shocking data points on there.

For example, there is no difference in sales between $7.99 and $9.99. And perhaps most shocking, books at $0.99 sell *less* than books priced at $3.99.

This actually brings me to my next point, which is a very important factor for pricing business and personal development books: **credibility.**

Books are, within certain ranges, Veblen goods. This means that people will often judge the quality of your book, at least partially, on the price of your book.

You can even see the impact of the Veblen goods effect in the book pricing data. The fact that there is no sales difference between $7.99 and $9.99 tells you that within certain price bands, the price actually does not have an impact on demand.

The data pretty clearly show that there are four price ranges:

E-BOOKS

High Price	$7.99–$9.99
Normal	$4.99–$6.99
Cheap	$2.99–$3.99
Dirt Cheap	$0.99–$1.99

Why does this matter?

Because for many authors, *pricing a book too low will hurt your credibility with your readers.*

This is how it works with many luxury goods. People assume you are worth what you ask, so if you ask a low price, they assume that is what you are worth.

(By the way, remember that most of our authors are not primarily focusing on making money through book sales but, rather, using the book to make money other ways.)

Given these two factors, for most authors, there are really three prices to choose from (at least for long-term pricing, not counting any promotions you do):

- **If you want to maximize units sold:** $3.99 (or possibly $0.99 in some rare cases)
- **If you want a good balance between sales and perception:** $6.99
- **If you want to maximize high status perception, and don't care about sales:** $9.99

PAPERBACK PRICING

At Scribe, we usually use KDP (Kindle Direct Publishing) for the paperback books we publish, as they are easy to use and produce high-quality books.

KDP pricing is so complicated that they actually built a calculator to help authors figure out what their royalties will be. It includes variations based on black and white versus color, length of book, bleed, and other factors.

The good news is that you don't need to use it, because almost all of the time, the royalty rate turns out to be around 40 percent. For example, if you sell your paperback for $10, then you will probably get about $4 in profit.

Paperback pricing is similar to e-book pricing, just add around $7–$10 to every price. So the chart would look like this:

PAPERBACKS

High Price	$17.99–$19.99
Normal	$14.99–$16.99
Cheap	$11.99–$13.99
Dirt Cheap	$7.99–$10.99

This rule of thumb has worked very well for our authors in pricing: whatever the e-book price is, add about $7–$10 for the paperback price.

HARDCOVER PRICING

It's almost impossible to give broad advice on hardcover pricing and royalties because so many factors impact the price, for example: color, printing price, size, niche, bleed, and many other factors.

Despite these variances, we've found a pretty solid rubric to use for hardcover book pricing that tracks pretty well with the paperback pricing: the hardcover should be $12–$15 more than the e-book.

And given this, you can expect a royalty rate of about 45 percent—but with HIGH variations depending on several factors.

There is an important exception to this: I would not price your hardcover above $27.99 unless you have a very specific reason.

HARDCOVER

High Price	$25.99–$27.99
Normal	$20.99–$24.99
Cheap	$16.99–$19.99
Dirt Cheap	$12.99–$15.99

HOW TO PRICE YOUR BOOK

So let's bring it all together and give you the best framework for pricing.

If you want to maximize units sold:

- $3.99 e-book (or $0.99 in some promotional cases) (royalty rate: 70 percent)
- $10.99–$12.99 paperback (royalty rate: ~40 percent)
- $14.99–$16.99 hardcover (royalty rate: ~45 percent)

If you want a good balance between sales and perception, there are two different options.

Option 1:
- $6.99 e-book (royalty rate: 70 percent)
- $13.99–$16.99 paperback (royalty rate: ~40 percent)
- $18.99–$21.99 hardcover (royalty rate: ~45 percent)

Option 2 (big spread): What this does is fix your paperback and/or hardcover as your "list price," so it stays high for perceived value. The e-book price is relatively low—but not too low—to maximize sales to that audience.

- $4.99 eBook (royalty rate: 70 percent)
- $16.99 paperback (royalty rate: ~40 percent)
- $24.99 hardcover (royalty rate: ~45 percent)

If you want to maximize high status perception:

- $9.99 e-book (royalty rate: 70 percent)
- $17.99–$19.99 paperback (royalty rate: ~40 percent)
- $24.99–$27.99 hardcover (royalty rate: ~45 percent)

PART 8

PUBLISH YOUR BOOK

HOW TO PICK THE RIGHT BOOK PUBLISHING OPTION

Many people are confused by the publishing landscape (which is understandable) and want a lot more background information before starting on their book publishing journey. This chapter is long and comprehensive, and answers questions like these:

- How does the book publishing business work?
- What are the most important things to know?
- What is "self-publishing"?
- What is "traditional publishing"?
- What is the difference and why does it matter?
- Should I self-publish or traditionally publish my book?
- How do I get a traditional publishing deal?
- How do I evaluate traditional publishers?
- What is professional versus amateur in publishing, and why does that matter?

HOW TO UNDERSTAND THE BOOK PUBLISHING LANDSCAPE

The book publishing landscape can be very confusing. This is for many reasons. The most relevant to you is that the business of book publishing has changed dramatically over the past decade, and most of the advice people give is dated and wrong.

Furthermore, most of the guides to book publishing are geared towards professional writers, novelists, or hobbyists. Entrepreneurs, business owners, executives, and other professionals who are writing business and personal development books should look at book publishing through a completely different lens than professional writers.

This piece will examine the three book publishing options commonly available, explain the pros and cons of each, and help you understand exactly which one you should select.

TRADITIONAL AND SELF-PUBLISHING

The first thing you have to understand is that there are two major publishing models: **traditional** and **self**.

I'll dive deeper into each publishing option, what the basic facts are, and the questions you need to ask for each so you can decide which one to use.

There is also a third option called hybrid publishing. In my opinion, hybrid is by far the worst of the three options, and I will briefly cover it at the end.

TRADITIONAL PUBLISHING

SUMMARY

In traditional publishing, an author must find a book agent to represent them to publishing companies. Then along with the agent, pitch a book publishing company (which are almost all based in New York City, such as HarperCollins or Simon & Schuster) with their book idea. If the pitch is successful and the publishing company offers the author a publishing deal, the publishing company purchases the ownership of the print license from the author in return for an advance on royalties (that the author does not have to pay back). The author is on their own to write the book, sometimes with editorial help from the publisher, sometimes not. The publisher then manages and controls the whole publishing and distribution process (the second and third steps).

OWNERSHIP AND RIGHTS

A publishing company always owns the print license (which includes digital), while the author always owns the copyright. All other rights (movie, excerpt, etc.) are negotiable.

This means the publishing company has final say over all aspects of that book.

TYPICAL ROYALTY RATE

15 percent hardcover, 7.5 percent trade paperback, 5 percent mass market.

ADVANCE AGAINST ROYALTIES

The amount varies greatly depending on the author.

WRITING AND EDITING

This is typically the author's job. Very little help, limited to some editing and copyediting. Make sure to note that a publishing company usually has the absolute right to change your content and writing as they wish.

PUBLISHING SERVICES AND DESIGN

They (usually) do everything, though the quality varies greatly. You don't get to choose paperback or hardcover or price, or most other decisions.

DISTRIBUTION

They do everything.

MARKETING

Usually, the publisher offers very little marketing. More often than not, they can inhibit marketing (explained below).

PRESTIGE AND PERCEPTION

Usually the highest of the three models, but fading prestige, and not at all relevant to readers.

TIME TO PUBLISH

Twelve to thirty-six months.

ADVANTAGES

1. Monetary advance before publishing
2. Highest potential for traditional media coverage
3. Social signaling/feeling of acceptance
4. Possible bookstore placement

DRAWBACKS

1. Very hard to get a deal
2. Huge time investment
3. Loss of ownership
4. Loss of marketing control
5. Loss of creative and content control
6. Limited financial upside

TRADITIONAL PUBLISHING PROBLEM #1: CAN YOU EVEN GET A TRADITIONAL PUBLISHING DEAL?

When considering traditional publishing, the first and MOST important question you need to ask yourself is: **can you even**

get a publishing deal from a traditional publisher? Most authors cannot, so there's no reason to waste time trying.

To get a publishing deal from a traditional publisher, you must go through these steps:

1. Find a book agent willing to represent you and your book idea to a publisher (this is very hard; most agents get thousands of inbound requests a week).
2. Write a book proposal (this is such a big task, authors often pay freelance writers $10k–$15k or more to do this for them).
3. Shop the book proposal around to publishers (through the agent).
4. Have a publisher make you an offer based on your proposal and pitch.
5. Negotiate and accept that offer.

That seems like a lot, but in some cases, it can be easy. A book publisher's decision hinges on one simple fact: ***do you have an existing audience that is waiting to buy a lot of copies of your book?***

If you do have a big audience—people who already follow you in some form, like an email list or social media, or something like that—most of that will be doable, if not easy. Usually publishers will need to be able to see a clear path to 25,000 book sales in the first month to even consider a book deal for an author.

If you do not have an existing audience that is ready to buy your book, then it is nearly impossible to get a traditional book deal.

The reason for this is because traditional publishers are terrible at selling and marketing books, and they now rely almost exclusively on authors to do this for them. I'm not just saying this. Book agent Byrd Leavell says this (he's repped several number one *New York Times* bestselling authors who have sold more than 10 million nonfiction books):

> Publishers aren't buying anything that doesn't come with a built-in audience that will buy it. They don't take risks anymore, they don't gamble on authors, they only want sure things. I won't even take an author out unless they have an audience they can guarantee 25k presales to.

If you do not have a built-in audience—people who follow you and are used to buying things from you—then you have almost no shot to get a deal.

TRADITIONAL PUBLISHING PROBLEM #2: IF YOU CAN GET A TRADITIONAL PUBLISHING DEAL, SHOULD YOU TAKE IT?

As recently as twenty-five years ago, this was a no-brainer: of course you took the deal, because you didn't really have any other options to get a book into the hands of readers.

The game has changed since then. In the modern world of

book publishing, traditional publishers are no longer the gatekeepers, they provide very little prestige or access, and the other self-publishing options are better than a traditional publisher for most authors.

At this time, there are really only three reasons for an author to sign with a traditional publisher:

1. You Need the Advance They Will Pay You

If you already have a big audience, then a publishing company will probably give you a big advance. A "big" advance can range from $100K–$1 million (or much more in rare cases), but the advance is directly tied to the expected book sales.

This is not charity. They will do this because they expect to make a lot of money when you sell your books to your audience. And if you do not have a big audience, your chance of getting an advance in this range is essentially zero (unless there is some other angle that makes the publisher confident you will sell many books).

The cool thing is that even if your book does not sell, you don't have to pay this advance back. It's yours. But make no mistake—you are paying for this money in other ways. You no longer own the print license for the book, which means you cannot do anything with this content other than have it in the book. It's not yours to use anymore, and if the book is a major hit, you only get a small fraction of the profits. You are selling the potential upside to the publisher.

2. You Must Have Mainstream Media Attention for the Book to Be Successful

If you absolutely NEED a lot of mainstream media attention for your book to be a success, then going with a traditional publisher really helps. When I say mainstream, I mean like *New York Times*, *Wall Street Journal*, media outlets like that.

The types of people who fall into this category tend to be celebrities, politicians, etc. They are the type of people whose time is extremely valuable and generally tend to be very, very rich. By the way, they have to pay for PR to get media as well. They do the whole song and dance, mainly because they are famous and do NOT have their own platform.

Let me be very clear: doing a book with a traditional publisher does not mean it will be covered in those outlets. In fact, the odds are small, even if you do get a traditional publishing deal. Each publisher puts out tens of thousands of books a year, and bookstores and retailers do not have the shelf space for all of them.

The reason it helps is because, while no book reader cares who the publisher is, journalists who work for major media companies still look at the publisher as a signal of credibility.

3. You Want the Social Signal and Feeling of
Acceptance That Comes from Being "Picked" by a
Traditional Publishing House

Let's be honest. This is the primary reason most people
want a deal from a traditional publisher. They want to feel
like they were "picked," that this selection is an unassail-
able signal of their importance and relevance.

I have gotten publishing deals from several major publishing companies (Simon & Schuster and Little Brown), so I
wish so much that this was true—that these deals meant I
am now unquestionably important. It doesn't.

Here's a great example: a Ferrari is a cool car. But what
do you think of the old guy who bought it? Compensating,
right?

It can work the same with traditional publishers. Having a
"fancy" publisher's name on the spine of your book doesn't
make you important. In the modern world, no reader
notices or cares who publishes your book.

In fact, in many circles (especially entrepreneurs and
forward thinkers), traditional publishing is starting to
be seen as a negative signal. Self-publishing used to be
seen as "vanity publishing" because the assumption was
that you could not get "picked" by a traditional publisher.
But in the modern book world, controlling the rights and
usage of your book is now seen as much more important

by most authors. In fact, traditional publishing is now the new "vanity" publishing because authors with traditional deals are looking for that ego boost and external validation rather than "picking" themselves and owning their book.

TRADITIONAL PUBLISHING PROBLEM #3: ARE THE TRADE-OFFS OF TRADITIONAL PUBLISHING WORTH IT?

So even if you can get a traditional publishing deal AND you fall into one of the three reasons to publish it, the trade-offs may still make it a bad choice for you. These are the major trade-offs with traditional publishing.

1. No Ownership of Rights and Profits

You are literally selling the publisher not only the upside profits of the book, but more importantly, *you are selling them control of your intellectual property*. Once they own the book, they ONLY care about selling copies. You can no longer do anything with that book that doesn't involve paying THEM for copies of it because that is how publishing companies make money.

2. Loss of Creative and Content Control

Make no mistake about this: once you take a deal from a publisher, they own the book and all the content in it, so they get to decide everything that goes in the book. They get final say over every word, the book cover, the author bio, everything.

I can tell you from my experience, as a group, publishers tend to make terrible aesthetic decisions. This is for many reasons, but the biggest is what I call "adverse selection." Though some people who work in publishing are deeply skilled and thoughtful editors whose work makes books much better, those people are rare, and tend to only work with the biggest authors. Most of the people working at publishing companies are doing that because they were not good enough to make a living as a writer. I don't say that as a put-down, I say it simply so you understand that someone who didn't make good enough decisions on their own about their writing is now in a position to hold *final decision-making power over your book.*

Furthermore their incentives do not always align with yours. Publishers ONLY care about selling books. They don't care about any of your other goals, and they will force creative decisions on you that you don't want. This most often plays out in marketing (below).

3. Loss of Marketing Control (and No Support)

Publishers do no marketing. I cannot emphasize this enough. Publishers expect YOU to do all the work of selling the book for THEM. They don't have a plan to sell 25,000 copies of your book. That's YOUR job.

This might be okay for a novelist with a big existing audience, but if you are someone like the authors my company works with and you want your book to promote you or your business, a traditional publisher greatly restricts your options.

For example, if you want to position yourself as an expert in something, what happens if they don't think your book topic appeals to enough people? They don't care about your business. They only care about selling copies of books, so they'll make you go broader with your topic, which means the book won't be as appealing to the specific audience you are trying to reach.

Even worse, because the ONLY way they make money is to sell copies of the book, you can't give copies away for free, you can't give the PDF away for free, you can't use your content in other places as a lead generator for your company. They now are going to force you to put all your promotion efforts on selling copies, which does not always help you reach as many people as possible.

Also, they give you ZERO price control, so your ability to make marketing deals with any number of people is none. This type of flexibility is critically important for so much marketing, and they won't do it.

4. Huge Time Investment

Even if you get a traditional book deal, it's a huge amount

of effort to put it all together. You have to find an agent to represent you to a traditional publisher, you have to do a book proposal that will appeal to a publisher, and then you have to shop the book deal.

From the start of the process to publishing, it's usually twenty-four months—often thirty-six. That's two to three YEARS, which is an incredibly long time in the modern media world, especially for a nonfiction author.

5. Bookstore Placement

A lot of people think traditional publishing is their preferred method because it's the best way to get into bookstores. This is not an accurate calculus. Traditional book publishers do not get most of their books into bookstores on any large scale. Furthermore, the ones they do get in tend to get pulled out quickly—unless they sell a lot of copies. And your book will not be on display until it has already proven it will sell a lot of copies.

Beyond that, the entire idea that bookstore distribution matters is just not true anymore. Bookstores account for less than 25 percent of book sales (and that number is falling), and the majority of that is fiction. Bookstore distribution tends to not benefit most authors.

SELF-PUBLISHING

SUMMARY

In the self-publishing model, the author retains ownership of their book and manages and controls the whole process. Self-publishing has many different forms, but at its core, the author does the publishing work (or manages freelancers or publishing services companies who do the work for a fee). There is no acceptance needed, no advance, and the author retains all rights.

OWNERSHIP AND RIGHTS

Author retains all rights.

ROYALTY RATE

Variable, usually between 40 percent and 100 percent, depending on the sales channel.

ADVANCE AGAINST ROYALTIES

None.

WRITING AND EDITING

Author must manage. Many variations of help exist, but all are paid.

PUBLISHING SERVICES

Author must manage. Many variations of help exist, but all are paid.

DISTRIBUTION

Author must manage. Many variations of help exist, but all are paid.

MARKETING

Author must manage. Many variations of help exist, but all are paid.

PRESTIGE AND PERCEPTION

Variable. Totally depends on quality of the book.

TIME TO PUBLISH

As fast as you can manage.

ADVANTAGES INCLUDE

- Full ownership of rights and royalties
- Completely customizable in all aspects
- Fast to market
- Total marketing control
- Total creative control

- Total freedom

DRAWBACKS INCLUDE

- It is a lot of work to do it right
- If it's unprofessional, will result in poor appearance and low status
- Time-consuming to learn and manage the process yourself
- If you hire excellent professionals to help you, it's expensive

SELF-PUBLISHING PROBLEM #1: CAN YOU DO A PROFESSIONAL JOB WITH YOUR SELF-PUBLISHED BOOK?

This is the absolutely crucial question for self-publishing—one that trumps every other. If you can do a professional job with your book, then self-publishing is almost always the best bet for most authors.

If you cannot do a professional job, then you may either not want to self-publish, or you may not want to publish a book at all.

The reason this is so crucial is because readers judge a book—and judge the author—not by who published it but by how professional and credible it is.

The saying is right: everyone judges a book by its cover. But not just the cover. The title, the book description, the author photo, the blurbs, even the author bio, all tell a story about how credible and authoritative that book and author are.

Whereas, a book that has a cover that looks like a child designed it, a book description with spelling and grammar errors, a poorly lit photo, or a bragging or incomplete bio all look bad.

It used to be that traditional publishers were the only ones who had the expertise and access to the talented people necessary to make books that looked professional. That was true thirty years ago, but not anymore. In fact, almost all of the best talent out there is freelance and can be hired for reasonable rates. Just in my company alone, we use writers, editors, proofreaders, copywriters, and book cover designers who all either used to work for traditional publishers and left to freelance, or are the same freelancers that the traditional publishers use.

Some people think there is still a stigma to self-publishing. Well, the data appears to say otherwise. Hugh Howey (self-published his novel *Wool*, which has sold millions of copies and is being made into a movie directed by Ridley Scott) did a study on 200,000 titles and showed that the self-published books on Amazon had, on average, a higher star ranking than traditionally published books.

This all boils down to the fact that if you're willing to put in the work to make sure your self-published book is super professional, then you're going to be well off. But if not, then your book, and you, will suffer.

SELF-PUBLISHING PROBLEM #2: WHAT IS THE MAJOR TRADE-OFF OF SELF-PUBLISHING?

There is really one major trade-off with self-publishing:

Professionally self-publishing a book requires you to put in either time or money (or both).

It's not hard to do all the steps necessary to make a professional book. This book clearly details every step. It just takes time. The way around that is to hire great people or, even better, hire a publishing services firm to manage the whole process for you. That takes money.

It's a pretty simple calculation: if you have money, spend it to save time.

If you don't have money, then your time isn't your most expensive asset, so use it to learn how to professionally publish your book and execute it (that's what this book is about).

HYBRID PUBLISHING

In the hybrid model, the publisher will tell you that they combine the advantages of a traditional publisher with the flexibility and upside of self-publishing. That's the theory, but it never works that way in practice.

Hybrid doesn't really exist. It's a made-up word so that publishing companies that use a variation of the traditional model can pretend they are something different.

They're basically just fee-for-service publishing companies. They pay little to no advance, still take a lot of the royalties, still control a lot of the process, and still do some part of the publishing work. They try to give authors the illusion of status from being "picked" by a publisher, but they make the author do all of the work, and they still own the rights, and they still get the upside—all while NOT paying an advance. It's a terrible deal.

The other problem is that in hybrid publishing, oftentimes the publishing company will try to retain copyright or other rights. One of the main attributes of old traditional publishing companies is that they ALWAYS reserve copyright to the author and almost always leave all other rights to the author (movie, TV, etc.). They only care about the rights involved around profiting from the printed word and related rights.

SUMMARY: WHICH SHOULD YOU PICK?
WHO SHOULD GO WITH TRADITIONAL PUBLISHING?

- Celebrities
- Athletes

- Musicians
- Actors
- Politicians
- Professional Writers (novelists, etc.)

WHO SHOULD GO WITH SELF-PUBLISHING?

- Entrepreneurs
- Businesspeople
- Executives
- Financial Planners
- Lawyers
- Doctors
- Business Owners
- Consultants
- Coaches
- Just about everyone else

WHO SHOULD GO WITH HYBRID PUBLISHING?

- Pretty much no one

NOW DO IT

"He who has a hundred miles to walk should reckon ninety as half the journey."

—AWA KENZO

After 75,000 words, there isn't much more to say about writing and publishing your book. Either you're going to do it, or you aren't.

Everything you need is in this book.

My hope—the reason I wrote this book—is that it will demystify the book writing and publishing process and turn it into a really digestible, easy-to-act-on set of steps—and that you *actually act on it*.

I hate the thought of people reading this and saying, "Yeah, it does sound totally doable," and then not doing anything about it.

Don't do that.

You read this book because you have something to say to the world and because you've already taken the hard step of writing it down.

But if you don't put it out to the world, then no one can hear it, and no one can benefit from you sharing your knowledge and wisdom. Not you or your reader.

And that is the point.

So write your book, then publish your book, and make sure the world hears what you have to say.

ABOUT THE AUTHORS

TUCKER MAX is the cofounder of Scribe Media, a company that helps people write, publish, and market their books.

He has written four *New York Times* bestsellers, which have sold over 4.5 million copies worldwide. He's credited with being the originator of the literary genre "fratire" and is only the third writer (after Malcolm Gladwell and Michael Lewis) to ever have three books on the *New York Times* nonfiction bestseller list at one time. He was nominated for the *Time* magazine 100 Most Influential list in 2009.

He received his BA from the University of Chicago in 1998, and his JD from Duke Law School in 2001. He currently lives in Austin, Texas, with his wife Veronica and three children.

ZACH OBRONT is the cofounder of Scribe Media, where he works to help authors write, publish, and market their books without the usual barriers.

As an expert in the changing publishing industry, he's spoken to crowds at Harvard, Yale, Google, and Adobe, and has worked with thousands of authors to professionally publish and promote their books, reaching millions of readers in the process.